THE FORBIDDEN IDEA

Hidden Truths About Individual Liberty,
Economic Freedom, Political Philosophy, and History

MARK A. MONOSCALCO

FOREWORD BY RON PAUL, M.D.

The Forbidden Idea
Hidden Truths About Individual Liberty,
Economic Freedom, Political Philosophy, and History

© 2026 by Mark A. Monoscalco

Paperback ISBN 979-8-9939715-2-0
Hardcover ISBN 979-8-9939715-0-6
EPUB ISBN 979-8-9939715-4-4
Kindle ISBN 979-8-9939715-5-1

The Root of Liberty Press LLC
Honolulu, Hawaii
www.TheRootOfLibertyPress.com

This book is a work of non-fiction. It reflects the author's research, analysis, and opinions. While every effort has been made to ensure accuracy, the author and publisher make no representations or warranties regarding the completeness or reliability of the information contained herein. Readers should exercise independent judgment and, where appropriate, consult qualified professionals before acting on any information in this book.

Printed in the United States of America
Library of Congress Control Number: 2026903605

ABOUT THE COVER

Some words are closely related in meaning, such as light and enlightenment or darkness and ignorance. Darkness cannot resist light—it disappears when light is present. In the same way, ignorance cannot resist enlightenment; it fades when understanding is introduced.

From the perspective shown on the book cover, you stand outside the gates, surrounded by darkness—a symbol of ignorance. The elites of society want to keep you there, unaware of the ideas that could set you free. Behind the gates, the books glow with light, representing knowledge that brings enlightenment—*The Forbidden Idea*. To escape the darkness, read this book.

DEDICATION

I was privileged to know Richard (Dick) Rowland, founder of the Grassroot Institute of Hawaii. Dick was a passionate and persuasive champion of individual liberty and was never without his pocket version of the Declaration of Independence. Dick's favorite motto was "upward to liberty," and he loved to remind us that "when government gets bigger, you get smaller."

With profound respect and heartfelt gratitude, I dedicate this book to Dick Rowland and his legacy of individual liberty.

**Liberty is not a means to a higher political end.
It is itself the highest political end.**

—Lord Acton[1]

AUTHOR'S NOTE

To download an audiobook or a digital version of this book, follow this link:

www.TheForbiddenIdea.com

Explore my website and blog:

www.DefendingCivilSociety.com

Research a curated reading list on individual liberty:

www.TheRootOfLiberty.com

Sign up for my newsletter:

www.DefendingCivilSociety.com/sign-up

Conventions used in this book:

- Footnotes are identified by Roman numerals and appear at the bottom of the page.

- Endnotes are identified by consecutive numbers and are compiled at the end of the book.

- Quotations and excerpts from other sources appear in an indented format.

CONTENTS

FOREWORD BY RON PAUL, M.D.

The United States of America has been through many changes in its relatively short existence as a nation. In what began as "the land of the free," and carried on as such for a good century, Americans now find themselves in a much different situation. The downward pull of bureaucracy and power eventually gained the upper hand, and today, the United States has the largest and most indebted government in history.

Today, it's not an exaggeration to state that Americans live in an Empire of Lies. And as I've repeated all too often, "Truth is treason in an Empire of Lies." Yet, despite the dangers, truth must continue to be told. In *The Forbidden Idea*, Mark A. Monoscalco sounds the alarm bells against the Empire of Lies.

In this book, you will not find the usual weak defenses of the *status quo*. Instead, you will march alongside Aristotle, Aquinas, Locke, Smith, Bastiat, Mises, Hayek, Rand, and Rothbard as living allies, not long-ignored authors. The book is stripped of academic jargon and sharpened with moral clarity. It has been written to prepare you for battle—a battle that all of us are a part of, whether we like it or not. The ideas of individual liberty need to be understood, but they also must be spoken.

Human flourishing is the product of unfettered minds and voluntary cooperation. Nothing short of that ideal is worthy of a free people. Page by page, Monoscalco restores the concepts that have been dulled in modern America: consent over coercion, spontaneous order over central planning, voluntary cooperation over legal plunder.

Each chapter is both a revelation and a call to arms, exposing the myths that continue to grow the size and scope of the U.S. federal government. In the era of "fake news," myths about the government are not in short supply. They are broadcast every day on the TV news. *The Forbidden Idea* will assist you in dispelling those myths.

Read it, absorb it, and above all, share it with others. America can once again be "the land of the free." The Empire of Lies need not last much longer. But it will take the conviction and courage of passionate individuals to turn the tide.

I invite you to join the battle of ideas.

Ron Paul, M.D.
Lake Jackson, Texas
June 6, 2025

PREFACE

Individual liberty resides at the pinnacle of human needs. Throughout history, it has faced opposition from tyrannical forces and has been valiantly defended by the ideas and courageous actions of its heroic champions.

Prepare to explore a series of ideas that offer the most profound understanding of the world. These ideas are among the most liberating yet historically suppressed, as they challenge established powers by asserting that human progress stems not from violence, coercion, or royal decrees, but from the creativity and freedom of ordinary individuals. Astonishingly, these brilliant and liberating ideas have been met with contempt. This book provides a concise yet comprehensive introduction to these crucial concepts—ideas that took millennia to fully develop—while honoring them with the respect they deserve.

You will be introduced to the philosophical foundations of individual liberty, along with the key events, individuals, writings, and quotations that have advanced its cause. While this book does not focus on the actions, usurpations, or responses of tyrants who have opposed the human pursuit of individual liberty, it does conclude with a discussion on the persistent challenges to individual liberty and the strategies required for its ultimate triumph. Once you have absorbed the ideas presented in this book, you will be equipped to think clearly about individual liberty and to advance its realization in your own lifetime.

Yours in Liberty,

Mark A. Monoscalco
Honolulu, Hawaii
September 27, 2025

INTRODUCTION

I've heard the frustration and despair expressed by many of my friends and acquaintances. This book is for the forgotten man or woman who wakes each day and works tirelessly to build a better life, yet feels trapped in a system that seems stacked against them.

I have also struggled with frustration, despair, and internal conflicts about political and economic issues. A deep unease churned within me about our society's political and economic trajectory, but I struggled to articulate my thoughts clearly. Unrelenting and consuming disquiet tormented my soul. Fortunately, I discovered the classic works on the philosophy of individual liberty. It felt as if I had put on a pair of glasses for the first time: everything suddenly became clear. The confusion and turmoil faded into understanding, and I gained a profound sense of inner peace.

This clarity inspired me to share what I had discovered. Though I had never written a book before, my background in engineering and business had given me a problem-solving mindset well-suited to exploring these ideas.

I hold a BS in Civil Engineering from the Illinois Institute of Technology and an MBA from the University of Chicago. I have always enjoyed the challenge of solving real-world problems, and my studies have taught me that it is nearly impossible to do so without the right tools.

In 2016, I joined the Board of Directors of the Grassroot Institute of Hawaii. We are a state policy think tank with a mission to educate people about the principles of individual liberty, economic freedom, and limited, accountable government. Joining this Board inspired me to expand my knowledge of the principles listed in our mission statement. Studying these principles changed my life. My work at the Grassroot Institute of Hawaii taught me that trying to solve real-world problems involving politics and economics requires understanding the fundamental philosophy of individual liberty.

Sometimes, when someone reacts hysterically to a political or economic issue, they ask how I remain so calm. I smile and reply, "Because I know I'm right." I explain that the philosophy of individual liberty is grounded in truths discovered by some of history's greatest intellectuals, and these truths have been proven over thousands of years. I don't say this to sound arrogant or superior, but to convey the quiet confidence that comes from understanding this fundamental philosophy. I feel, quite literally, above the fray. You can achieve this as well.

I wrote this book to present the principles of individual liberty in clear, concise language, stripped of anything unnecessary. My goal is to provide not only a deeper understanding of these ideas but also the inspiration to defend them. For too long, you have been denied the opportunity to learn the fundamental principles of human flourishing.

The forbidden idea is this: Individual liberty, grounded in natural law that predates government, is essential to a rational human life. Without it, we are reduced to slaves or beasts of burden.

The first six chapters of this book examine perspectives on individual liberty from some of our most influential philosophers and historical figures. Each chapter is structured around key quotations; these will be a foundation for exploring the topic in depth and building a deeper understanding. Use these first six chapters as a reference, revisiting topics when questions arise or when you're looking for answers and counterarguments in political discussions.

In Chapter 7, you'll explore the struggles of our ancestors and their greatest achievement: breaking free from the chains of tyranny. I assure you, as you read this chapter, you'll come across historical events you've never encountered before. Some sections may even make you think, *This can't be true.* All sources are cited so you can review the original material for yourself. You were not taught these things in school because they challenge the prevailing narrative of submission to a higher political authority. Yet you need to know them, because the history of individual liberty is an essential component of the Forbidden Idea.

Chapter 8 outlines the three core philosophies embraced by advocates of collectivism and centralized control, which together constitute the primary threat to individual liberty today.

Finally, Chapter 9 presents a range of practical tools to help overcome tyranny and secure individual liberty within our lifetime.

As government spending and regulation continue to grow, we are accelerating down the road to serfdom. However, by working together as advocates for individual liberty, we can change our society's trajectory, defeat the forces of tyranny, and rise upward to liberty!

1

AND WHAT IS LIBERTY?

And what is liberty, whose name can make every heart beat, and which can agitate the world… —Frédéric Bastiat[2]

We begin by seeking a definition of individual liberty, following the path of countless students before us in pursuit of fundamental truth. From this foundation, we will explore the elements that lead to human flourishing. Our path will be illuminated by the words and ideas of great scholars who have come before us.

Aristotle once said, "All men by nature desire to know," and this is where our story begins.[3] He argued that this innate quality distinguishes humans from all other species. This idea became a cornerstone of Western philosophy, shaping various schools of thought and guiding intellectual pursuits for generations.

Driven by the desire to know, as described by Aristotle, humanity has spent nearly 2.5 millennia contemplating what it means to lead a good life and to live freely. One of the most influential thinkers in this tradition is Saint Thomas Aquinas, a thirteenth-century Dominican friar, theologian, and philosopher whose synthesis of Christian doctrine with Aristotelian philosophy shaped much of Western thought. Aquinas argued nine centuries after Aristotle that this desire to know is not only a natural human inclination but also a path to understanding divine truth and virtue:

> The chief part of virtue is choice, which cannot exist without voluntariness, to which violence is opposed.[4]

Aquinas places the responsibility for virtue on the individual, asserting that a person can only choose virtue freely, without coercion. However, when violence is present, the capacity for voluntary choice is destroyed, making the attainment of virtue impossible.

Over four centuries later, John Locke, an English philosopher and political theorist, who is widely regarded as the father of classical liberalism and the person who laid the groundwork for the Declaration of Independence and the American Revolution.[i] In his *Second Treatise on Government* (1689), he provides us with a definition of liberty that many people today would recognize:

> The natural liberty of man is to be free from any superior power on Earth, and not to be under the will or legislative

---

[i] Classical liberalism, which emerged in the 17th and 18th centuries, centered on the principles of individual liberty, private property, limited government, and free markets. Thinkers such as John Locke, Adam Smith, and John Stuart Mill shaped these ideas, which in turn inspired movements like the American Revolution. Their focus was on minimizing government control over individuals' lives, fostering voluntary exchanges to promote economic freedom.

Over time, however, the term liberalism began to shift in meaning, particularly in the 19th and 20th centuries. Many classical liberals began to support government intervention to address economic and social inequalities. This led to what is now termed modern liberalism, which emphasizes welfare programs, regulatory policies, and a more prominent government role in economic affairs.

In response to these changes, a group of thinkers—many inspired by the Austrian School of Economics, including figures like Ludwig von Mises, F.A. Hayek, and Murray Rothbard—sought to revive and advance the original ideals of classical liberalism for a new era. To distinguish their approach from the new direction of modern liberalism, they began to use the term "libertarianism."

authority of man, but only to have the law of nature for his rule.[5]

This concept, "the law of nature," forms the core of a theory we will explore in Chapter 3. It is a set of universal moral principles inherent in human nature and discoverable by reason, providing an objective benchmark for judging what is just and unjust that exists independently of—and should guide—human-made laws. No earthly ruler has the authority or ability to override the law of nature.

Henry David Thoreau, a nineteenth-century philosopher, also had a profound influence on political thought. His focus on personal conscience and nonviolent resistance inspired figures like Mahatma Gandhi and Martin Luther King Jr. During an 1848 debate, Thoreau emphasized individual liberty with a striking observation:

> Disobedience is the true foundation of liberty. The obedient must be slaves.[6]

This statement reinforces the concept that a person is obligated only to follow the law of nature. Obeying a despotic ruler who issues commands that violate natural law amounts to slavery. To achieve individual liberty under tyranny, one must resist and disobey.

Over the course of a meaningful life, you will face a choice: Obey to avoid confrontation and punishment; or resist and disobey, breaking the chains that bind you to tyranny and opening the way upward to individual liberty. By the end of this book, you will be prepared to choose wisely.

Now, armed with the knowledge we have gained from the above paragraphs, let us examine the quotation with which we began this chapter, drawn from a statement made by Frédéric Bastiat in his essay "The Law" (1850). Bastiat was a prominent political and economic thinker of the early nineteenth century. For him, liberty was an indivisible whole:

> And what is liberty, whose very name makes the heart beat faster and shakes the world? Is it not the union of all

> liberties—liberty of conscience, of education, of association, of the press, of travel, of labor, of trade? In short, is not liberty the freedom of every person to make full use of his faculties, so long as he does not harm other persons while doing so? Is not liberty the destruction of all despotism—including, of course, legal despotism? Finally, is not liberty the restricting of the law only to its rational sphere of organizing the right of the individual to lawful self-defense, of punishing injustice?

In this paragraph, Bastiat outlines various actions a person can choose when free from the grip of despotism. He also examines the issue of legal despotism, asserting that the sole purpose of law should be to protect the individual from injustice.

An important, if underrated, twentieth-century political thinker, Bertrand de Jouvenel, penned his book *On Power: The Natural History of Its Growth* (1945), which includes this definition:

> Liberty is the direct, immediate, and concrete sovereignty of man over himself.[7]

With this single sentence, de Jouvenel introduces the idea that personal sovereignty is essential for achieving individual liberty. In other words, to achieve individual liberty, a person must exercise complete control over themselves.

Ludwig von Mises, one of the great economists of the twentieth century, warned about the dangers of totalitarianism, the most terrifying threat to individual liberty. Fleeing the Nazis, Mises made his way to America in 1940. When he arrived, he struggled to find an academic position because the left-wing socialists liked him no more than the right-wing socialists did. Mises's masterpiece, *Human Action*, published in 1949, contains this brief reflection on the meaning of liberty:

> Liberty and freedom are terms employed for political conditions under which the individual citizen is in a position to choose how he wants to integrate himself into the totality of society. He is not subject to violent intervention by an

autocratic power. He is not obliged to yield to the arbitrary will of a dictator.[8]

Here, we see Mises integrating Aquinas's ideas of choice and freedom from violent intervention with Thoreau's concept of disobedience.

F.A. Hayek, Mises's most accomplished student, was awarded the Nobel Prize in Economics in 1974. Beyond his economic achievements, Hayek was deeply engaged in political philosophy. In his book *The Constitution of Liberty* (1960), he offers the following definition of individual liberty (although he uses the words freedom and liberty interchangeably):

> The state in which a man is not subject to coercion by the arbitrary will of another or others is often also distinguished as "individual" or "personal" freedom.[9]

In this definition, Hayek emphasizes that liberty is an individual attribute.

During the Great Depression and the New Deal, it became common and widely accepted to expect government to address economic inequalities. The utilitarian idea that the government's role was to provide "the greatest amount of good for the greatest number" was gaining traction. Observing this growing government intervention in individual lives, Ayn Rand, the bestselling novelist, was having none of it. For her, human beings were not to be used as pawns in someone else's political or economic game:

> Man—every man—is an end in himself, not a means to the ends of others; he must live for his own sake, neither sacrificing himself to others nor sacrificing others to himself; he must work for his rational self-interest, with the achievement of his own happiness as the highest moral purpose of his life.[10]

In Rand's best-known work, *Atlas Shrugged* (1957), John Galt declares:

> I swear by my life and my love of it that I will never live for the sake of another man, nor ask another man to live for mine.[11]

With these statements, Rand emphatically rejects the notion that any individual or group should be forced to suffer for the sake of others. When she speaks of rational self-interest, she incorporates the concept of reason as a distinctive human trait, a concept rooted in Aristotle's philosophy.

In her 1966 book *Capitalism: The Unknown Ideal,* Rand included this observation:

> Foggy metaphors, sloppy images, unfocused poetry, and equivocations such as "a hungry man is not free" do not alter the fact that only political power is the power of physical coercion and that freedom in a political context has only one meaning: the absence of physical coercion.[12]

Milton Friedman, another Nobel Prize–winning economist and author, reflected deeply on these issues. In his 1962 book *Capitalism and Freedom,* he argued that freedom is indivisible, asserting that economic and political freedom cannot be separated:

> Economic freedom is an essential requisite for political freedom. By enabling people to cooperate with one another without coercion or central direction, it reduces the area over which political power is exercised. The combination of economic and political power in the same hands is a sure recipe for tyranny.[13]

Reflecting on Friedman's argument, it becomes apparent that economic freedom requires fundamental human rights, including speech, assembly, association, transit, private property, and the enforcement of contracts. These foundational rights are essential for individuals to engage in meaningful economic interactions, such as exchanging ideas, forming businesses, and moving goods and labor. Without these rights, true economic freedom cannot be realized, as individuals would lack the ability to express themselves, organize, and operate freely.

Moreover, these fundamental rights not only support economic interactions but also lay the groundwork for broader political freedoms. When these rights are safeguarded in the economic sphere, they naturally expand into a more comprehensive protection of political liberties. Thus, economic freedom, rooted in these fundamental human rights, is not just a component of political freedom but a mechanism through which political structures that respect and uphold individual autonomy can develop and thrive.

Individual liberty, of course, stands in direct philosophical and political opposition to tyranny. In his 1964 speech titled *A Time for Choosing*, which marked the beginning of his political career, Ronald Reagan introduced his view of the political spectrum as follows:

> You and I are told increasingly that we have to choose between a left or right, but I would like to suggest that there is no such thing as a left or right. There is only an up or down: up to a man's age-old dream, the ultimate in individual freedom consistent with law and order, or down to the ant heap of totalitarianism. And regardless of their sincerity, their humanitarian motives, those who would trade our freedom for security have embarked on this downward course.[14]

Reagan thereby introduced a new way to measure political philosophy: an axis that moves upward toward liberty and downward toward tyranny, rather than the traditional left-to-right, liberal-to-conservative spectrum.

Drawing on his extensive knowledge of economics, philosophy, and history, Murray N. Rothbard authored his masterpiece, *For a New Liberty: The Libertarian Manifesto*, in 1973. In this seminal work, he insists that the same moral law applies to every person and every institution, with no exceptions:

> Libertarians make no exceptions to the golden rule and provide no moral loophole, no double standard, for government. Hence, we are on the side of the liberty of every individual to

be free from aggression, whether it is aggression by a criminal or aggression by the police or by the state as master.[15]

Rothbard's many philosophical works make it clear that he seeks to eliminate aggression as if it were a plague.

Dr. Ron Paul, a twelve-term U.S. congressman and three-time presidential candidate who also wrote the foreword to this book, has addressed countless audiences on the meaning and importance of liberty. He summarized his definition of liberty as follows:

> Liberty means to exercise human rights in any manner a person chooses, so long as it does not interfere with the exercise of the rights of others.[16]

In this definition, Dr. Paul emphasizes that every person has an obligation not to interfere with the individual liberty of others.

Contemporary authors Carl Barney and Craig Biddle remind us that the only alternative to liberty is force and violence. They emphasize the need to decide how we want to live:

> Liberty is the political condition in which individuals are free to act on their own judgment and to keep and use the product of their own effort. It is the condition in which individuals deal with one another by persuasion and all interactions with other people are consensual. The alternative is people dealing with one another by coercion—by physical force. "Free" means free from physical force or compulsion by other people, groups, and governments.[17]

This passage reinforces the earlier discussions in this chapter, emphasizing choice, consent, and the absence of coercion.

On Libertarianism.org, a project of the Cato Institute, we find this definition of liberty:

> Liberty means being free to make your own choices about your own life, that what you do with your body and your property ought to be up to you. Other people must not forcibly interfere with your liberty, and you must not forcibly interfere with theirs.[18]

This definition emphasizes the absence of force against one's body or property.

The Mises Institute, whose website likely holds the world's largest collection of writings on individual liberty, defines it elegantly and concisely:

> Liberty is the freedom of individuals from outside compulsion or coercion.

You might have noticed that I always use the term "individual liberty" instead of simply "liberty." This is an intentional and important distinction. Liberty is an individual property, not a collective property. We will justify this statement by researching the scholarly work of some of our great philosophers.

Ludwig von Mises recognized that the essence of economics is rooted in the study of human action. He never concentrated on aggregate data or collective outcomes. In *Socialism* (1922), he emphasizes the centrality of the individual:

> All rational action is in the first-place individual action. Only the individual thinks. Only the individual reasons. Only the individual acts.[19]

Mises' observation lays the groundwork for analyzing the core of human interactions, focusing solely on individuals.

Murray Rothbard expanded on Mises's observation in his 1973 book, *For a New Liberty: The Libertarian Manifesto*:

> Since men can think, feel, evaluate, and act only as individuals, it becomes vitally necessary for each man's survival and prosperity that he be free to learn, choose, develop his faculties, and act upon his knowledge and values.
>
> A group or society is simply a collection of individuals. "Society" is an abstract concept that does not exist independently of the individuals who make it up. Only individuals act, and their actions lead to aggregate outcomes. The individual is a unique, autonomous being with personal rights and responsibilities, whereas society is a collective entity that reflects the interactions and relationships among these individuals.[20]

By framing liberty as inherently individual, we distinguish it from collective or utilitarian goals, ensuring that each person's rights and autonomy remain the highest priority.

Individual liberty is achieved when each person has control over their life, body, and property. Equally crucial is the need for each individual to take responsibility for their own decisions and actions.

Our intellectual journey from ancient Greece through the twentieth century has provided the details and definitions necessary for us to answer Bastiat's question. What, then, is liberty? The common theme among the authors and works discussed above is that individual liberty is defined as the absence of coercion against individuals and their property.

With this answer, we have defined individual liberty, the fundamental principle that nurtures human flourishing. In the next chapter, we will examine the meaning behind another essential concept: "the absence of coercion."

2

THE ABSENCE OF COERCION

In Chapter 1, we established, with a series of basic and introductory arguments, that the most convincing definition of individual liberty is "the absence of coercion." In this chapter, we will build on this definition by gaining a deeper understanding of coercion itself and by drawing on additional insights from influential thinkers.

Without a clear understanding of coercion, it's easy to get lost in the details of political debates. You'll encounter arguments that try to justify or conceal coercion, which can be frustrating. But you can avoid this issue by recognizing coercion for what it is.

After defining coercion, we'll explore how it undermines individual liberty. You'll read a range of quotations from various thinkers discussing the relationship between liberty and coercion. When reading each quotation, consider how it supports or relates to our definition: "Individual liberty is the absence of coercion."

It is, of course, essential to understand what we mean when we use the term "coercion." Murray N. Rothbard provides a clear and concise definition of coercion in his 1962 treatise, *Man, Economy, and State*:

Coercion is the invasive use of physical violence or the threat thereof against someone else's person or (just) property.

This is an intentionally narrow definition that limits coercion to actual or threatened physical violence against person or property. This definition can be broken down into its primary components:

1. "Invasive use of physical violence": This refers to an act of aggression in which physical force is used in a way that intrudes upon someone's bodily autonomy or personal space. It involves actions that directly harm an individual's body.

2. "Or the threat thereof": The threat of violence can be just as coercive as actual physical violence. A person doesn't need to experience physical harm to be coerced; the mere threat of it can compel someone to act against their will.

3. "Or (just) property": The inclusion of "just property" indicates that coercion also encompasses acts of violence or threats against a person's possessions or assets. This could involve threats to destroy, damage, or take property unless certain demands are met. Property here is considered an extension of the individual, and violence against property is viewed as indirect violence against the person. The addition of the qualifying term "just" highlights that the property in question is legitimate or rightfully owned by the person, and that person has a moral or legal claim to ownership. This is an important distinction because violence or threats of violence against unjustly held property might not be considered coercion.

With this concise definition of coercion in place, we can now examine the interplay between coercion and individual liberty.

Because individual liberty has not been the norm in human history, it can be hard for us to conceive what it would look like in practice. Leonard E. Read discussed this problem in his essay "Students of Liberty", published in 1950:[21]

Let it be said that this is a subject not easily mastered. Liberty—the absence of coercion or violence—is not readily comprehended. Relatively few among those who have lived on this earth have been able to visualize any order in society, or any progress by those who compose it, except as the will of some has been imposed on the actions of others.

History, for the most part, is a record of violence. Present-day talk and writing—history in the making—for the most part is an argument for the rearrangement of the rules of violence. An appreciation that progress is possible only when human energy is freed of restraint, has been gained by but few men.

The reason for this difficulty in understanding liberty is that liberty, like truth, is an object of infinite pursuit, a quest without end, ever. Liberty does not lend itself to objective definition except to say that liberty is the absence of its opposites—restraint or coercion. These, to some degree, can be observed and talked about descriptively.

Once the reliance on self is removed, once the responsibility for a portion of our being has been assumed by another—be that other a person, a set of persons, or the police force—we cease to think about or apply our ingenuity to the activities thus transferred. When the agency to which the transfer is made is the state, an agency of coercion, is it any wonder that creative thought diminishes to near non-existence? Creative thought is abandoned by man as a free and thus a creative agent, and assumed by man as an agent of coercion. Coercion, by its nature, is incapable of creativeness. One minus one plus zero equals zero![ii] Understanding lib-

---

[ii] When he says, "One minus one plus zero equals zero," Read is using a mathematical metaphor to emphasize that coercion (the "minus one") only negates what already exists (the creative or productive efforts of individuals) and adds nothing new (the "plus zero"). In this sense, coercion does not generate wealth, innovation, or positive outcomes; instead, it stifles them. Only in a free society, where

erty requires that we think in these lost areas, in areas where there is no longer incentive for thinking except for the seemingly unrewarding and abstract objective of replacing violence with voluntary action.[iii]

Read is using a mathematical metaphor to emphasize that coercion (the "minus one") only negates what already exists. In the last paragraph, by "lost areas," he refers to realms of thought and social organization where coercion, force, or state intervention have become so ingrained that people no longer question them.

Throughout history, there have been many students of liberty around the world working to define individual liberty. One such student was Islamic philosopher and historian Ibn Khaldun, who discussed individual liberty in his book *Muqaddimah* (1377):

> Those who, of their own free will and without any compulsion, act according to the Qur'ān and the Sunna wear the turban of freedom…

---

individuals are free to pursue their own creative and productive endeavors, can progress and prosperity emerge.

[iii] Read is emphasizing the importance of thinking deeply and critically about liberty, especially in areas where the discussion or pursuit of liberty may have become neglected or unpopular. By "lost areas," he refers to realms of thought and social organization where coercion, force, or state intervention have become so ingrained that people no longer question them. In such areas, individuals may no longer feel the need to think critically about or challenge the use of coercion, as it has become the accepted norm.

Read suggests that understanding liberty requires deliberate intellectual effort in these neglected spaces, even though there may be no immediate or obvious rewards for doing so. He acknowledges that thinking in these areas can seem "unrewarding" because it is abstract and may not yield quick or tangible benefits. However, the long-term objective—replacing violence (coercion or force) with voluntary action—is vital for a truly free and peaceful society.

For an example from Japan, Fukuzawa Yukichi's book *Gakumon no Susume (An Encouragement of Learning), Part I* (1872) defines individual liberty as the following:

> The true meaning of freedom is to act according to one's own mind without obstructing the freedom of others.

In Europe, the study of individual liberty flourished. John Locke, an English philosopher whose political thought was highly regarded by the American Founding Fathers, was an enormously influential Enlightenment thinker whose book *Two Treatises of Government* (1689) was a pivotal text in the development of classical liberal political philosophy. In this text, Locke challenges the prevailing notions of absolute monarchy and divine right, arguing instead for a government based on the consent of the governed and the protection of natural rights—life, liberty, and property.

Locke speaks about individual liberty using the same kind of language employed so far in this book:

> Liberty is to be free from restraint and violence from others.[22]

Building on John Locke's foundational ideas about natural rights and the role of government in protecting individual liberty, we turn to Frédéric Bastiat, who further developed these principles in the context of economic freedom.

Frédéric Bastiat was a nineteenth-century French economist and writer, as well as a staunch advocate of classical liberalism and free-market principles. Known for his sharp wit and clarity of thought, Bastiat passionately argued against the expansion of state control and abuses of government power. His most famous work, *The Law*, published in 1850, is a concise yet powerful critique of socialism and the misguided uses of law. In this book, Bastiat argues that the proper role of law is to protect individual rights—namely, life, liberty, and property—rather than to redistribute wealth or grant privileges to special interests. He warns against the perversion of law into a tool of plunder, urging a return to its legitimate function of ensuring justice. He also defines individual liberty thus:

> Liberty is the freedom of every person to make full use of his faculties, so long as he does not harm other persons while doing so.[23]

A century later, F.A. Hayek expanded on this insight, arguing that what made coercion wrong was precisely its encroachment on the individual's right to the full use of his faculties. He offered the following compelling analysis of the detrimental effects of coercion:

> Coercion is evil precisely because it thus eliminates an individual as a thinking and valuing person and makes him a bare tool in the achievement of the ends of another. We rob people of their moral agency when we force them to follow our plans and work towards our goals against their will.[24]

Hayek's contemporary, Milton Friedman, another economist advocating for individual liberty, argues in *Capitalism and Freedom* (1962) that economic freedom is a necessary condition for political freedom and that the two are, in fact, deeply interconnected. He contends that true political freedom entails the absence of coercion, emphasizing that the greatest threat to individual liberty stems from the power to coerce, regardless of its source:

> Political freedom means the absence of coercion of a man by his fellow men. The fundamental threat to freedom is power to coerce, be it in the hands of a monarch, a dictator, an oligarchy, or a momentary majority.[25]

Murray Rothbard, a contemporary of both F.A. Hayek and Milton Friedman, was a leading figure in the Austrian School of Economics and a prominent advocate of libertarianism. He further developed his philosophical and ethical arguments for a free society in his influential book *The Ethics of Liberty* (1982). Here, Rothbard delves into the moral foundations of a libertarian social order, arguing that individual rights and self-ownership are the cornerstones of a just society.

Rothbard critiques both state intervention and coercion, positing that true liberty can only be achieved through a strict adherence to the principles of non-aggression and voluntary interaction. His vision of society is one grounded in natural rights and self-ownership:

> Liberty is defined as "The absence of molestation of a man's just property," with justice implying, once again, ownership title to one's own self, to one's own transformed property, and to the fruits of voluntary exchanges built upon them. ... Consider the universal status of the ethic of liberty, and of the natural right of person and property that obtains under such an ethic. For every person, at any time or place, can be covered by the basic rules: ownership of one's own self, ownership of the previously unused resources which one has occupied and transformed; and ownership of all titles derived from that basic ownership—either through voluntary exchanges or voluntary gifts. These rules—which we might call the "rules of natural ownership"—can clearly be applied, and such ownership defended, regardless of the time or place, and regardless of the economic attainments of the society.[26]

Hayek and Rothbard were both students of economist Ludwig von Mises. During a lecture at Princeton University in October of 1958, at the 9th Meeting of the Mont Pelerin Society (later published as an essay titled *Liberty and Property*), Mises stressed the significance of individualism in Western civilization:

> The distinctive principle of Western social philosophy is individualism. It aims at the creation of a sphere in which the individual is free to think, to choose, and to act without being restrained by the interference of the social apparatus of coercion and oppression, the State. All the spiritual and material achievements of Western civilization were the result of the operation of this idea of liberty.[27]

F. A. Harper, a prominent economic educator, author, and founder of The Institute for Humane Studies, gave a brilliant summary of the philosophy of individual liberty at the 8th Meeting of the Mont Pelerin Society in St. Moritz, Switzerland, on September 4, 1957:

> Liberty stems from *liber*, which means "to be free." And so, the definition of liberty I would propose is this:
>
> Liberty is the absence of coercion of a human being by any other human being; it is a condition where the person may do whatever he desires, according to his wisdom and conscience.
>
> This means that to have liberty, one must be free without qualification or modification, so far as his social relationships are concerned. Nature will still impose its restrictions on him, of course; but his fellow men shall impose none.
>
> This, as I see it, is the sequence of rights which flow from the assumption of a right to life:
>
> 1. The right to life.
>
> 2. If one has the right to life, he then has the right to sustain his life with his own time and means, so long as in so doing he does not infringe on the same right of others.
>
> 3. If one has the right to thus sustain his life, he then has the right to have whatever he is able to produce with his own time and means.
>
> 4. If he has the right to whatever he is able to produce, he then has the right to keep it for any period of time—the right of private property.
>
> 5. If he has the right of private property, he then has the right to exchange it, sell it, or give it away on any terms acceptable to the recipient. No third party, be it one person or any combination of persons, has any right to intercede in the process or dictate its terms.[28]

Harper's discussion of individual liberty provides the final reinforcement to answer Bastiat's opening question in Chapter 1: "And what is liberty?" Indisputably, individual liberty is the absence of coercion.

In the first two chapters, we have examined the meaning and necessity of individual liberty. We have also established that individual liberty can only exist in the absence of coercion. In our next chapter, we will examine the philosophy and methods that allow us to live without coercion.

3

NATURAL LAW

To promote individual liberty, a framework must exist to guard against coercion—this is the role of natural law. Without natural law, human interaction collapses into primal instincts governed only by brute force.

We are born into this life naked and helpless, dependent on our parents for survival. As we mature, we come to depend less on our parents and more on ourselves. During our development, we depend on our ability to reason, to understand the world around us, and to modify it for our benefit. If we are to survive and flourish, we must be allowed to explore and create using our ability to reason. As noted earlier, Aristotle famously observed that "all men by nature desire to know."

Peaceful coexistence among human beings requires a framework that allows each individual to occupy space and control resources. Otherwise, conflict will arise as multiple people attempt to control the same physical space or objects simultaneously. This necessary sovereignty over self and property is established by natural law.

Natural law is the concept that a universal standard of justice applies to everyone. This standard, which can be discovered through reason and intuition, binds all individuals and serves as the benchmark against which human-made laws should be measured. According to this principle, there exists an eternal standard of justice that should guide our moral reasoning. This standard transcends all human authority; even the most powerful rulers are subject to it. If a king's law is unjust by the principles of natural law, then natural law prevails. This higher law, to which we must adhere morally, holds greater significance than any legislation crafted by lawmakers. Without a foundation in natural law, laws become arbitrary, oppressive, and disconnected from principles of justice and human rights.

Most importantly, natural law predates government. Frédéric Bastiat explained this in his book *The Law* (1850):

> Life, liberty, and property do not exist because men have made laws. On the contrary, it was the fact that life, liberty, and property existed beforehand that caused men to make laws in the first place.[29]

You may be wondering, how are these universal standards of justice discovered? Several methods are presented by various philosophers:

> Saint Thomas Aquinas concluded that "good is to be done and pursued, and evil avoided." From that self-evident rule, he reasons outward, asking what goods our rational-animal nature tends toward (life, procreation, knowledge, sociability, etc.).

> John Locke treats every human as a free and equal "workmanship" of God. Because no one has a natural authority over another, pure practical reason tells us that each must respect the life, liberty, and property of all. The "law of nature," therefore, is a rule of reciprocal restraint that reason can formulate without appealing to any enacted statute.

> John Finnis sets aside abstract theory and asks: What ends do people inevitably recognize as worth having for their own sake? Careful introspection, he argues, reveals seven such

basic goods—life, knowledge, play, aesthetic experience, friendship, practical reason, and religion.[iv]

Of course, the concept of natural law has also had its share of critics. In his 1795 essay "Anarchical Fallacies—a critique of the French Declaration of the Rights of Man and of the Citizen," Jeremy Bentham declared that "natural and inalienable rights" were "rhetorical nonsense ... nonsense upon stilts."[v]

Natural law has also been criticized by postmodernist philosophers, who question the authority and foundations of claims to universal truth. They argue that language plays a crucial role in shaping culture and even our understanding of reality.

Yet the concept of natural law cannot be dismissed as mere nonsense or a private delusion derived from linguistic interpretations. Instead, it is a discipline aimed at identifying the moral constants that enable human flourishing and the creation of just laws. Natural law offers a general consensus on core principles that define a fulfilling, purposeful, and moral life, as well as procedural standards for evaluating laws, thereby refuting claims of subjectivity.

The existence of natural law is borne out by empirical observation. Across cultures and eras, humans display strikingly consistent patterns of moral belief and behavior. Anthropologists have documented

---

[iv]   John Finnis (b. 1940) is an Australian-born legal philosopher best known for revitalizing natural law theory in the late twentieth century. He taught at the University of Oxford as Professor of Law and Legal Philosophy from 1989 to 2010 (now Emeritus) and has been a long-time faculty member at Notre Dame Law School in the United States.

[v]   Jeremy Bentham (4 February 1747 – 6 June 1832) was an English philosopher, jurist, and social reformer regarded as the founder of the modern utilitarianism philosophy. According to utilitarianism, an action is right if it tends to promote happiness or pleasure and wrong if it tends to produce unhappiness or pain, not just for the performer of the action but also for everyone else affected by it. The philosophy of utilitarianism is summarized with the slogan "the greatest happiness for the greatest number."

hundreds of universal human traits across all societies studied. Among these are explicit moral rules, including prohibitions against murder, rape, incest, assault, and robbery, as well as praise for promise-keeping, recognition of private property, and admiration for fairness.

Although natural law has at times been derived from divine revelation, Murray Rothbard suggests that reason alone is sufficient to establish it:

> The natural law philosopher maintains that man can attain knowledge of the basic principles of morality and justice by the use of his reason, without relying on arbitrary "faith," "intuition," or "revelation."[30]

The Romans popularized the idea of natural law, though its roots can be traced even further back to the Greeks, particularly in Plato's philosophy. Plato's concept of the Form of Justice holds that justice is an eternal and perfect ideal, discoverable through rational thought, while human laws are imperfect attempts to reflect that ideal. Natural law continued to be developed throughout the early ages of Western civilization and into the modern world.

During the Enlightenment, John Locke had much to say about natural law and how it should guide our behavior toward ourselves and one another:

> But though this be a state of liberty, yet it is not a state of license: though man in that state have an uncontrollable liberty to dispose of his person or possessions, yet he has not liberty to destroy himself, or so much as any creature in his possession, but where some nobler use than its bare preservation calls for it. The state of nature has a law of nature to govern it, which obliges every one: and reason, which is that law, teaches all mankind, who will but consult it, that being all equal and independent, no one ought to harm another in his life, health, liberty, or possessions ... being furnished with like faculties, sharing all in one community of nature, there cannot be supposed any such subordination among us, that may authorize us to destroy one another, as if we were made

for one another's uses, as the inferior ranks of creatures are for ours. Every one, as he is bound to preserve himself, and not to quit his station willfully, so by the like reason, when his own preservation comes not in competition, ought he, as much as he can, to preserve the rest of mankind, and may not, unless it be to do justice on an offender, take away, or impair the life, or what tends to the preservation of the life, the liberty, health, limb, or goods of another.[31]

Locke begins by distinguishing between liberty and license. The "state of liberty" means individuals have the right to control their own actions and property, but this right is not unrestricted. In other words, liberty does not imply the freedom to do anything one pleases (the "state of license"), especially actions that would harm others. This idea precludes the right to needlessly destroy what is under one's control.

He then asserts that the state of nature is governed by a "law of nature," which obligates all individuals to act according to reason. This law is accessible to everyone who "will but consult it," suggesting that moral truths are self-evident to those who exercise rational thought. Thus, natural law upholds the equality and independence of all human beings, meaning that no one has inherent authority to dominate or harm another ("no one ought to harm another in his life, health, liberty, or possessions").

He reinforces the principle of human equality, namely that all people share the same faculties and exist within a "community of nature." There is no natural hierarchy among human beings, unlike the hierarchical relationships that exist between human beings and animals. This equality entails a mutual obligation to refrain from harming each other's life, health, liberty, or possessions.

Locke allows one exception to the duty "to preserve the rest of mankind": justice against an offender. If an individual violates the natural law by harming others, then it is permissible to impair or take away that person's life or property to administer justice.

A century and a half before Locke was writing, a noteworthy appeal to natural law had occurred when Saint Thomas More was tried for treason. More questioned the ability of man to create laws that attempted to circumvent nature's laws. During his trial in 1535, he asked the following questions:

1. Can a temporal prince—by his own laws and statutes—make any change in the law of God and the Church, which is universal and for all time?

2. Is it right to follow the dictates of one's conscience, informed by natural law and divine law, even if it conflicts with the commands of temporal authority?

3. Can any human law or authority supersede the universal and eternal principles of natural law?[32]

Natural law serves as the foundation for understanding and defining natural rights. It outlines a framework of moral principles that distinguishes between what is just and what is unjust. From these principles, natural rights are derived. The foundation of individual liberty lies in these natural rights, which originate from humanity's capacity for reason.

Natural rights are universal and inalienable, meaning they cannot be surrendered, transferred, or taken away. Natural rights are not granted by governments, societies, or "social contracts" but are inherent in human nature itself. Examples of natural rights are the rights to life, liberty, and property.

Respecting natural rights is a matter not only of practical governance but also of moral obligation. Any political or social system that violates natural rights is fundamentally unjust and illegitimate. A just legal system must protect natural rights.

Since these rights are universal, everyone must be able to exercise them simultaneously and equally. If this is not possible, the claimed right cannot be considered a natural right. (We will return to this point in Chapter 6.)

In *The Virtue of Selfishness* (1964), Ayn Rand discusses the meaning of rights:

> Rights are conditions of existence required by man's nature for his proper survival. If man is to live on earth, it is right for him to use his mind, it is right to act on his own free judgment, it is right to work for his values and to keep the product of his work. If life on earth is his purpose, he has a right to live as a rational being, nature forbids him the irrational.[33]

In *For a New Liberty: The Libertarian Manifesto* (1973), Murray Rothbard examines natural rights and their relationship to natural law:

> "Natural rights" is the cornerstone of a political philosophy which, in turn, is embedded in a greater structure of "natural law." Natural law theory rests on the insight that we live in a world of more than one—in fact, a vast number—of entities, and that each entity has distinct and specific properties, a distinct "nature," which can be investigated by man's reason, by his sense perception and mental faculties. The nature of man is such that each individual person must, in order to act, choose his own ends and employ his own means in order to attain them. Possessing no automatic instincts, each man must learn about himself and the world, use his mind to select values, learn about cause and effect, and act purposively to maintain himself and advance his life. Since men can think, feel, evaluate, and act only as individuals, it becomes vitally necessary for each man's survival and prosperity that he be free to learn, choose, develop his faculties, and act upon his knowledge and values. This is the necessary path of human nature; to interfere with and cripple this process by using violence goes profoundly against what is necessary by man's nature for his life and prosperity. Violent interference with a man's learning and choices is therefore profoundly "antihuman"; it violates the natural law of man's needs.[34]

Thus, both Rand and Rothbard define man's natural rights as being based on reason. They are building on the Aristotelian foundation we mentioned earlier: "All men by nature desire to know." Human survival and flourishing depend on the freedom to think and act on one's knowledge. Natural rights are moral principles grounded in the nature of a reasoning being.

In summary, natural law holds that a universal and eternal standard of justice—discoverable through reason and intuition—governs all people and should guide human laws. Rooted in ideas like Plato's Form of Justice, it rejects unrestrained license and forbids actions that harm others. Natural rights, such as life, liberty, and property, are inherent, inalienable, and not granted by governments. They must be exercisable equally by all, and any system that violates them is unjust and illegitimate.

In the next chapter, we will explore your most fundamental natural right: ownership of your own body, mind, and labor.

4

THE PRINCIPLE OF SELF-OWNERSHIP

The principle of self-ownership is a logical extension of natural law and natural rights, asserting that you alone claim ownership over your life, as well as your labor (and the product of your labor, your property). No other person or group can rightfully claim authority over your life, just as you have no rightful claim over the lives of others. This principle is the moral safeguard that protects you from being enslaved.

In *The Ethics of Liberty* (1982), Murray Rothbard argues compellingly that self-ownership is the cornerstone of individual liberty. He asserts that to be fully human requires complete ownership of oneself:

> The right to self-ownership asserts the absolute right of each man, by virtue of his (or her) being a human being, to "own" his own body; this means the absolute right to control that body free of coercive interference. If every man does not have this right, then what does it mean to say that a man is fully human? If each man is not a self-owner, then this means that he is, in fact, the property of someone else—an alien despot, the "world," the collective, or the state. But if

every man is owned by someone else, then human history
is necessarily a state of unending despotism. And if each
person has a rightful master, then no person can be fully
human, because to be fully human is to be a self-owner.[35]

Owning your life enables you to experience events and activities as
they unfold through time—past, present, and future. This passage
through time is reflected in your life, your liberty, and the property
you create and acquire utilizing that life and liberty.

Losing your life means losing your future. Losing your liberty means
losing your present. And losing the products of your life and liberty—
your property—means losing a part of your past that was invested in
creating them.[36]

In *Two Treatises of Government* (1689), John Locke presents his theory
of property rights:

> Though the earth and all inferior creatures be common to
> all men, yet every man has a property in his own person.
> This nobody has any right to but himself. The labor of his
> body and the work of his hands, we may say, are properly
> his. Whatsoever then he removes out of the state that nature
> hath provided and left it in, he hath mixed his labor with,
> and joined to it something that is his own, and thereby
> makes it his property. It being by him removed from the
> common state nature placed it in, it hath by this labor some-
> thing annexed to it that excludes the common right of other
> men. For this labor being the unquestionable property of the
> laborer, no man but he can have a right to what that is once
> joined to, at least where there is enough, and as good, left in
> common for others.[37]

In this passage, Locke explains that when a person applies their
labor to something in nature—such as farming land or collecting
resources—they change it from a shared good into private property.
This transformation happens because they have "mixed" their personal labor, which belongs to them, with natural resources. However,

this mixing of labor must result in a substantial transformation; for instance, pouring a can of tomato juice into the Pacific Ocean does not make you the owner of the ocean.

Another way to acquire private property is by being the first to use or claim it, a process known as homesteading. When a person invests their labor in something unowned—such as cultivating a field, building a structure, or extracting minerals—they transform it and impart value to it. This transformation establishes a rightful claim to the resource, thereby justifying the laborer's ownership of the property.

Property also includes what you receive from others through voluntary exchange and mutual consent. When two people voluntarily exchange property, both benefit; otherwise, the exchange wouldn't occur. Only they have the rightful authority to make that decision for themselves.

Rothbard believed that private property is an essential component of individual liberty. He explores the origins of private property in *The Ethics of Liberty*:

> The key to the theory of liberty is the establishment of the rights of private property, for each individual's justified sphere of free action can only be set forth if his rights of property are analyzed and established. "Crime" can then be defined and properly analyzed as a violent invasion or aggression against the just property of another individual (including his property in his own person).

> The individual man, in introspecting the fact of his own consciousness, also discovers the primordial natural fact of his freedom: his freedom to choose, his freedom to use or not use his reason about any given subject. In short, the natural fact of his "free will." He also discovers the natural fact of his mind's command over his body and its actions: that is, of his natural ownership over his self.

> As long as an individual remains isolated, then, there is no problem whatever about how far his property—his

> ownership—extends; as a rational being with free will, it extends over his own body, and it extends further over the material goods which he transforms with his labor.
>
> In contrast, the society of absolute self-ownership for all rests on the primordial fact of natural self-ownership by every man, and on the fact that each man may only live and prosper as he exercises his natural freedom of choice, adopts values, learns how to achieve them, etc. By virtue of being a man, he must use his mind to adopt ends and means; if someone aggresses against him to change his freely selected course, this violates his nature; it violates the way he must function. In short, an aggressor interposes violence to thwart the natural course of a man's freely adopted ideas and values, and to thwart his actions based upon such values.[38]

In *For a New Liberty: The Libertarian Manifesto* (1973), Rothbard evaluates the necessity of private property for human flourishing:

> If a man has the right to self-ownership, to the control of his life, then in the real world he must also have the right to sustain his life by grappling with and transforming resources; he must be able to own the ground and the resources on which he stands and which he must use. In short, to sustain his "human right."[39]

Self-ownership is an inseparable component of individual liberty. While it may seem obvious and indisputable that you own your life, many members of our society argue against your right to own private property. However, an attack on private property is an attack on natural rights and, ultimately, a denial of your right to self-ownership.

In the next chapter, you will be presented with the fundamental principle that protects life and property from coercion.

5

THE NON-AGGRESSION PRINCIPLE

We now turn to this book's most important concept. If everyone upheld the non-aggression principle, we all would enjoy a life of peace and prosperity.

The non-aggression principle is an ethical axiom that forms the foundation for the philosophy of individual liberty. The principle forbids "aggression," which is understood to be all forcible interference with any individual's person or property except in self-defense.

The non-aggression principle was first articulated in a modern context by Ayn Rand and Murray Rothbard, though its roots can be traced to earlier ideas in natural law.

Rothbard is generally credited with formalizing the non-aggression principle. He described it as the foundation of libertarian ethics, arguing that the initiation of force or coercion against another individual's person or property is inherently illegitimate. In his works, particularly *For a New Liberty: The Libertarian Manifesto* and *The Ethics of Liberty*, Rothbard outlined the case for the non-aggression principle as the moral foundation for a free society, emphasizing absolute property rights and self-ownership. He stated this fundamental principle in one sentence:

> No man or group of men may aggress against the person or property of anyone else.

Although Rothbard provided the clearest articulation of the non-aggression principle, the concept is also closely associated with Ayn Rand's philosophy of Objectivism. She argued that the use or threat of force is immoral, as it violates the autonomy of individuals. Rand's belief in a "ban on physical force" in human relations provided an intellectual backdrop for the development of the non-aggression principle:[40]

> No man may initiate the use of physical force against others. … Men have the right to use physical force only in retaliation and only against those who initiate its use.

These versions of the non-aggression principle are often viewed as a restatement of Herbert Spencer's law of equal freedom, which was formulated over a century earlier in his book *Social Statics* (1851):

> Every man has freedom to do all that he wills, provided he infringes not the equal freedom of any other man.[41]

The law of equal freedom, the principle of self-ownership, and the non-aggression principle all define protected boundaries around each individual. These boundaries typically encompass not only a person's mind and body but also their legitimately acquired external property. Within these boundaries, individuals are entitled to full freedom from coercive interference by others, with each person's liberty limited only by the similar rights of others.

Philosophy professor Roderick T. Long argues that applying the non-aggression principle to human interactions reveals a key distinction: When we resort to coercion instead of persuasion, we abandon our humanity and behave like beasts:

> If we are rational creatures, then we must adopt the view that we will not initiate violence against other people and instead deal with others on the basis of reason and persuasion.

> The virtue of justice defines the appropriate human attitude toward violence. A maximally human life will give central place to distinctively human faculty of reason; and one's life more fully expresses this faculty to the extent that one deals with others through reason and persuasion rather than through violence and force. To choose cooperation over violence is to choose a human mode of existence over a bestial one. Hence the virtuous person will refrain from initiating coercion against others.[42]

In *The Machinery of Freedom: Guide to a Radical Capitalism* (1973), economist David D. Friedman expresses his opinion on the use of force:

> The direct use of physical force is so poor a solution to the problem of limited resources that it is commonly employed only by small children and great nations.[43]

The non-aggression principle establishes a foundation for peaceful coexistence, individual autonomy, and voluntary cooperation, which are essential for personal development and social progress. By prohibiting the initiation of force or coercion against others, the non-aggression principle ensures that individuals are free to pursue their goals, express their creativity, and make choices that align with their values, without fear of interference. This freedom encourages innovation, trade, and collaboration, which contributes to the advancement of civil society.

When individuals are protected from aggression, they can focus on productive activities, build mutually beneficial relationships, and create wealth, all of which contribute to overall well-being. The non-aggression principle promotes respect for individual liberty and individual rights, establishing trust and stability within a community. This, in turn, reduces conflict and allows people to thrive.

In summary, by upholding the non-aggression principle, we can create a society free from coercion—which will promote individual liberty. This safeguards self-ownership and natural rights, allowing us to flourish in a society that never infringes upon life, liberty, or property.

In the next chapter, we'll explore the final component of the philosophy of liberty: "rights." The discussion may seem obscure at first, but with your careful consideration, its significance will become clear.

6

NEGATIVE RIGHTS AND POSITIVE RIGHTS

Political discussions often include the term "rights." Before we can make a meaningful and persuasive contribution to these discussions, we must first have a clear definition of "rights."

In his 1974 essay "Private Property and Collective Ownership," James A. Sadowsky, S.J., concisely defines rights:

> Lest there be any confusion, it would be well to define exactly the manner in which we are employing the term "right." When we say that one has the right to do certain things, we mean this and only this: that it would be immoral for another, alone or in combination, to stop him from doing this by the use of physical force or the threat thereof.[44]

Sadowsky's definition is based on morality. It would be immoral for someone to steal from me an item of property that I had justly acquired, as that would violate my right to property. Likewise, it would be immoral for someone to murder me, as that would destroy my right to life.

Rights can be divided into two categories: negative rights and positive rights. The term "negative rights" may seem to imply that those rights are undesirable, while "positive rights" sound like something beneficial. However, in this context, "negative" and "positive" do not denote value judgments about the rights themselves.

A negative right imposes no obligation on you to take any action. Instead, it demands that you refrain from certain actions—e.g., do not steal, do not cause physical harm. My right to life, for example, does not require you to bring me food, build me a house, or buy me a kidney dialysis machine if I should ever need one. My right to life means simply that you shall not deprive me of my life.

Likewise, my right to property does not obligate you to provide me with property. It means simply that you will not steal my legitimately acquired property. We may say that my right to property tells us not so much what I may properly do but rather what others may not properly do to me. In short, it is fundamentally a right not to be interfered with.

Negative rights do not demand anything from others except that they refrain from interfering with you. The inclusion of "not" in these statements reflects their negative nature. Negative rights protect your freedom to live and enjoy your property without external intrusion.

In contrast, positive rights do impose an obligation on people to provide certain benefits to others. Unlike negative rights, which require others only to refrain from interfering with you, positive rights necessitate that others take action on your behalf.

For instance, the right to healthcare is a positive right because it obliges others to provide you with healthcare services. When someone claims a right to healthcare, they mean that others, such as doctors, must allocate their time and resources to fulfill this right. Thus, positive rights involve compelling others to act—often through the use of force or coercion.

Positive rights—such as the rights to food, to shelter, to healthcare, to education, and to earn a living wage—require others to provide services or resources. This, in turn, necessitates enforcement and, potentially, the use of coercion to ensure compliance.

As is likely evident from these definitions, there is an inherent conflict between positive and negative rights. If someone claims a positive right to healthcare, that claim infringes upon others' negative rights to individual liberty and personal property. There is no way to implement positive rights without interfering with the ability of some individuals to enjoy their negative rights, as it requires taking resources or labor from one person to provide for another.

Positive rights not only violate the negative rights of others, but also violate fundamental principles of natural law and natural rights that we have been discussing in this book. As we have seen, natural rights are, by definition, inherent to all human beings simply by virtue of their being human and possessing the ability to reason. Since these rights are universal, everyone must be able to exercise them simultaneously and equally. If this is not possible, the claimed right cannot be considered a "natural" right.

For example, the right to healthcare cannot satisfy this criterion. It involves one person demanding services or resources from another, which means that not all people can exercise it equally at the same time. One person exercising this right would result in another person being obligated to provide care, rather than both people exercising the right equally.

Consider the case of two people living on a desert island. If one person claims a right to healthcare, the other person must provide it, leading to an imbalance in which one person's right overrides the other's autonomy. The person claiming the right to healthcare could offer payment to the other person for their services, but if the payment is considered inadequate, no services will be provided. The only remaining option is coercion; the first person could force the other person to provide healthcare by using or threatening violence. This contradiction illustrates why the right to healthcare cannot be a natural right, as it cannot be applied universally without infringing on others' freedoms.

Thus, the concept of positive rights must always and everywhere be rejected. Positive rights are inherently inconsistent and impractical because they cannot be universally exercised simultaneously by everyone. Enforcing positive rights necessitates the threat or use of violence to ensure compliance. As a result, positive rights cannot be regarded as natural to human beings. Positive rights, by requiring coercion, violate all fundamental principles of individual liberty.

In contrast, negative rights align with individual liberty, natural law, self-ownership, and the non-aggression principle, as they do not rely on coercion or aggression.

Some of the most frustrating discussions center on claims to positive rights. If the argument demands that one individual or group provide goods or services to another individual or group, then it asserts a positive right and undermines individual liberty. Recognizing this allows you to respond calmly and confidently—without frustration or anger—by making a persuasive case that positive rights are illegitimate and contrary to individual liberty.

Congratulations! By reading this far, you've completed your introduction to the core philosophy of individual liberty. Don't worry if you don't feel like an expert yet—this book is intentionally concise, and we've covered a lot in a short space. As was discussed in the introduction, you can use these first six chapters as a reference, revisiting topics when questions arise or when you're looking for answers and counterarguments in political discussions. (Interestingly, the table of contents of this book unintentionally outlines the fundamental principles of individual liberty. If you need a refresher, a quick glance at the first six chapter titles may help jog your memory.)

In the next chapter, we'll explore the history and key figures that helped shape the philosophy of individual liberty.

7

A BRIEF HISTORY OF LIBERTY

The pursuit of individual liberty dates back to the beginning of human history. There is a longing within all people to be free of coercion and to retain and benefit from the fruits of their labor. In this chapter, we will explore significant events and influential figures, writings, and quotations that have shaped and promoted the cause of individual liberty.

As you read on, you'll see that more than four thousand years ago, our ancestors grappled with many of the same political and economic challenges we face today. Some of history's brightest minds studied these issues and offered enduring insights. By standing on the shoulders of these giants, we can deepen our understanding of individual liberty and explore how to apply its principles in our own time.

As promised in the introduction, this chapter presents historical events that may be unfamiliar to you—some of which may even seem unbelievable. Again, all sources are cited for you to review the original materials for yourself. Many of these historical events have been deliberately suppressed to silence the call of individual liberty and nurture the pestilence of tyranny. The history of individual liberty is an essential component of the Forbidden Idea.

Our exploration of the evolution of individual liberty begins with the earliest surviving texts of ancient civilizations (3000 B.C. – 600 B.C.). We then examine the transformative ideas of the Classical Era (600 B.C. – 476 A.D.), navigate the complexities of the Middle Ages and the early stirrings of the Renaissance (476 – 1450 A.D.), and witness the revolutionary shifts of the Early Modern Era during the height of the Renaissance (1450 – 1750 A.D.). The journey continues with the groundbreaking ideas of the Enlightenment, also known as the Age of Reason (1637 – 1815 A.D.), and the rise of individual liberty in Colonial America (1585 – 1776 A.D.) and during the American Revolution (1750 – 1790 A.D.). From the pivotal transformations of the Modern Era (1790 – 1900 A.D.) to the sweeping advancements of the twentieth and twenty-first centuries, this narrative traces humanity's enduring pursuit of individual liberty.

7.1 Ancient Civilizations

Several ancient societies developed systems and practices that, while not fully aligned with modern conceptions of individual liberty, laid essential foundations for its principles. These societies introduced ideas and methods that established legal protections, property rights, the rule of law, and social mobility.

2350 B.C., Mesopotamia

More than two millennia before Christ, Urukagina, the leader of Girsu/Lagash in Sumeria (Mesopotamia, modern-day Iraq), led a popular movement that resulted in the reform of the oppressive city-state's legal and governmental structures.[45]

Urukagina's immediate predecessor was Lugalanda, who had a reputation for greed and corruption. Lugalanda seized control of the most important temples, those of the gods Ningirsu and Shulshagana and the goddess Bau. He placed them under the administration of his own appointed official, who was not, as was formerly the case, a priest. Lugalanda also appointed himself, his wife Baranamtarra, and other family members as administrators of the temples. He referred to the temples as the private property of the *ensi* (rulers or governors). He no longer mentioned the names of deities in temple documents, and he levied taxes on the priesthood.

Lugalanda and his wife became the largest landholders in the region. His wife shared in the *ensi's* power, managing her private estates and those of the temple of Bau. She sent diplomatic missions to neighboring states, and she bought and sold slaves.

Tensions between the *ensi* and the community increased. On his foundation cones, Urukagina describes the prevailing conditions for the common people:[vi] "Their boats were seized by the chief of the boatmen. Their sheep were appropriated by the head herdsman, and their fish stores were confiscated by the fisheries inspector." The "men of the *ensi*" cut down the orchards of the poor, and they conscripted workers to labor in their fields.

Lugalanda inserted his bureaucrats into all aspects of society, which Urukagina recounts as "court officials were everywhere." The *ensi* took the best land for himself and used the sacred oxen from the temples to plow his fields. The temple officials were also greedy and corrupt: They charged excessive fees to perform their religious rituals and to bury the dead. They took bribes; they levied onerous taxes, which they shared with the *ensi*; and they likewise used the temple oxen to plow their fields. Although these conditions had existed to some degree since time immemorial ("from distant days"), they seemed to become much worse during the reign of Lugalanda.

[vi]   A foundation cone is a cone-shaped stone with inscriptions. These were used as memorial stones in the construction of important buildings, functioning much like cornerstones.

The oppressive conditions were recorded on the stone tablets:

> "From the borders of Ningirsu to the sea, there was the tax collector," the tablets said.[46]

In seizing power, Urukagina claimed he was acting on behalf of boatmen, shepherds, fishermen, and farmers, and he implied he was aided by the priests.

During his reign, Urukagina implemented a sweeping set of laws that guaranteed the rights of property owners, reformed the civil administration, and instituted moral and social reforms.

He banned both civil and ecclesiastical authorities from seizing land and goods for payment, eliminated most of the state tax collectors, and ended state involvement in matters such as divorce proceedings and perfume-making (perfumes were a valuable commodity in those times). He even returned land and other properties his predecessors had seized from the temple.

Urukagina enacted reforms to eliminate the abuse of the judicial process used to extract money from citizens, and he took great pains to ensure the public nature of legal proceedings. As far as we know, Urukagina was the first ruler to reverse the growth of government power. He reduced the financial and regulatory burden on his citizens. This is, of course, the fundamental message of the philosophy of individual liberty: Eliminate coercion, and civil society will thrive.

1750 B.C., Babylon

Hammurabi, sixth king of the First Dynasty of Babylon (also located in Mesopotamia, modern-day Iraq), is credited with creating a legal code consisting of 282 laws, now known as "The Code of Hammurabi." The code includes many types of law, including criminal, family, property, and commercial law.[47] It is often cited as one of the earliest legal codes and is thought to be the first to enshrine the presumption of innocence.

Before Hammurabi's reign, laws were often arbitrary and inconsistent, dependent on the whims of rulers or local authorities. Hammurabi's code established a standardized set of laws that applied equally to all his subjects, regardless of social class, thereby limiting the arbitrary use of power. This predictability in the law provided citizens with a form of security and stability. The Code of Hammurabi begins with a prologue, which describes the time that Hammurabi first became king:

> Anu (King of Anunaki) and Bel (Lord of Heaven and Earth) called by name me, Hammurabi, the exalted prince ... to bring about the rule of righteousness in the land to destroy the wicked and the evildoers so that the strong should not harm the weak, so that I should rule over the black-headed people like Shamash and enlighten the land to further the well-being of mankind.[48]

Hammurabi's code dealt extensively with property rights, including regulations on trade, contracts, and property ownership. By establishing clear rules on ownership and commercial practices, the code provided individuals with the ability to conduct business and own property under a stable legal framework, which provided the king's subjects with the first instance of economic freedom.

1100 B.C., Samuel and the Old Testament

Yes, there are even stories from the Bible that describe the struggle for individual liberty!

In the Old Testament, Samuel was a prophet and a judge.[49] As the story is told in 1 Samuel 8 (NLT), Israel requested a king:

> 1 As Samuel grew old, he appointed his sons to be judges over Israel.
>
> 2 Joel and Abijah, his oldest sons, held court in Beersheba.

3 But they were not like their father, for they were greedy for money. They accepted bribes and perverted justice.

4 Finally, all the elders of Israel met at Ramah to discuss the matter with Samuel. 5 "Look," they told him, "you are now old, and your sons are not like you. Give us a king to judge us like all the other nations have."

6 Samuel was displeased with their request and went to the Lord for guidance.

7 "Do everything they say to you," the Lord replied, "for they are rejecting me, not you. They don't want me to be their king any longer.

8 Ever since I brought them from Egypt they have continually abandoned me and followed other gods. And now they are giving you the same treatment.

9 Do as they ask, but solemnly warn them about the way a king will reign over them."

The Israelites sought a king because they desired the security, stability, and centralized power that they believed would protect them from their enemies and give them a sense of national identity. This demand reflects a willingness of a people to trade a measure of their freedom for what they see as the benefits of strong, centralized authority.

Samuel warned against a kingdom:

10 So Samuel passed on the Lord's warning to the people who were asking him for a king.

11 "This is how a king will reign over you," Samuel said. "The king will draft your sons and assign them to his chariots and his charioteers, making them run before his chariots.

12 Some will be generals and captains in his army, some will be forced to plow in his fields and harvest his crops, and some will make his weapons and chariot equipment.

13 The king will take your daughters from you and force them to cook and bake and make perfumes for him.

14 He will take away the best of your fields and vineyards and olive groves and give them to his own officials.

15 He will take a tenth of your grain and your grape harvest and distribute it among his officers and attendants.

16 He will take your male and female slaves and demand the finest of your cattle and donkeys for his own use.

17 He will demand a tenth of your flocks, and you will be his slaves.

18 When that day comes, you will beg for relief from this king you are demanding, but then the Lord will not help you."[50]

This story has profound implications concerning governance and individual liberty. It asks whether people prefer the uncertainties of freedom or the predictability of hierarchy and centralized power. It also suggests that the cost of surrendering individual liberty may not be immediately apparent but becomes painfully obvious as the burdens of autocracy accumulate over time.

In many ways, this story anticipates later political debates about the nature of sovereignty, the balance between liberty and order, and the limits of government power. It can be seen as a warning against the allure of power and the dangers of trading freedom for the promises of protection and prosperity.

From the earliest recorded history, humanity has struggled against coercion and fought to advance individual liberty. Even the Bible contains a passage warning about the danger of trading individual liberty for the promise of security. Needless to say, the stories laid out in this section are only the beginning.

7.2 Classical Era

As civilization moved forward into the Classical Era and population centers grew, the idea of individual liberty began to take shape in diverse regions around the world. These explorations of liberty were deeply influenced by the distinct cultural, social, and political contexts of each society.

500 B.C., Taoism

Taoism, founded 500 years before Christianity, embraced many principles that align with individual liberty, prosperity, and happiness.

Its philosophical founder, Lao Tzu, included in his book, *Tao Te Ching*, advice about abolishing tyrannical institutions:

> If social institutions hampered the individual's flowering and happiness, then those institutions should be reduced or abolished.

He also analyzes how the size and scope of government hinders society:

> Government, with its laws and regulations more numerous than the hairs of an ox, is a vicious oppressor of the individual, and more to be feared than fierce tigers.

> The more artificial taboos and restrictions there are in the world, the more the people are impoverished.
> The more that laws and regulations are given prominence, the more thieves and robbers there will be.[51]

> The more prohibitions you make, the poorer people will be.
> The more weapons you possess,

the greater the chaos in your country.
The more knowledge that is acquired,
the stranger the world will become.
The more rules and regulations,
the more thieves and robbers.
If a government is unobtrusive,
the people become whole.
If a government is repressive,
the people become treacherous.
When people go hungry,
the government's taxes are too high.
When people become rebellious,
the government has become too intrusive.[52]

Lao Tzu is often regarded as the first libertarian, embodying the curiosity and rejection of tradition that would later define classical liberalism and the Enlightenment. Importantly, Lao Tzu and his philosophy are entirely independent of Western civilization and have no roots in Judeo-Christian thought; he was Chinese, and his ideas emerged from Asian traditions. Keep this in mind whenever you hear claims that the philosophy of individual liberty is merely a relic of Western civilization.

500 B.C. – 1600 A.D., Early Gaelic Civilizations

The early Gaelic civilizations of Ireland were each known as a *túath* (also spelled "tuath").[53] The *túath* was a social and political unit, often translated as "tribe" or "territory." A *túath* was a kingdom, or the land ruled by a chieftain, consisting of several extended families or clans bound together by social, economic, and kinship ties. Each *túath* operated as a purely stateless society, with no legislature, no sheriff, no police, and no public enforcement of justice.

During this time, Ireland was not in any sense a "primitive" society; it was a highly complex society that was, for centuries, the most advanced, most scholarly, and most civilized in all Western Europe.

All "freemen" who owned land, as well as professionals and crafts-men, were entitled to become members of a *túath*. The members of each *túath* formed an annual assembly that decided on common pol-icies, declared war or peace on other *túatha*, and elected or deposed their "kings." Unlike primitive tribes, individuals were not bound to a given *túath* by kinship or geographical location. Members were free to secede from a *túath* and join another, and it was common for individ-uals to do so. Additionally, two or more *túatha* often chose to merge into a single, larger unit.

During this period, the law was based on a body of ancient customs, passed down through oral (and later written) traditions by a class of professional jurists known as *brehons*. The *brehons* were not public or governmental officials; rather, they were chosen by parties to disputes based on their reputations for wisdom, their knowledge of customary law, and the integrity of their decisions.

The decisions of the *brehons* were enforced through sureties: an elabo-rate, voluntarily developed system of "insurance." Individuals were con-nected through various surety relationships, in which they guaranteed one another the rectification of wrongs and the enforcement of justice and the *brehons'* decisions.

The *túath* system gradually succumbed to English colonization and was ultimately obliterated during the Cromwellian conquest of Ireland in the mid-seventeenth century. The extensive time required for the English to conquer Ireland was largely due to the decentralized nature of the *túath* system. It offered no central government for the English to defeat and co-opt to dominate the Irish people.

The society that thrived under the *túath* system for almost 2,000 years demonstrated that it is entirely possible to have efficient and cour-teous police, competent and learned judges, and a body of systematic and socially accepted law—all without being provided by a coercive government.

427 – 348 B.C., Plato

In ancient Athens, Plato's most famous contribution is the theory of forms (or ideas),[54] which has been interpreted as advancing a solution to what is now known as the problem of universals.[vii]

Plato formulated a theory of natural law that was rooted in his belief that there exists a higher, eternal realm of Forms or Ideas, which represents the true, unchanging reality beyond our physical world. According to Plato, natural law is derived from these ideal Forms, particularly the Form of the Good, which serves as the ultimate source of all truth, justice, and order in the universe.

For Plato, justice and moral values are not subjective human constructs but objective truths that exist independently of human perception. He believed that humans should align their actions and societies with these universal principles to achieve harmony and justice.

The idea that Justice exists as a perfect Form inspired societies to judge their laws and institutions by higher principles rather than mere tradition or custom. Justice and rights are seen not as human inventions but as eternal truths that all political authority must uphold. This concept sets the groundwork for natural law theories that later philosophers, like Aristotle, Aquinas, and Locke, would develop further.

384 – 322 B.C., Aristotle

Aristotle, the Greek philosopher and polymath, accepted and expanded on natural law theory but also criticized the collectivist ideal of his mentor, Plato, arguing that the best constitution promotes the interests of each citizen—and, hence, protects individual rights.

[vii] Whether universal qualities (such as "redness," "beauty," or "justice") exist independently of the objects that exemplify them. The theory of forms seeks to understand the nature of properties, types, and general concepts that can be shared by multiple things.

Aristotle is credited with establishing the fundamental concepts of natural law. He provided a broad outline:

> Law is either special or general. By special law, I mean that written law which regulates the life of a particular community; by general law, all those unwritten principles which are supposed to be acknowledged everywhere.[55]

Aristotle also championed private property:

> We may define happiness as prosperity combined with virtue; or as independence of life; or as the secure enjoyment of the maximum of pleasure; or as a good condition of property and body, together with the power of guarding one's property and body and making use of them.[56]

Some of Aristotle's constitutional theory will sound familiar if you are an heir of European classical liberalism and familiar with the U.S. Constitution:

> He must, therefore, know how many different forms of constitution there are; under what conditions each of these will prosper and by what internal developments or external attacks each of them tends to be destroyed. When I speak of destruction through internal developments, I refer to the fact that all constitutions, except the best one of all, are destroyed both by not being pushed far enough and by being pushed too far. Thus, democracy loses its vigor, and finally passes into oligarchy, not only when it is not pushed far enough, but also when it is pushed a great deal too far....[57]

In *An Austrian Perspective on the History of Economic Thought* (1995), Murray Rothbard offers high praise for Aristotle's theory of private property:

> Perhaps influenced by the private-property arguments of Democritus, Aristotle delivered a cogent attack on the communism of the ruling class called for by Plato. He denounced

Plato's goal of the perfect unity of the state through communism by pointing out that such extreme unity runs against the diversity of mankind, and against the reciprocal advantage that everyone reaps through market exchange. Aristotle then delivered a point-by-point contrast of private as against communal property. First, private property is more highly productive and will therefore lead to progress. Goods owned in common by a large number of people will receive little attention, since people will mainly consult their own self-interest and will neglect all duty they can fob off on to others. In contrast, people will devote the greatest interest and care to their own property.

Second, one of Plato's arguments for communal property is that it is conducive to social peace, since no one will be envious of, or try to grab the property of, another. Aristotle retorted that communal property would lead to continuing and intense conflict, since each will complain that he has worked harder and obtained less than others who have done little and taken more from the common store. Furthermore, not all crimes or revolutions, declared Aristotle, are powered by economic motives. As Aristotle trenchantly put it, "men do not become tyrants in order that they may not suffer cold."

Third, private property is clearly implanted in man's nature: His love of self, of money, and of property are tied together in a natural love of exclusive ownership.

Fourth, Aristotle, a great observer of past and present, pointed out that private property had existed always and everywhere. To impose communal property on society would be to disregard the record of human experience, and to leap into the new and untried. Abolishing private property would probably create more problems than it would solve.

Finally, Aristotle wove together his economic and moral theories by providing the brilliant insight that only private

property furnishes people with the opportunity to act morally,
e.g. to practice the virtues of benevolence and philanthropy.
The compulsion of communal property would destroy that
opportunity.[58]

When sharing is coerced, it produces compliance, not virtue. True
generosity arises only within a system of private property where individuals are free to give—or not give. This makes private property not
merely an economic institution, but a moral one—a condition essential
for genuine human flourishing.

470 – 391 B.C., Mozi and *Condemnation of Offensive War I*

Mozi was a Chinese philosopher and the founder of Mohism, a school
of thought that emerged during the Warring States period. He advocated universal love (*jian ai*), meaning impartial care for all individuals, challenging Confucian emphasis on familial loyalty. His philosophy emphasized meritocracy, frugality, and practical governance,
which shaped early Chinese thought on ethics and social order. In his
book *Condemnation of Offensive War I*, he explores the irrationality of
justifying war:

> To kill one man is to be guilty of a capital crime, to kill ten
> men is to increase the guilt tenfold, to kill a hundred men
> is to increase it a hundredfold. This the rulers of the earth
> all recognize, and yet when it comes to the greatest crime—
> waging war on another state—they praise it! ... If a man on
> seeing a little black were to say it is black, but on seeing a lot
> of black were to say it is white, it would be clear that such
> a man could not distinguish black and white. ... So those
> who recognize a small crime as such but do not recognize the
> wickedness of the greatest crime of all ... cannot distinguish
> right and wrong.

Mozi exposes the hypocrisy of rulers who condemn individual violence while glorifying war, revealing their inability to consistently judge
good and evil. His critique highlights how societies punish murder by

individuals yet celebrate it when carried out by nations—showing how power and scale can distort our moral judgment.

369 – 286 B.C., Zhuangzi and *The Zhuangzi*

Zhuang Zhou, also known as Zhuangzi, was the author of the self-titled book *The Zhuangzi*, one of the foundational texts of Taoism. The Chinese philosopher's dissertations are the first known explorations into the concept of "spontaneous order," a notion popularized in the twentieth century by economist and philosopher F.A. Hayek:

> There has been such a thing as letting mankind alone; there has never been such a thing as governing mankind [with success]. In fact, the world simply does not need governing; in fact, it should not be governed.[59]

He revealed his inclinations toward individual liberty in short, witty statements:

> Good order results spontaneously when things are let alone.

> A petty thief is put in jail. A great brigand becomes a ruler of a State.

Zhuangzi believed that society could function well without rulers. True peace and order, he argued, arise naturally when people are left to themselves. He saw government as often little more than a criminal enterprise disguised by titles and rituals to appear legitimate. Unlike other Chinese thinkers of his time, who trusted strict laws or moralizing rulers to create harmony, Zhuangzi held that real harmony comes only when people are free from control.

106 – 43 B.C., Cicero and Natural Law

Cicero was a Roman statesman, lawyer, scholar, philosopher, and "academic skeptic" who, during the chaotic middle period of the first century B.C., championed natural law and republican government.

In a period marked by civil wars and the dictatorship of Julius Caesar, Cicero stated his case for natural law in his book *De Officiis* (On Duties):

> If nature prescribes that one man should want to consider the interests of another, whoever he may be, for the very reason that he is a man, it is necessary, according to the same nature, that what is beneficial to all is something common. If that is so, then we are all constrained by one and the same law of nature; and if that is also true, then we are certainly forbidden by the law of nature from acting violently against another person.[60]

In his book *De Legibus* (The Laws, written between 52 and 43 B.C.), Cicero argued that "howsoever one defines man, the same definition applies to us all,"[61] and articulated the idea of a universal legal order. Those ideas, both directly and indirectly, deeply influenced the tradition of natural law.

Law is not merely a product of government decree; it arises from human nature and applies equally to all. A single law of nature binds everyone. Justice is not relative or culture-specific; it reflects principles that hold true across all societies. Since human nature is the same everywhere, law must be grounded in that common foundation, not in the whims of rulers or the traditions of any one community.

56 – 120 A.D., Tacitus and *The Annals of Imperial Rome*

Tacitus was a Roman historian and politician. His writings are considered some of the greatest sources of historical knowledge about the early Roman Empire, providing detailed narratives, insightful critiques, and a perspective that often questioned the morality and stability of imperial power. He presented this insight in his book *The Annals of Imperial Rome*:

> The more corrupt the state, the more numerous the laws.[62]

When a state becomes corrupt, rulers multiply laws not to serve justice but to conceal their wrongdoing and tighten control. More laws don't necessarily bring more justice; instead, they produce less individual liberty and more tyranny. As morality and virtue decline, governments try to replace character and freedom with coercion and regulation. A corrupt regime reveals itself by overwhelming society with rules—because when justice and virtue are gone, power is maintained through control, not principle, which deepens oppression.

312 A.D., Constantine and the Solidus

Roman emperor Constantine I introduced an influential gold coin: the gold solidus. It became a cornerstone of Byzantine and European economies for over seven centuries, and it was sometimes referred to as the "bezant" in Western Europe.

The solidus was created to stabilize the economy, replacing the increasingly debased aureus (another Roman gold coin). It was minted at key mints across the empire, such as Constantinople, Rome, and Antioch.

Weighing about 4.5 grams of pure gold, the solidus became the foundation of Roman and Byzantine currencies because of its reliability in weight and purity, which never changed throughout the entire time of its circulation. This stable and reliable currency stimulated an expansion of commerce and prosperity.

Money serves three classic functions: a medium of exchange, a unit of account, and a store of value. It's the store of value that makes money more than a simple token—it allows people to save today and spend tomorrow with confidence. When money is stable, it protects savings, ensures fair trade, and fosters trust. It links present efforts with future plans, enabling families to prepare, businesses to invest, and societies to build lasting wealth.

Beyond a mere economic instrument, stable money is a moral commitment. It guarantees that what you earn honestly today retains its worth tomorrow. When money is weakened through inflation or debasement, that promise is broken. It becomes a hidden tax that punishes savers and rewards the powerful, quietly shifting wealth from the many to the few. In short, inflation or debasement of money is a violation of property rights.

354 – 430 A.D., Saint Augustine of Hippo

Saint Augustine of Hippo was a significant Christian theologian and philosopher whose writings have profoundly shaped Western Christianity and philosophy. Born in Tagaste (present-day Algeria), Augustine was raised by a Christian mother, Saint Monica, and a pagan father, Patricius. His early years were marked by a search for truth, leading him to study rhetoric and philosophy in Carthage.

Augustine described his internal conflict with leaving behind his previous indulgent lifestyle. In Book 8 of *Confessions*, he famously expresses a prayer-like sentiment: "Grant me chastity and continence, but not yet." This captures the tension between his intellectual conviction about the truth of Christianity and his lingering attachment to worldly pleasures.

After converting to Christianity, he returned to North Africa and was ordained a priest, eventually becoming the Bishop of Hippo. (Hippo Regius, an ancient city located in what is now Annaba, Algeria, was a thriving Roman port city situated in the North African province of Numidia.) He spent the rest of his life writing extensively on theology, philosophy, and pastoral care. His works—including *Confessions*, a profound spiritual autobiography, and *The City of God*, which addresses the relationship between the divine and secular realms amidst the decline of the Roman Empire—remain foundational to Christian thought.

Augustine did not subscribe to a theory of the "divine right" of rulers, nor did he believe that legislation or decrees should pass unquestioned. He maintained that "an unjust law is no law at all." To Augustine, government was, at best, a necessary evil that only grows more evil the bigger it becomes. In *The City of God*, he questioned the legitimacy of government itself:

Justice being taken away, then, what are kingdoms but great robberies? For what are robberies themselves but little kingdoms? The band itself is made up of men; it is ruled by the authority of a prince, it is knit together by the pact of the confederacy, the booty is divided by the law agreed on. If, by the admittance of abandoned men, this evil increases to such a degree that it holds places, fixes abodes, takes possession of cities, and subdues peoples, it assumes the more plainly the name of a kingdom, because the reality is now manifestly conferred on it, not by the removal of covetousness, but by the addition of impunity. Indeed, that was an apt and true reply that was given to Alexander the Great by a pirate who had been seized. For when that king had asked the man what he meant by keeping hostile possession of the sea, he answered with bold pride, "What thou meanest by seizing the whole earth; but because I do it with a petty ship, I am called a robber, whilst thou who doest it with a great fleet art styled an emperor."[63]

Augustine warned against tyranny and taught that rulers are not above moral law. By contrasting the eternal "City of God" with the flawed "City of Man," he showed that no earthly state has ultimate legitimacy. His ideas shaped natural law theory and influenced the American Founders' commitment to limited government.

527 – 565 A.D., Justinian and *The Institutes*

Emperor Justinian I, ruler of the Byzantine Empire, implemented a policy of separation of church and state to reduce the influence of the Roman Senate and Roman law on the church. This policy was known as caesaropapism, and it was intended to strengthen the authority of the Byzantine emperor by limiting the power of the clergy. Under this policy, the emperor was the ultimate authority in both secular and spiritual matters, and the clergy were expected to serve the state. However, Justinian's policy of caesaropapism was not a complete separation of church and state, as the emperor still maintained a great deal of control over the church.

Justinian also oversaw a codification of Roman law, which produced *The Institutes.* This document lays out the essence of legal obligation thus:

> ...to live honestly, to injure no one, and to give every man his due.[64]

By the end of the Classical Era, intellectual giants from widely diverse cultures had articulated core principles of individual liberty. They argued that law and order can exist without coercive rulers, that justice and rights are superior to custom, and that private property is essential to genuine virtue. They exposed the hypocrisy of states that punish small crimes but glorify war, and they warned that governments often resemble criminal enterprises. True law, they taught, flows from human nature itself, while corrupt rulers multiply laws to disguise injustice and tighten control. The philosophers of this era bestowed upon us these immutable truths: Power breeds corruption, stable money secures property rights, and church and state must remain separate.

7.3 Middle Ages

The fall of the Western Roman Empire in 476 A.D. eliminated the central state from its previously conquered territories. Kingdoms and independent city-states arose out of the splintered remnants.

Competition among the kingdoms and city-states promoted innovation in governance, law, and military tactics. Kings and rulers, needing the support of their populations to wage wars or maintain power, often granted concessions—such as town charters, parliaments, and legal protections for merchants—to secure loyalty and funding.

This period also witnessed the beginnings of legal protections for individuals, notably through common law in England and the early development of constitutional frameworks.

The lack of central authority allowed the Church to rise as a powerful institution, but even within the Christian regions, the competition between secular rulers and the papacy created opportunities for alternative movements and doctrines to emerge.

The pursuit of knowledge and the competition between regions sparked an era of intellectual and creative achievement known as the Renaissance.

1215, The Magna Carta

After losing the Battle of Bouvines in northern France in 1214, King John of England (1166–1216) was forced by his rebellious nobles to recognize a long list of liberties that the monarchy henceforth had to respect. These became known as the "traditional rights of Englishmen," also known as the Magna Carta.[65]

While the Magna Carta contains sixty-three clauses that address a variety of feudal issues, several key principles were significant in the advancement of individual liberty:

Rule of Law

The Magna Carta established that the king and his government were not above the law. This principle, encapsulated in Clause 39, stated: "No free man shall be seized or imprisoned, or stripped of his rights or possessions, or outlawed or exiled, or deprived of his standing in any other way, nor will we proceed with force against him, or send others to do so, except by the lawful judgment of his equals or by the law of the land."

This clause laid the foundation for the principle that the law is supreme over all individuals, including the sovereign—a revolutionary concept at the time that would influence the development of constitutionalism and the concept of a government limited by laws.

Due Process and Habeas Corpus

By asserting that no one could be deprived of liberty or property without "the lawful judgment of his peers or by the law of the land," the Magna Carta introduced a rudimentary form of what would later be known as due process. This principle evolved into the right to a fair trial and the protection against unlawful detention, later expressed in the development of habeas corpus, a fundamental legal concept that prevents arbitrary imprisonment.

Consent to Taxation

The Magna Carta addressed the issue of "scutage" and other forms of arbitrary taxation, asserting that certain taxes could not be levied without the consent of the barons (later interpreted as consent by the broader community of the realm). This principle established the idea that the monarch could not unilaterally impose taxes without the agreement of his subjects.

Checks on Arbitrary Power

Clauses 12 and 61 provided mechanisms to limit royal authority. Clause 61, known as the "security clause," allowed a council of 25 barons to meet and override the king's decisions if he violated the charter. This was an early attempt to institutionalize the concept of checks and balances— placing restraints on royal power through mechanisms of accountability.

Protection of Church Rights

The Magna Carta protected the rights and privileges of the Church, setting a precedent for the separation of church and state. Although primarily concerned with preventing royal interference in ecclesiastical appointments, this clause contributed to the broader tradition of limiting the absolute power of the state.

Rights of Nobility and Commoners

While the original Magna Carta was primarily a feudal document concerned with baronial rights, certain clauses (such as protections against arbitrary justice) would later be interpreted as applying to "all free men," thereby planting the seeds for broader applications of individual rights and liberties.

Over time, the Magna Carta's principles were reinterpreted, expanded, and universalized. The document's significance lies in its assertion that even the highest authority must be bound by the law. This was a radical idea at the time that paved the way for modern concepts of constitutional governance and civil liberties. By establishing the rudimentary idea that rulers should be subject to the law and that rights must be respected, it set the stage for the centuries-long evolution of individual liberty and justice.

1217 – 1293, Doctor Solemnis

Henry of Ghent was a scholastic philosopher, known as Doctor Solemnis (the "Solemn Doctor"), Henricus de Gandavo, and Henricus Gandavensis. He was the most prominent figure at the Faculty of Theology in Paris during the last quarter of the thirteenth century.

Henry of Ghent did not develop a theory of self-ownership in the modern sense. However, he did defend the idea of individual liberty and autonomy, which he saw as grounded in human nature and the image of God in which humans were created. He argued that individuals had a natural right to use their own abilities and resources to pursue their own well-being, but this did not imply absolute or unrestricted ownership of oneself or one's possessions. Instead, he believed that these rights and freedoms had to be tempered by moral and social obligations, including the duty to use them in ways that promoted the common good and the well-being of others.

1225 – 1274, Saint Thomas Aquinas

Saint Thomas Aquinas was born into a noble family in Roccasecca, Italy. Aquinas joined the Dominican Order against the wishes of his family and dedicated his life to the study of Christian doctrine, integrating the works of ancient Greek philosophers, especially Aristotle, into a Christian framework. In his book *Summa Contra Gentiles* (1265), he contended that human laws cannot create virtuous men "since the main thing in virtue is choice, which cannot be present without voluntariness to which violence is opposed."[66]

Similarly, in his book *Summa Theologica* (1274), Aquinas argued that "human laws do not forbid all vices, from which the virtuous abstain, but only the more grievous vices … without the prohibition of which human society could not be maintained; thus, human law prohibits murder, theft and the like."[67]

Individuals, therefore, have a private "sphere of action which is distinct from that of the whole." According to Aquinas, this private sphere should be left to voluntary choice, although vice may be the consequence. Human laws do not make men good but rather establish the outward conditions in which a good life can be lived. Rather than prescribing a uniform goal for everyone, human laws should prescribe rules of external conduct that enable individuals to pursue their separate goals.

If conscience tells us that human laws are unjust, then such laws "do not bind in conscience," he said, and may be disobeyed.

Aquinas made a distinction between a good citizen and a good man. One can possess the virtues necessary for citizenship, such as abstaining from theft, while being morally deficient in other respects.

Aristotle introduced this distinction, but Aquinas expanded on it in ways Aristotle had not. It later became the foundation for a jurisdiction of individual liberty beyond the state's influence.

In the Middle Ages, the principles of individual liberty began to take legal form. The Magna Carta marked the first and most influential milestone. Thinkers further developed the concept of self-ownership, recognizing that laws should not dictate a single goal for all but instead set rules of conduct that allow individuals to pursue their own purposes.

7.4 Early Modern Era

This period was characterized by profound cultural, political, scientific, and economic changes that reshaped the world.

It was the height of the Renaissance, which began in Italy and spread throughout Europe. The movement promoted humanism—a focus on human potential and achievements—drawing inspiration from the enduring masterpieces of ancient Greece and Rome.

Innovations in art (e.g., Leonardo da Vinci, Michelangelo) and literature (e.g., Shakespeare, Cervantes) flourished. European explorers, such as Christopher Columbus and Vasco da Gama, ventured across the globe, leading to the discovery of new continents and trade routes, which in turn marked the beginning of European colonialism.

This period, often referred to as the Columbian Exchange, initiated global exchanges of goods, plants, animals, people, and (unfortunately) diseases.

Martin Luther's Protestant Reformation challenged the authority of the Catholic Church, sparking religious wars and the rise of Protestant denominations. The Catholic Counter-Reformation responded with reforms, including the Council of Trent and the creation of the Jesuit order.

Advances in mathematics, astronomy, and physics reshaped views of the universe, with figures such as Copernicus, Galileo, and Newton challenging traditional beliefs and laying the groundwork for modern science.

1469 – 1527, Machiavelli and *The Prince*

Machiavelli was an Italian statesman and political scientist. In his renowned work *The Prince*, he shared his insights on politics:

> That politics is about power, that politicians talk about justice as a gambit to maintain their power.[68]

Machiavelli argued that politics is ultimately about power, not moral ideals. Rulers don't invoke justice and virtue from genuine morality; most often, they are used as instruments to secure loyalty and preserve authority. Rulers use moral language and symbolic acts to justify their actions and gain the trust of their subjects. By appearing just, merciful, and virtuous, they project an image of legitimacy that inspires loyalty and obedience, even when their true motives are self-preservation and control. Public rituals, laws framed as "for the common good," and appeals to divine or moral authority all serve to cloak coercion in the guise of righteousness, allowing rulers to preserve their power while maintaining the people's faith in their rule. By cutting through illusions and exposing the realities of power, Machiavelli directly confronted the tension between morality and political necessity.

1483 – 1546, The School of Salamanca

The School of Salamanca was an influential group of sixteenth-century theologians and scholars based at the University of Salamanca in Spain. Their work, often associated with Catholic scholasticism, spanned multiple fields—particularly law, economics, ethics, and theology.

Key figures such as Francisco de Vitoria, Domingo de Soto, and Francisco Suárez applied the achievements of Thomas Aquinas (remember him from the section on the Middle Ages?) to contemporary issues like just war, human rights, political governance, and economic regulation. By challenging prevailing notions of empire, sovereignty, and commerce, the School of Salamanca helped lay the intellectual foundations for modern international law and economics. Their scholarship anticipated many of the themes later found in the works of Adam Smith and the Austrian School of Economics. They emphasized natural law as the basis of property and contracts, recognized subjective value and the role of supply and demand in setting prices, and warned against inflation through the early quantity theory of money. They argued that just prices arise from voluntary exchange, defended free trade over government controls, and tied economics to moral responsibility.

The colonization of South America prompted Vitoria to condemn the Spanish enslavement of the Indians in the New World in terms of individualism and natural rights:

> Every Indian is a man and thus capable of achieving salvation or damnation. ... Inasmuch as he is a person, every Indian has free will and, consequently, is the master of his actions. ... Every man has the right to his own life and to physical and mental integrity.[69]

Vitoria and his colleagues also developed natural law doctrine in such areas as private property, profits, interest, and taxation.

The idea that all humans—regardless of economic status, religion, or abilities—possess a right to life and to physical and mental integrity marked a dramatic break from prevailing practice. Historically, slavery and domination were widespread. The School of Salamanca challenged this tradition, advancing a bold new declaration of individual liberty.

1552, La Boétie and *Discourse on Voluntary Servitude*

Étienne de La Boétie, a French magistrate, classicist, writer, poet, and political theorist, circulated a manuscript titled *Discourse on Voluntary Servitude*. In this book, La Boétie presented radical and sweeping conclusions on the nature of tyranny, the liberty of the people, and what is needed to overthrow a tyrant and secure liberty.

His fundamental insight was that every tyranny must necessarily be grounded upon general popular acceptance. In short, the bulk of the people themselves, for whatever reason, comply with their own subjection. If this were not the case, no tyranny—indeed, no governmental rule—could long endure. Hence, a government does not have to be popularly elected to enjoy public support, for general public support is in the very nature of all governments that endure, including the most oppressive of tyrannies.

Discourse on Voluntary Servitude provides timeless insights into the structure of subjection:

> I should like merely to understand how it happens that so many men, so many villages, so many cities, so many nations, sometimes suffer under a single tyrant who has no other power than the power they give him; who is able to harm them only to the extent to which they have the willingness to bear with him; who could do them absolutely no injury unless they preferred to put up with him rather than contradict him. Surely a striking situation! Yet it is so common that one must grieve the more and wonder the less at the spectacle of a million men serving in wretchedness, their necks under the yoke, not constrained by a greater multitude than they....

> Roman tyrants ... provided the city wards with feasts to cajole the rabble. ... Tyrants would distribute largesse, a bushel of wheat, a gallon of wine, and a sesterce;[viii] and then everybody would shamelessly cry, "Long live the King!" The fools did not realize that they were merely recovering a portion of their own property, and that their ruler could not have given them what they were receiving without having first taken it from them. A man might one day be presented with a sesterce and gorge himself at the public feast, lauding Tiberius and Nero for handsome liberality, who on the morrow, would be forced to abandon his property to their avarice, his children to their lust, his very blood to the cruelty of these magnificent emperors, without offering any more resistance than a stone or a

------

[viii]   A Roman coin.

tree stump. The mob has always behaved in this way—eagerly open to bribes…

Resolve to serve no more, and you are at once freed. I do not ask that you place hands upon the tyrant to topple him over, but simply that you support him no longer; then you will behold him, like a great Colossus whose pedestal has been pulled away, fall of his own weight and break in pieces.[70]

La Boétie struck a raw nerve by showing that a small group—or even a single ruler—can control the many only with their consent. In this sense, people are responsible for their own enslavement, since no one can rule without the submission of the governed.

1559, Sir Thomas Gresham and "Bad" Money

In his letters to Queen Elizabeth I, Sir Thomas Gresham addressed the issues of coinage and monetary policy in England. He emphasized the impact of "bad" money, or debased coinage, on the economy. The primary points he made in his letters can be summarized as follows:

1. **Debasement of Coinage**: Gresham highlighted the problems caused by the debasement of coinage, a practice in which the intrinsic value of coins (the value of the metal they contained) was reduced by mixing in less valuable metals. This practice was often used by monarchs to stretch their resources, but it led to a loss of confidence in the currency.

2. **Bad Money Drives Out Good**: He observed that in a government-monopoly monetary system, the circulation of both debased and full-value coins led people to hoard the full-value coins ("good money") and spend the debased ones ("bad money"). Consequently, good money vanished from circulation—a phenomenon later termed Gresham's Law.

3. **Economic Stability**: Gresham advised that maintaining the integrity of the coinage was crucial for economic stability

and public confidence in the currency. He argued that restoring the full value of coins would help stabilize prices and improve trade.

4. **Policy Recommendations**: He recommended that the Crown take measures to recall and remint debased coins, ensuring that all coinage in circulation had a consistent and reliable value.

As discussed earlier in Chapter 7.2, "312 A.D., Constantine and the Solidus," money serves three classic functions: a medium of exchange, a unit of account, and a store of value. Inflation or debasement undermines the store of value function, violating your property rights and eroding your individual liberty. Gresham added an important insight: When multiple currencies circulate, people tend to hoard the one they consider more valuable. His insight enhances the concept that stable money is essential to advance individual liberty.

1563 – 1638, Althusius and *Politica*

Johannes Althusius was a German political theorist and philosopher whose ideas on federalism, natural law, and communal governance significantly influenced early modern political thought. Often regarded as one of the founding fathers of modern federalism, Althusius developed a comprehensive theory of social organization and governance that emphasized the importance of associations and communities, from the family unit to larger political bodies, as the foundation of political life.

In his book *Politica* (1603), Althusius argued that true political authority derives from the collective will of the people, expressed through a series of interlocking associations rather than a single centralized power. His concept of "consociationalism" promoted a decentralized political structure in which power is distributed among various societal groups, advocating a bottom-up approach to governance that respects the autonomy of smaller communities while maintaining cohesion through shared values and agreements.

Althusius's ideas resonate with themes of self-governance, local autonomy, and the protection of individual liberties within a structured society. His theories laid the early groundwork for later thinkers who would expand upon ideas of federalism, republicanism, and subsidiarity, shaping the development of constitutional and democratic thought in Europe and, eventually, influencing political theory in the United States.

1506 – 1582, Buchanan and *De Jure Regni apud Scotos*

George Buchanan was a prominent Scottish scholar, humanist, and political theorist. He is best known for his contributions to the Scottish Reformation, his role in shaping political thought, and his mastery of Latin prose and poetry. Buchanan was a tutor to James VI of Scotland (later James I of England) and one of the leading intellectual figures of his time. He produced influential works that contributed to the development of political theory, emphasizing the limitations of monarchical power and advocating for popular sovereignty.

A staunch advocate of Protestantism and a fierce critic of Catholicism, Buchanan's works often explored the nature of governance and the relationship between rulers and the governed. His political treatises placed him in the forefront of Renaissance thinkers advocating constitutional limitations on monarchy and for the rights of citizens to resist tyrannical rulers.

De Jure Regni apud Scotos (*The Right of the Kingdom in Scotland*), published in 1579, is Buchanan's most famous political work. Written in the form of a dialogue, it is a radical treatise on political theory, arguing that the power of the king is derived from the people and that sovereignty ultimately resides with the people, not the monarch. The book rejects the idea of the divine right of kings and asserts that a king who becomes tyrannical may justifiably be resisted or deposed.

Buchanan argued that the authority of kings is not absolute. Instead, it is a trust granted by the people, who are the original source of all political power. This concept is known as popular sovereignty. The book emphasizes the idea that the relationship between a ruler and his subjects is contractual: If a monarch fails to uphold his duties, he forfeits his right to govern.

For when a king becomes tyrannical and violates his task to safeguard individual rights, this means "that the whole body of the people, and even individual citizens, may be said to have the authority to resist and kill a legitimate ruler in defense of their rights." Buchanan, for the first time, presented a truly individualist theory of natural rights and sovereignty and, therefore, a justification for individual acts of tyrannicide. Thus, in a highly individualist and even anarchic view of political resistance, Buchanan stressed the following:

> It is lawful for the people to shake off whatever imperium they may have imposed on themselves, the reason being that anything which is done by a given power can be undone by a like power.[71]

Buchanan advocated for a form of government in which power is shared and checked, reflecting early ideas of constitutionalism.

The book was groundbreaking for its time, as it questioned the foundations of absolute monarchy and set a precedent for later political thinkers, such as John Locke, in advocating constitutional limits and the rights of citizens. Although the treatise was specifically focused on Scotland, its arguments had broader implications, influencing political thought in Britain and Europe for centuries. Some historians believe Buchanan's work secularized politics into an independent "political science." More precisely, he freed political theory from the religious focus of the church founders, grounding it instead in natural law and natural rights.

1590, St. Robert Bellarmine and *De Laicis*

St. Robert Bellarmine, a Jesuit priest, published a book titled *De Laicis*, which presented a position that political authority is vested in the people. He asserted that kings do not rule by divine right but through the consent of the governed:

Secular or Civil authority (saith he) is instituted by men; it is in the people unless they bestow it on a Prince. This Power is immediately in the Multitude, as in the subject of it; for this Power is in the Divine Law, but the Divine Law hath given this power to no particular man. If the Positive Law be taken away, there is left no Reason amongst the Multitude (who are Equal) one rather than another should bear the Rule over the Rest. Power is given to the multitude to one man, or to more, by the same Law of Nature; for the Commonwealth cannot exercise this Power, therefore it is bound to bestow it upon some One man or some Few. It depends upon the Consent of the multitude to ordain over themselves a King or other Magistrates, and if there be a lawful cause, the multitude may change the Kingdom into an Aristocracy or Democracy.[72]

Bellarmine argued that civil power originates in the people, who delegate it to rulers for the sake of order. Because authority comes from the people, they also retain the right to alter their form of government when necessary. This argument marked a sharp break from the belief that monarchs ruled by God's direct will, and it helped lay the foundation for later theories of popular sovereignty, natural rights, and constitutional government.

1598, Mariana and *De Rege et Regis Institutione*

Juan de Mariana, a Spanish Jesuit priest and historian, published *De Rege et Regis Institutione* (*The King and the Education of the King*). This treatise is significant because it discusses the principles of monarchical government and the rights and responsibilities of kings. Echoing themes similar to those of George Buchanan, it controversially argues that it is justifiable to overthrow or even assassinate a tyrant if they violate the fundamental rights of their subjects. This radical idea led to its censure by both the Spanish monarchy and the Catholic Church.

This book also implicitly deals with the concept of natural rights. Mariana argued that the authority of a ruler is derived from the people and that if a ruler becomes a tyrant by violating the natural rights of his subjects, the people have the right to resist and depose him. This idea aligns with the notion of natural rights, suggesting that certain rights are inherent; they are not granted by governments or rulers but are instead fundamental to human nature.

The Early Modern Era marked the rise of political philosophy as a distinct field of study. Thinkers advanced the idea that all humans—regardless of status, religion, or ability—possess a right to life and to physical and mental integrity. They argued that rulers, whether a single monarch or a small group, can govern only with the consent of the governed. They also reiterated that stable money is essential for securing individual liberty.

Concepts of federalism, republicanism, and subsidiarity began to take shape, influencing the growth of constitutional and democratic thought. These ideas challenged the foundations of absolute monarchy and paved the way for later thinkers, such as John Locke, who supported constitutional limits and the rights of citizens. Some even held that the people as a whole—or individual citizens—may resist and even kill a ruler who violates their rights. In the broader context, authority originates from the people; they retain the right to alter their form of government when necessary.

7.5 The Enlightenment

Enlightenment philosophers like John Locke, Voltaire, Condorcet, Denis Diderot, David Hume, Adam Smith, Thomas Jefferson, and Thomas Paine (many names you've likely heard before) championed reason as the ultimate source of authority and legitimacy. They advocated for foundational ideals, including individual liberty, natural rights, economic freedom, scientific inquiry, and intellectual progress. Believing in the power of rational and scientific thought to understand and elevate society, they prioritized reason over tradition and rejected superstition as a barrier to progress.

These thinkers contended that all individuals are born with inherent, inalienable natural rights of life, liberty, and property, which precede and transcend government authority. To safeguard individual liberty and prevent tyranny, they proposed separating government power into legislative, executive, and judicial branches.

The philosophers of the Enlightenment strongly supported civil liberties, such as freedom of speech and expression, and they opposed censorship and religious intolerance. They called for a society where people could speak and publish without fear of persecution, and they advocated for secularism—the separation of church and state.

Their vision included promoting religious tolerance and rejecting any religion's monopoly on truth or influence over governance. They believed that advancing knowledge and moral development would ultimately lead to a better future, and they emphasized the importance of individual entrepreneurship and economic freedom.

1628, The Petition of Right

The Petition of Right is a foundational document in English constitutional history that outlines specific liberties and rights of subjects while restricting the powers of the monarchy.[73] Drafted by Sir Edward Coke and others, it was presented to King Charles I by Parliament in response to perceived abuses of royal authority. The petition sought to reaffirm principles of governance rooted in earlier laws, such as the Magna Carta.

This petition

- demanded that taxes and levies (e.g., forced loans) not be imposed without the consent of Parliament, reaffirming the principle of "no taxation without representation."

- challenged the use of arbitrary imprisonment without cause, citing the right to habeas corpus. Citizens could not be detained without being charged and tried under the law.

- opposed the practice of forcing individuals to house soldiers in their homes without their consent, as this was seen as a violation of property rights.

- objected to the imposition of martial law in peacetime, arguing it undermined civil liberties and the authority of common law.

King Charles I initially accepted the Petition of Right to secure funding from Parliament, but largely ignored its provisions afterward.

His disregard for the petition, along with other abuses of power, contributed to the political and constitutional crises that led to the English Civil Wars (1642–1651).

1642, The Levellers

The Levellers were a political movement active during the English Civil Wars (conflicts between the Royalists and the Parliamentarians). The Royalists supported King Charles I and the monarchy, believing in the king's divine right to rule and the importance of hierarchy and tradition. The Parliamentarians, in contrast, supported Parliament's authority over the king, favoring limits on royal power and supporting the rule of law and greater representation of the people in government.

The Levellers were committed to individual liberty, democratic governance, equality before the law, popular sovereignty, extended suffrage, and religious tolerance. The hallmark of Leveller thought was its populism, as shown by its emphasis on equal natural rights and the group's practice of reaching the public through pamphlets, petitions, and vocal appeals to the crowd.

The Levellers came to prominence at the end of the First English Civil War (1642–1646) and were most influential before the start of the Second Civil War (1648–1649).

Although the Levellers were considered allies of the Parliamentarian cause, Oliver Cromwell and other Parliamentarian leaders viewed the Levellers as a threat to stability. By 1649, key Leveller leaders were imprisoned, and their ideas were suppressed. In the same year, a Leveller mutiny in the army was crushed at Burford, effectively marking the end of the movement's political influence.

With the Levellers out of the way, Cromwell consolidated power, disbanded parliament, and ruled as a dictator. The Levellers had provided enough opposition to keep the flame of individual liberty burning in England, but the darkness of tyranny returned when they were defeated.

1643, Louis XIV

Inspired by the work of Copernicus, who proved that the planets revolve around the sun, Louis XIV declared himself *le Roi Soleil*, the "Sun King," believing he was the center of life in France. He famously declared, "L'etat, c'est moi" ("I am the state"). This epic level of arrogance and tyranny produced dire consequences for his great-great-grandson, Louis XVI, who was executed by guillotine on January 21, 1793.

Louis XIV embodied the belief in the divine right of kings. He regarded all of France as his personal property, with its people existing solely to serve him. As far as he was concerned, individual liberty was a plague to be eliminated.

1644, Milton and *Areopagitica*

John Milton published *Areopagitica*, a powerful argument for freedom of religion and against official licensing of the press. Dealing with the relationship between freedom and virtue, Milton wrote, "Liberty is the best school of virtue." Virtue, he said, is only virtuous if chosen freely.

On freedom of speech, he wrote, "Whoever knew Truth put to the worse in a free and open encounter?"[ix]

Milton passionately defended the right to free speech and freedom of religion at a time when both were strictly controlled by government. His ideas were expanded on and eventually incorporated into the Bill of Rights in the U.S. Constitution.

1646, Overton and *An Arrow Against All Tyrants*

Richard Overton's book *An Arrow Against All Tyrants* argued that every individual has a "self-propriety"—that is, everyone owns himself and thus has rights to life, liberty, and property: "No man hath power over my rights and liberties, and I over no man's."

Overton's writings made him a target for both Royalists and Parliamentarians, who viewed his ideas as dangerous. He was imprisoned multiple times for his radical views, including a significant stint in the notorious Newgate Prison. Even in confinement, he continued to smuggle out pamphlets and writings.

During his imprisonment in Newgate Prison, Overton published *The Commoners' Complaint* (1647), in which he expressed his beliefs that law without equity becomes meaningless and that fairness and justice must be the guiding principles of any legitimate legal system:

[ix]   Here, Milton is asserting that truth, when freely debated and tested in an open exchange of ideas, will ultimately prevail over falsehood. He is making a case for free speech and intellectual liberty, arguing that suppressing ideas out of fear of falsehood is unnecessary because truth is strong enough to withstand scrutiny and emerge victorious in a fair contest.

He is implicitly challenging the idea that authorities need to "protect" people from dangerous ideas. He suggests that truth should not need government enforcement—it should be allowed to compete in the marketplace of ideas.

> The Law taken from its originall reason and end is made a
> shell without a kernel, a shaddow without a substance, a cark-
> esse without life.[74]

One of the most famous episodes in Overton's life involved his imprisonment alongside fellow Levellers John Lilburne and William Walwyn in 1649. This act of repression only heightened public sympathy for the Leveller cause.

Overton and his Leveller compatriots paid a heavy price for their commitment to individual liberty. Tyranny, by its nature, must crush all opposition, and propaganda must find a method to censure opposing views. Cromwell and his minions imprisoned many, but they were not able to dislodge the ideas of individual liberty.

1632 – 1704, Locke and *The Second Treatise of Government*

John Locke, an English philosopher and political theorist, is widely recognized as a pivotal figure of the Enlightenment and a key architect of classical liberalism. His concepts of natural rights, government by consent, and religious tolerance profoundly shaped Western thought, inspiring major political revolutions—most notably in America and France—and laying the groundwork for modern democracies.

In *The Second Treatise of Government* (1690), John Locke posed a fundamental question: What is the purpose of government? His answer was that people possess inherent rights—natural rights—that exist independently of government. The only legitimate role of government, he argued, is to protect these rights.

He defended the natural law tradition, asserting that rulers are bound by moral laws and cannot govern arbitrarily. "Reason, which is that Law," Locke declared, "teaches all Mankind, who would but consult it, that being all equal and independent, no one ought to harm another in his Life, Health, Liberty, or Possessions."

Thomas Jefferson was influenced by Locke's ideas, which are evident in the Declaration of Independence's reference to "unalienable Rights," namely "life, liberty, and the pursuit of happiness."

Locke believed that people form a government to protect their rights. They could protect them without government, but not as reliably or securely. And if government exceeds that role, people are justified in revolting. He asserted that natural law is universal, applying to all individuals equally:

> "A Government is not free to do as it pleases. ... The law of nature stands as an eternal rule to all men, legislators as well as others."[75]

The Second Treatise of Government is one of the most influential books on political philosophy; its ideas even heavily inspired the American Revolution.

1623 – 1683, Sidney and *Discourses Concerning Government*

Algernon Sidney, another English philosopher, wrote the posthumously published *Discourses Concerning Government* (1698), which Thomas Jefferson described as "probably the best elementary book of the principles of government, as founded in natural right, which has ever been published in any language."

Sidney's advice is timeless:

> All human constitutions are subject to corruption and must perish unless they are timely renewed and reduced to their first principles.

> No man can confer upon others that which he has not in himself. ... Equality of right and exemption from the dominion of any other is called liberty. ... He, who enjoys it, cannot be deprived of it unless by his own consent, or by force. ... A multitude, consenting to be governed by one man, doth confer upon him the power of governing them;

the powers therefore that he has, are from them; and they who have all in themselves can receive nothing from him, who has no more than every one of them, till they do invest him with it.

Every man ought to be just, true, and charitable; and if they were so, laws would be of no use....

One owes no more to another than another to him, unless for some benefit received, or by virtue of some promise made. The duty arising from a benefit received must be proportionable to it: that which grows from a promise is determined by the promise or the contract made, according to the true sense and meaning of it.

It is not therefore the king that makes the law, but the law that makes the king.

Property is also an appendage to liberty; and it is impossible for a man to have a right to land or goods, if he has no liberty, and enjoys his life only at the pleasure of another, as it is to enjoy either, when he is deprived of them.

If the safety of the people be the supreme law, and this safety extend to, and consist in, the preservation of their liberties, goods, lands, and lives, that law must necessarily be the root and the beginning, as well as the end and the limit, of all magisterial power, and all laws must be subservient and subordinate to it.

The Liberty of a people is the gift of God and nature.

The only ends for which governments are constituted, and obedience rendered to them, are the obtaining of justice and protection; and they who cannot provide for both give the people a right of taking such ways as best please themselves, in order to their own safety.

> Those who delegate powers, do always retain to themselves more than they give, they [the people] who send these men [representatives], do not give them an absolute power of doing whatsoever they please, but retain to themselves more than they confer upon their deputies: they must therefore be accountable to their principals....
>
> The legislative power is always arbitrary, and not to be trusted in the hands of any who are not bound to obey the laws they make.[76]

In the above passages, Sidney argues that legitimate political authority originates in the people, who naturally possess individual liberty and cannot give to a ruler any power they do not first hold themselves. Governments exist only with the consent of the governed, and their purpose is to secure the safety, property, and freedoms of the people. Because these ends derive from fundamental "laws of nature and God," they supersede any human law or decree—even those of a king.

He emphasizes that no government is permanent or infallible; like all human institutions, it must be periodically "reduced to first principles" so that it protects rather than destroys individual liberty. In outlining the limits of power, he explains that law is superior to the king, that property is inseparable from individual freedom, and that citizens retain a right to resist or alter a government that fails to safeguard their lives, goods, and liberties. In addition, elected officials remain accountable to those who appoint them.

Sidney's overarching message is that just rule depends on respecting the people's fundamental rights and remains valid only as long as it fulfills the primary purpose of securing their well-being and freedom.

Unfortunately, he was implicated in the Rye House Plot of 1683, an alleged conspiracy to assassinate King Charles II and his brother, James (the future King James II). Although evidence of his involvement was weak, Sidney was tried and executed for treason. His writings were used as evidence during his trial, further cementing his status as a martyr for individual liberty.

1680 – 1734, Cantillon and Inflation

Richard Cantillon was an Irish-French economist and banker, often credited as a pioneer of modern economics. His work laid the foundations for both classical economics and Austrian economics, influencing later figures like Adam Smith and Jean-Baptiste Say. Cantillon's treatise, *Essai sur la Nature du Commerce en Général* (*Essay on the Nature of Trade in General*, 1730), is considered one of the first systematic analyses of economic theory.

You might wonder why discussions of economics appear in a book about individual liberty. It is because individual liberty requires the protection of property rights, and there can be no property rights without economic freedom. Thus, we must understand economic principles and how they apply to our everyday lives. There is no economic phenomenon that has a greater impact on individuals than inflation. Fortunately, Cantillon has provided us with a brilliant observation concerning inflation that is more relevant today than it was in his time.

Cantillon introduced the concept of the entrepreneur as a risk-taker who engages in economic activity by buying at certain prices with the uncertainty of selling at higher prices. This definition places risk and uncertainty at the heart of entrepreneurship. Unlike wage earners with fixed pay or landowners collecting rent, the entrepreneur's income depends entirely on how well they anticipate and adapt to market conditions.

Earlier thinkers emphasized land, labor, and capital as the sources of wealth, but Cantillon shifted the focus to decision-making under uncertainty, presenting the entrepreneur as the agent who coordinates production and exchange. In this view, the entrepreneur is not merely a participant in but the driving force of the market economy.

Cantillon's insight remains highly relevant: Every business, from a street vendor to a multinational firm, survives by bearing the uncertainty of tomorrow's market. This explains why entrepreneurship is both risky and indispensable for economic vitality. When policymakers overlook the vital role of entrepreneurs, they often implement taxes, regulations, or subsidies that discourage risk-taking, diminish its rewards, or insulate others from failure—ultimately stifling growth and innovation. Cantillon also developed an early version of supply-and-demand theory, distinguishing between an item's "intrinsic value" (essentially its cost of production, determined by land and labor) and its "market price" (the actual price at which a good is bought and sold). When demand for a product exceeds its supply, prices rise above the intrinsic value, incentivizing producers to increase supply. Conversely, if supply surpasses demand, prices drop below the intrinsic value, prompting producers to reduce output over time.

He explained the inefficiencies of barter-based exchange, where a trade can only occur if both parties desire what the other offers. And he illustrated how money emerged to solve this challenge, later termed the "double coincidence of wants" problem.

Cantillon recognized that money, in and of itself, does not constitute genuine wealth; rather, it serves as a medium of exchange that facilitates trade. He drew a sharp distinction between "real wealth" (the goods, services, and productive resources that actually improve well-being) and "nominal wealth" (the amount of money circulating in the economy). In his view, increasing the money supply can influence prices, but it does not automatically create new wealth if the underlying production of goods and services remains unchanged.

He argued that newly introduced money spreads through the economy gradually, not uniformly or instantaneously. Instead, it enters specific channels first—such as through government spending on civil servants, the military, or public infrastructure—and eventually works its way through the broader economy. Those who receive the new money early on are able to make purchases at existing (lower) prices, giving them a distinct advantage. As these early recipients spend their new money, demand increases and prices begin to rise for goods and services—often before wages or other incomes have adjusted. By the time the later recipients access the new money, they face higher prices, reducing their purchasing power.

This sequential process means that increases in the money supply change the distribution of income and wealth in non-neutral ways, creating winners and losers depending on where one sits in the chain of monetary circulation. This insight is now referred to as the Cantillon Effect, often discussed in the context of inflation.

The creation of money and the subsequent inflation it causes is the millstone that grinds the working class into dust. Cantillon realized that not all people are hurt by this process and that those who receive the new money first actually benefit, but it is a process that diminishes the value of personal property for most individuals and, therefore, represses individual liberty.

1680, Laissez-faire

The French finance minister Jean-Baptiste Colbert asked a merchant named M. Le Gendre what the state could do to promote industry. According to legend, the reply came: "Laissez-nous faire." ("Let it be.")

The slogan was later codified in the words of Vincent de Gournay: "Laissez-faire et laissez-passer, le monde va de lui même!" ("Let it be and let goods pass; the world goes by itself.")

These quotations are the source of the term "laissez-faire," the economic philosophy of minimal government intervention in the marketplace. The core idea is that economies function best when individuals and businesses are free to operate according to their own interests, without regulation, taxation, or other government intervention.

The concept of laissez-faire means granting the greatest possible economic freedom: the ability to engage in voluntary exchange and cooperation without interference. This provides you with the maximum flexibility to make use of your labor and personal property, advancing your individual liberty.

1685, Rumbold

Richard Rumbold (1622–1685) was an English Parliamentarian soldier and political radical, exiled for his role in the 1683 Rye House Plot and later executed for taking part in the Argyll's Rising rebellion of 1685. His speech from the scaffold included this statement:

> None comes into the world with a saddle on his back, neither any booted and spurred to ride him.

Can you imagine being led to the gallows and still having the composure to make such an eloquent statement? Rumbold was telling us that no one is naturally superior; we are all equal at birth. This is an excellent reminder that individual liberty requires that no one exert aggressive coercion.

1694 – 1774, Quesnay and the Physiocrats

François Quesnay was the leading figure of the Physiocrats, scholars generally considered to be the first school of economic thinking. The name "Physiocrat" derives from the Greek words *phýsis*, meaning "nature," and *kràtos*, meaning "power."

The Physiocrats believed that an economy's power derived from its agricultural sector. They wanted the government of Louis XV, who ruled France from 1715 to 1774, to deregulate and reduce taxes on French agriculture so that poor France could emulate wealthier Britain, which had a relatively laissez-faire policy. That Quesnay had such a seminal influence on economics is more surprising, since he served under Louis XV in Versailles not as an economist, but as a medical doctor.

Once again, we find in this era of history an ardent supporter of laissez-faire economic policy. Allowing each individual the maximum flexibility to utilize their labor and property to engage in economic exchange advances individual liberty for all.

1694 – 1778, Voltaire and Civil Liberties

Voltaire (the pen name of François-Marie Arouet) was an outspoken advocate of civil liberties, and he was at constant risk from the strict censorship laws of the Catholic French monarchy. He is credited with the following quotations:

> It is forbidden to kill; therefore, all murderers are punished unless they kill in large numbers and to the sound of trumpets.

> Those who can make you believe absurdities can make you commit atrocities.

> It is dangerous to be right in matters on which the established authorities are wrong.

> It is better to risk saving a guilty person than to condemn an innocent one.

> Our wretched species is so made that those who walk on the well-trodden path always throw stones at those who are showing a new road.

Voltaire was able to convey the philosophy of individual liberty in concise, poetic phrases. Have you yet found a better criticism of war than "unless they kill in large numbers and to the sound of trumpets"?

1689, The Bill of Rights

The Bill of Rights was a landmark constitutional document in British history that established limits on the powers of the monarchy and laid out the rights of Parliament and individuals. Passed after the Glorious Revolution, which deposed King James II and brought William III and Mary II to the throne, it laid the foundation for constitutional monarchy in England. The document enumerated the following rights and laws:

The monarch cannot suspend or create laws without Parliament's consent.

Taxation requires parliamentary approval.

Free elections to Parliament.

Freedom of speech within parliamentary proceedings (parliamentary privilege).

Regular sessions of Parliament.

Protestants have the right to bear arms for self-defense (subject to laws).

No cruel or unusual punishments.

No excessive bail or fines.

The right to petition the monarch without fear of retribution.

The prohibition of standing armies during peacetime without Parliament's consent.

This Bill of Rights built on previous laws designed to restrict the actions of the king. By removing powers from the king, it advanced individual liberty for the people.

1713 – 1784, Diderot

Denis Diderot, a French philosopher and author, is credited with this quotation:

Man will never be free until the last king is strangled with the entrails of the last priest.

In Diderot's time, individuals were subservient to both the King and the Church, and he wished for a day when individuals had neither as their ruler. This quotation is an example of humor that would be considered both treason and blasphemy.

1720, Cato's Letters

Cato's Letters is a collection of political essays written by John Trenchard and Thomas Gordon, published between 1720 and 1723. These writings became a significant influence on eighteenth-century political thought. Written under the pseudonym "Cato"—a homage to Cato the Younger, a Roman statesman famous for his resistance to Julius Caesar—the letters passionately advocated for individual liberty, limited government, and freedom from tyranny. The *Letters* were collected and printed in four volumes in 1737 as *Essays on Liberty, Civil and Religious*.

Through these essays, Trenchard and Gordon argued for the natural rights of individuals, freedom of speech, and the dangers of unchecked government authority. They drew from classical natural law ideals, claiming that liberty is constantly under threat from those who seek power.

Their work resonated widely, especially in the American colonies, where it influenced revolutionary leaders like John Adams and Thomas Jefferson. *Cato's Letters* thus served as a foundation for the principles of liberty and limited government that later shaped the political ideologies underlying the American Revolution.

Here are some of Trenchard and Gordon's significant insights, presented in their original order:

Liberty allows all other blessings.

Freedom of speech is the great bulwark of liberty; they prosper and die together.

Few men have been desperate enough to attack openly, and barefaced, the liberties of a free people. ... Even when the enterprise is begun and visible, the end must be hid or denied.

Government executed for the good of all, and with the consent of all, is liberty; and the word government is profaned, and its meaning abused, when it signifies anything else.

I know not what treason is if sapping and betraying the liberties of a people be not treason.

Only government founded upon liberty is a public blessing; without liberty, it is a public curse.

Free government is the protecting of the people in their liberties by stated rules: Tyranny is a brutish struggle for unlimited liberty to one or a few, who would rob all the others of their liberty and act by no rule but lawless lust.

The love of liberty is an appetite so strongly implanted in the nature of all living creatures that even the appetite of self-preservation … seems to be contained in it; since by liberty they enjoy the means of preserving themselves, and of satisfying their desires in the manner which they themselves choose and like best.

Where liberty is lost, life grows precarious, always miserable, often intolerable. Liberty is to live upon one's own terms; slavery is to live at the mercy of another.

Civil governments were instituted by men, and for the sake of men … men have a right to expect from them protection and liberty, and to oppose rapine and tyranny wherever they are exercised.

The security of property and the freedom of speech always go together … where a man cannot call his tongue his own, he can scarce call anything else his own.

The truth is, if the people are suffered to keep their own, it is the most that they desire: But even this is a happiness which in few places falls to their lot; they are frequently robbed by those whom they pay to protect them.

The two great laws of human society, from whence all the rest derive their course and obligation, are those of equity and self-preservation: By the first, all men are bound alike not to hurt one another; by the second, all men have a right alike to defend themselves.

Government, therefore, can have no power, but such as men can give. ... No man can give to another what is none of his own.

It is a mistaken notion of government that the interest of the majority is only to be consulted. ... Otherwise, the greater number may sell the lesser and divide their estates among themselves, and so, instead of a society where all peaceable men are protected, become a conspiracy of the many against the minority.

Every man is in nature and reason the judge and disposer of his own domestic affairs. ... Government being intended to protect men from the injuries of one another, and not to direct them in their own affairs.

Let people alone, and they will take care of themselves and do it best; and if they do not, a sufficient punishment will follow their neglect without the magistrate's interposition and penalties.

Indeed, liberty is the divine source of all human happiness. To possess, in security, the effects of our industry, is the most powerful and reasonable incitement to be industrious: And to be able to provide for our children, and to leave them all that we have, is the best motive to beget them. But where property is precarious, labor will languish. The privileges of thinking, saying and doing what we please, and of growing rich as we can, without any other restriction, than that by all this we hurt not the public, nor one another, are the glorious privileges of liberty; and its effects, to live in freedom, plenty, and safety.

Choose whether you will be freemen or vassals; whether you will spend your own money and estates, or let others worse than you spend them for you: Methinks the choice should be easy.

Government is only the union of many individuals for their common defense.

The product of the whole people's labor and sustenance is not suffered to be devoured by a few.

Political power ... This is the greatest trust that can be committed by men to one another; and contains in it all that is valuable here on earth, the lives, the properties, the liberties, of your countrymen. ... This great trust, Gentlemen, is not committed to you for your own sakes but for the protection, security, and happiness of those whom you represent.

These quotations are a small sample of the passionate message of individual liberty conveyed by *Cato's Letters*, which were an essential component of the independence movement in Colonial America.

1727 – 1781, Turgot and Reform

Anne Robert Jacques Turgot, Baron de l'Aulne, commonly known as Turgot, was a French economist, statesman, and philosopher, best known for his role as an early advocate of economic liberalism and free-market policies. His ideas significantly influenced both classical economics and revolutionary thought in France and beyond.

Turgot was an advocate of laissez-faire economics, arguing that economies function best with minimal government interference. He believed that free trade and competition were essential to prosperity, and he opposed state monopolies and heavy regulations. He conveyed these beliefs in a single sentence:

> In all matters of commerce, the sole function of government is to secure freedom of trade, to suppress monopolies—in short, to ensure that no artificial advantage be given to one citizen over another.

Influenced by the Physiocrats, Turgot expanded on their ideas by emphasizing the importance of capital and innovation. He supported the notion that society progresses through stages, from barter- to money-based economies, which foreshadowed later economic theories.

Turgot served as Controller-General of Finances under King Louis XVI (1774–1776). In this role, he implemented several reforms aimed at reducing government spending and stimulating economic growth, such as eliminating guild monopolies and promoting free grain trade. However, opposition from vested interests led to his resignation after just two years.

Though his reforms were largely undone after his resignation, Turgot's ideas deeply influenced both economic theory and political reformers of the time. He formulated early versions of the subjective theory of value and the concepts of capital and interest—ideas that later became central to the Austrian School of Economics. In contrast to the mercantilists, who viewed wealth as stemming from hoarded gold or government privilege, Turgot argued that true wealth arises from productive activity, particularly agriculture and enterprise. He showed how savings and investment fuel economic growth, laying the foundation for modern capital theory. His work foreshadowed the ideas of later classical economists like Adam Smith, particularly in promoting the division of labor and free markets.

Turgot understood that the policies in place restricted the individual liberty of French citizens, so he worked to remove those restrictions on economic activity. His reforms were short-lived, but they set the stage for future like-minded thinkers to advance individual liberty.

1743 – 1794, Condorcet and *Sketch for a Historical Picture of the Progress of the Human Mind*

Marie Jean Antoine Nicolas de Caritat, Marquis of Condorcet, known simply as Condorcet, was a French philosopher, mathematician, economist, and political thinker. He is best known for his ideas on progress, human rights, and democracy, as well as his role in advocating gender equality and abolitionism.

Condorcet believed in the indefinite improvement of society through reason, science, and education. His most famous work, *Sketch for a Historical Picture of the Progress of the Human Mind* (1795), presents an optimistic view of human development and argues that humanity could continue improving morally and intellectually. He tempered this optimism with a condition, the necessity of individual liberty:

> All that we are and all that we have comes from the improvement of our reason, and its development depends upon freedom.[77]

He supported universal suffrage and fought for the inclusion of women and minorities in political life. His progressive ideas on equality and democracy were ahead of his time and would influence later democratic movements.

During the French Revolution, Condorcet championed a republic grounded in law, reason, and equality while rejecting absolute or dictatorial power. He sought reform through rational principles rather than violent upheaval. A staunch advocate of universal human rights, he defended freedom of speech, religious liberty, and political participation, and he was among the first to call for women's suffrage. He saw education as essential to both liberty and equality, envisioning a society advancing through science, reason, and moral progress—a distinctly Enlightenment vision.

Politically, Condorcet aligned with the Girondins, who favored reform and republican government but opposed the radical centralization and violence of the Jacobins. He condemned Robespierre's Reign of

Terror, warning that fear and executions would destroy individual liberty rather than safeguard it. In place of mob rule or authoritarian control, Condorcet promoted a democratic republic guided by reason and natural rights.

After falling out of favor with the radical Jacobins, Condorcet was arrested and imprisoned in 1794. He died under mysterious circumstances in prison, likely by suicide, though some accounts suggest he may have been poisoned because of his opposition to the Jacobins and Robespierre.

1756 – 1836, Godwin and *An Enquiry Concerning Political Justice*

William Godwin was a British writer, philosopher, and political thinker. His works challenged traditional power structures and promoted rationality, individualism, and the progressive evolution of society through reason and ethical behavior. Godwin's philosophical ideas emphasized the perfectibility of human beings and the idea that social institutions, particularly the government, impeded moral and intellectual progress.

In his landmark work, *An Enquiry Concerning Political Justice* (1793), Godwin argued that government inherently corrupts people by fostering dependency, inequality, and violence. He proposed that a society organized around voluntary cooperation, rather than coercive institutions, would better promote individual liberty and social harmony. This book positioned Godwin as a radical voice, making him a prominent figure among Enlightenment thinkers who influenced later movements toward socialism, anarchism, and liberalism.

Godwin also had a profound impact on literature. He authored the influential novel *Things as They Are; or, The Adventures of Caleb Williams* (1794), which explored themes of tyranny, justice, and personal freedom. His radical philosophy of liberty, justice, and human perfectibility had a significant influence on the Romantic writers of his time.

His daughter, Mary Shelley, wove these themes into her novel *Frankenstein*, exploring the moral dilemmas of unchecked ambition, the responsibilities that come with knowledge, and the corruption of natural goodness by society. Victor Frankenstein's refusal to take responsibility for his creation reflects Godwin's warnings about the misuse of power and the moral obligations of individuals.

Godwin's son-in-law, Percy Shelley, carried these ideas into his poetry, turning Godwin's philosophy into a passionate call for freedom and human progress.

Through these works, Godwin's vision endured in the Romantic movement's fusion of imagination, rebellion, and moral inquiry.

1767 – 1830, Constant and "The Liberty of the Ancients Compared with That of the Moderns"

Henri-Benjamin Constant de Rebecque, also known as Benjamin Constant, delivered a lecture in 1819 that was later published as an essay: "The Liberty of the Ancients Compared with That of the Moderns." Constant contrasted two forms of liberty that shaped ancient and modern societies and argued that the liberty valued by ancient societies—by which he meant Greece and Rome—differs significantly from the liberty cherished in modern times.

For the ancients, liberty meant active participation in collective, public life. Citizens were expected to be deeply involved in political decisions and direct governance, which included duties like voting on laws and serving in public offices. This form of liberty emphasized collective power over individual autonomy; citizens sacrificed personal interests for the good of the community. However, individual liberty in personal life was limited, as ancient societies often heavily regulated private conduct and personal choices.

In contrast, Constant argues, modern liberty prioritizes individual autonomy and individual rights. This includes freedom of thought, religion, economic choice, and private life without interference from the government. Modern liberty values protection from the state and is more focused on ensuring individuals can pursue their own happiness and interests.

Constant attributes this shift to changes in society, the economy, and the sheer scale of modern states, which make direct civic participation impractical for all citizens.

1776, Smith and *The Wealth of Nations*

Adam Smith published a groundbreaking book, *An Inquiry into the Nature and Causes of the Wealth of Nations*, commonly referred to as *The Wealth of Nations*. Through this book, he claimed he was describing "the simple system of natural liberty."

A condensed description of Smith's conclusions could be described as: Capitalism is what happens when you leave people alone. He described how individuals pursuing their own personal gain in production and trade are unknowingly guided by an "invisible hand" to ultimately benefit the broader community, even if they do not intend to do so. To obtain a job or to sell something for money, each person must discover what others would like to have.

The Wealth of Nations, Book IV, Chapter II contains this celebrated passage:

> It is not from the benevolence of the butcher, the brewer, or the baker that we expect our dinner, but from their regard to their own interest. We address ourselves not to their humanity but to their self-love, and never talk to them of our necessities but of their advantages.[78]

Thus, free markets let individuals pursue their own goals in ways that also benefit others, resulting in more goods, more choice, and higher living standards than any system based on privilege, monopoly, or state control.

Smith demonstrated how specialization, or the division of labor, greatly increases output. In a free market, individuals can specialize according to their skills and trade for what they lack. This multiplies productivity, lowers costs, and makes goods more abundant, so that comforts once reserved for the wealthy become accessible to ordinary people.

He observed that when individuals act in their own self-interest—pursuing profit, better work, or cheaper goods—they unintentionally advance the welfare of others. Through the "invisible hand" of competition, private ambition is redirected into public benefit, expanding choices and reducing prices.

Every market exchange occurs only when both parties expect to gain. Unlike systems rooted in coercion—such as feudalism or mercantilism—free markets enable people to improve their lives through consent rather than force, broadening opportunities for more individuals to fulfill their desires.

While mercantilism and heavy state control hoard resources, monopolize privilege, and suppress innovation, free markets reward creativity, efficiency, and responsiveness to consumer needs, continually raising the general standard of living.

Smith offered additional insights into economic activity and political agendas:

> By pursuing his own interest [the individual] frequently promotes that of the society more effectually than when he really intends to promote it. I have never known much good done by those who affected to trade for the public good....

> Labour was the first price, the original purchase—money that was paid for all things. It was not by gold or by silver, but by labour, that all wealth of the world was originally purchased....

> The uniform, constant, and uninterrupted effort of every man to better his condition, the principle from which public

and national, as well as private opulence is originally derived, is frequently powerful enough to maintain the natural progress of things towards improvement, in spite both of the extravagance of government and of the greatest errors of administration. Like the unknown principle of animal life, it frequently restores health and vigor to the constitution, in spite, not only of the disease, but of the absurd prescriptions of the doctor.[79]

The Wealth of Nations is one of the most influential books in economic history. It challenged mercantilism by arguing that wealth comes not from government control or hoarded gold but from productive labor, free markets, and voluntary exchange. Smith explained how the division of labor, competition, and the "invisible hand" of self-interest create prosperity and raise living standards. His work laid the foundation for modern economics, inspired free-market policies, and shaped the ideas of individual liberty and limited government, which influenced both the Industrial Revolution and political reform movements like the American Revolution.

The Enlightenment set the stage for sweeping political and economic reforms, igniting revolutions that reshaped the modern world. During this era, the philosophy of individual liberty was not only discovered and refined but also widely disseminated through books, pamphlets, and public debates, inspiring people to challenge entrenched authority and demand governments grounded in reason, justice, and personal rights.

7.6 Colonial America

The American colonies became a refuge for Europeans fleeing tyranny, particularly religious persecution. Many sought freedom from economic hardship, drawing them to the promise of a new, more prosperous life across the Atlantic.

Despite the land's natural abundance, early settlers faced immense challenges. Success required relentless effort and continual adaptation. Over time, the economic and political struggles of these colonies produced a powerful expression of individual liberty that would eventually captivate the world.

1585 – 1587, Roanoke, the "Lost Colony"

An English attempt to settle on Roanoke Island (modern-day North Carolina) failed mysteriously. The colony, known as the "Lost Colony," was discovered abandoned, with no clear explanation of what happened to the original 115 settlers.

Sponsored by Sir Walter Raleigh under a royal charter, the Roanoke settlements were joint ventures, organized collectively rather than on the basis of individual private property. Colonists were expected to work together for the survival of the community and for the interests of investors back in England. Supplies and resources were pooled, and the venture's success depended on the colony producing valuable exports for England.

The colony could have failed because of a lack of productive agriculture and animal husbandry. The collective nature of the ownership of land and resources failed in similar later colonies. In contrast, the Jamestown and Plymouth colonies saved themselves from starvation and failure by rejecting collective ownership and instituting private property.

Recent archaeological excavations have revealed strong evidence that the colonists moved to Croatoan Island, now known as Hatteras Island, and assimilated into the local Native American population.

1607, Jamestown

The first permanent English colony in North America was founded in Jamestown, Virginia. The early settlers initially experimented with a system of communal living—a form of collective ownership of resources and labor. This arrangement, driven by idealism and pragmatism, quickly proved problematic, leading to severe hardships for the colonists.

Jamestown was established under the charter of the Virginia Company of London, which sought to generate profit through exploration and resource extraction.

The company mandated that all resources, food, and labor be shared by the colony, creating a common store system. All colonists were required to contribute to the communal efforts, and the output—whether food or profit—was distributed equally among all.

Under this system, the colonists were required to work for the good of the group, and food was drawn from a shared storehouse, regardless of individual contribution.

Personal ownership of land or private agriculture was not initially allowed, as everything produced was considered communal property.

Many settlers withheld their full effort, expecting to depend on the labor of others. This phenomenon is often referred to as the "tragedy of the commons."

Because labor was inefficiently allocated, food production was insufficient. The winter of 1609–1610, known as the "Starving Time," was catastrophic. Out of 500 settlers, only sixty survived until the spring. There are even reports of cannibalism during this period.

In response to the colony's failures, Governor Sir Thomas Dale implemented significant reforms. He divided land into private plots, allowing colonists to own and cultivate their own parcels. Each family received three acres of land, and they could keep the food they produced after paying a small share to the colony's storehouse as tax.

The new policies unleashed market forces, leading to a dramatic rise in food production. Over time, tobacco became the colony's primary cash crop. The example of Jamestown—where most colonists starved under a system of collective ownership—demonstrates that private property is not optional. Individual liberty depends on it, and human flourishing depends on individual liberty.

1620, Plymouth

Plymouth Colony in Massachusetts was founded by the Pilgrims. Just as in Jamestown, a common store system was implemented and food and resources were shared among all colonists. Everyone worked the land collectively, and the harvest was distributed equally. As in Jamestown, many settlers lacked incentives to work hard, leading to poor harvests and widespread starvation. Only fifty-three of the original 102 passengers survived until spring.

In 1623, Governor William Bradford divided the land among families, giving each household control over its own crops. Productivity increased dramatically, and the colony survived as a result.

Bradford reflected on the failure of communalism, observing that individual ownership served better to foster industry and hard work. The collapse of communal ownership in the Plymouth colony once again underscores the essential role of private property in individual liberty and, by extension, the need to protect property rights.

1635, Williams and Providence Plantations

Roger Williams was an influential figure who developed dissenting views on religious freedom and the separation of church and state. He was banished from the Massachusetts Bay Colony for his unorthodox views.

Williams argued that civil authorities had no right to enforce religious practices. This idea was radical at the time and challenged the colony's blending of religious and civil governance.

After his banishment, Williams founded Providence Plantations (later part of Rhode Island) in 1636, a colony based on religious tolerance. It established, for the first time in colonial America, a community grounded explicitly in freedom of religion and conscience. This was radical in a world where most colonies were founded on established churches and conformity to a single faith.

Williams believed that faith—and to a broader extent, all social and political arrangements—must be genuine, not coerced, and his colony reflected that ideal of a civil society. By refusing to let government dictate religious practice, he affirmed that each person has a natural right to follow their own conscience in matters of belief. This was an early application of the principle that individual liberty means freedom from coercion—especially in the personal sphere of religion.

Although Williams's immediate concern was religion, the model of Providence Plantations set a precedent for broader concepts of individual liberty: property rights, limited government, and respect for the autonomy of each person. It demonstrated that a society could thrive without uniformity imposed from above.

His advancement of the separation of church and state had a lasting impact on the other colonies and, eventually, the United States.

1636 – 1638, Hutchinson and the Purpose of Government

Anne Hutchinson was a Puritan spiritual leader who challenged the religious orthodoxy of the Massachusetts Bay Colony. She held meetings in her home, criticizing the colony's ministers for preaching a covenant of works (salvation through deeds) rather than a covenant of grace (salvation through faith). Her religious views and outspoken criticism of the clergy were seen as a threat to the colony's stability. In 1637, she was put on trial for heresy and sedition, and she was eventually banished from the colony.

After her banishment, Hutchinson and her followers helped establish a settlement in what is now Rhode Island, which became a haven for religious dissenters.

Hutchinson spent the remainder of her life contemplating the purpose of religion and government. She eventually persuaded her husband to resign from his office as an assistant in the government, as she had decided that all government coercion is immoral.

1641, The Massachusetts Body of Liberties

The Massachusetts Body of Liberties is one of the earliest legal codes in colonial America and a foundational document for the development of American constitutional law. Drafted by Nathaniel Ward, a Puritan minister and lawyer, it codified individual rights, responsibilities, and protections for residents of the Massachusetts Bay Colony.

The document included ninety-eight specific liberties that outlined the rights of individuals in the colony, providing a framework for justice and governance. It addressed various aspects of life—including civil liberties, property rights, family law, and criminal justice—and specifically incorporated the following individual liberties:

> No person could be deprived of life, liberty, or property without due process.

> Guaranteed trial by jury, and the right to defend oneself in court.

> Prohibited "barbarous" punishments, such as torture, unless specifically allowed by law.

> Recognized the right to private property and its protection from unjust seizure.

> Allowed colonists to petition the government and express grievances.[80]

The Massachusetts Body of Liberties advanced individual liberty by transferring authority from arbitrary magistrates to the rule of written law. It recognized due process, protected property, and framed rights as God-given rather than granted by government. It reflected the Puritan belief that liberty meant obedience to God's law, not freedom from it. Rights were protected, but only within the moral framework of Puritan orthodoxy, where civil and religious authority were intertwined and dissent was punished. By contrast, Roger Williams's Providence Plantation embodied a revolutionary idea: liberty of conscience for all and a strict separation of church and state. Massachusetts sought order through moral conformity; Providence sought peace through individual freedom.

1676, Berkeley, Bacon, and Rebellion

Discontent spread among frontier settlers in Virginia over Governor William Berkeley's refusal to protect them from Native American attacks, as well as frustration with the colony's elite-controlled government. Frontier farmers, many of whom were recently freed indentured servants, struggled with economic hardship, lack of representation in government, and restricted access to fertile land.

During this time, Nathaniel Bacon, a wealthy but disgruntled planter, emerged as the leader of a rebellion. Despite being a member of the elite, he aligned himself with the discontented settlers on the frontier. Bacon led unauthorized raids against Native American tribes and demanded that the colonial government take more aggressive action. When Governor Berkeley refused to grant Bacon a military commission, Bacon raised his own militia and marched on Jamestown, forcing the governor to flee. The rebels briefly took control of Jamestown and burned the settlement to the ground.

The rebellion collapsed when Nathaniel Bacon died suddenly of dysentery in October 1676. Without Bacon's leadership, the rebels were unable to maintain control. Governor Berkeley, with support from British forces, suppressed the remaining rebellion. After the rebellion, twenty-three rebels were executed, and Berkeley was recalled to England because of criticism for his harsh response.

The rebellion exposed the instability of relying on indentured servants who could become rebellious after gaining their freedom. As a result, Virginia's elite increasingly turned to African slaves for labor, believing they would be easier to control.

By rising against an entrenched political elite, the rebellion revealed a growing belief among colonists that government should serve all people, not just the wealthy planter class. It laid early groundwork for the principle of government accountability. The rebels opposed Governor Berkeley's concentration of power and the lack of fair representation for frontier settlers—grievances that echoed later demands of the American Revolution: that government must reflect the will of the governed, not a privileged few.

Though sparked by disputes over land and frontier defense, the rebellion's core reflected a recurring theme in the history of individual liberty: the demand for secure property and protection from both external threats and a government that fails to defend its people. The colonists' insistence that government safeguard life and property reinforced the foundational link between property rights and individual liberty.

1677 – 1678, Culpeper's Rebellion

In Carolina, a rebellion was sparked primarily by opposition to the Navigation Acts, which required that colonial goods—particularly tobacco—be shipped exclusively through English ports using English ships, limiting the settlers' trade opportunities.

Many settlers relied on smuggling to trade with other colonies and foreign powers. The enforcement of the Navigation Acts threatened their livelihoods.

The Proprietors of the Carolina colony appointed Thomas Miller as customs collector and governor. Miller was highly unpopular, as he strictly enforced the Navigation Acts and imposed new taxes.

Many settlers resented the government's interference and Miller's authoritarian leadership. Led by John Culpeper and George Durant, a group of settlers seized and imprisoned Thomas Miller and other officials.

The rebels formed a new government, with Culpeper acting as the de facto leader. They held an Assembly and effectively governed the colony for about two years, collecting taxes and organizing trade.

In 1679, Culpeper was arrested by the English authorities and brought to trial in England for treason. However, he was acquitted, as the English government did not want to risk alienating the colonists further by enforcing harsh penalties.

Thomas Miller did not return to power. The rebellion had exposed the weakness of the Proprietary government in Carolina.

Culpeper's Rebellion was an early example of colonial resistance to English trade policies, foreshadowing later revolts. It demonstrated the colonists' growing frustration with both economic restrictions and authoritarian governance.

1689, The Glorious Revolutions

The Glorious Revolution in America refers to a series of uprisings in the American colonies triggered by the events of the Glorious Revolution in England. In 1688, King James II was overthrown by William of Orange and his wife, Mary, who established a constitutional monarchy.

This political upheaval in England had immediate consequences in the colonies; the overthrow of James II led to the collapse of colonial royal governments and the assertion of colonial self-governance. Several colonies took part in uprisings to remove officials associated with the deposed king.

The Dominion of New England, established by King James II in the late 1680s, aimed to centralize royal control and reduce colonial self-governance by replacing local governments. It was widely unpopular among colonists and quickly unraveled after news of the Glorious Revolution reached America in 1689.

- **Massachusetts Bay Colony:** In April 1689, armed colonists in Boston, led by Captain John Leverett, arrested Governor Sir Edmund Andros and dissolved the Dominion. Massachusetts reinstated its previous government, though it later received a new royal charter in 1691.

- **New York (Leisler's Rebellion)**: With Governor Francis Nicholson absent and tensions high, Jacob Leisler, a German-born merchant, seized control in May 1689, claiming to rule in the name of William and Mary. Backed by small merchants, artisans, and Dutch colonists—but opposed by the English elite—Leisler ruled for nearly two years. In 1691, royal governor Henry Sloughter arrived, arrested Leisler, and executed him and his son-in-law for treason.

- **Maryland**: In July 1689, Protestant settlers, inspired by the Glorious Revolution, overthrew the Catholic-led government of Charles Calvert. They removed Catholics from power and placed Maryland under royal control until 1715, when the Protestant Calverts regained authority.

- **Connecticut and Rhode Island**: Both colonies swiftly restored their previous governments with minimal resistance.

- **New Hampshire**: Briefly absorbed into the Dominion, New Hampshire reverted to separate colonial status shortly afterward.

The Glorious Revolution in America was another early example of colonial resistance to overreaching authority, which laid the groundwork for the American Revolution.

This marked a significant moment in colonial history, as it reinforced the colonies' expectation of local self-rule and autonomy from royal interference. Though this revolutionary movement did not call for independence, the experience contributed to the evolving relationship between the colonies and the British Crown, sowing seeds of discontent that would grow in the decades leading to the American Revolution.

1763, The Paxton Boys

In Pennsylvania, frustration grew among frontier settlers regarding the colonial government's leniency toward Native Americans. The

Paxton Boys massacred peaceful Conestoga Indians and marched on Philadelphia. Colonial authorities averted further violence by negotiating with the marchers.

Once again, this rebellion highlighted tensions between frontier settlers and colonial elites. It advanced individual liberty by highlighting the need for equal protection, accountable government, and fair representation for frontier settlers—concerns that later fueled revolutionary sentiment. Yet it also revealed a darker side, including a turn toward aggressive violence, ethnic hostility, and mob rule.

1765, The Regulators

Backcountry settlers in the Carolinas, frustrated by corrupt local officials and a lack of representation, sought reforms in colonial governance. A large group of farmers protested economic injustices and the abuses of county officials. They aimed to "regulate" the government, demanding reforms to reduce corruption and lower fees imposed by officials. These farmers became known as the Regulators.

The Regulators were defeated by militia forces in the Battle of Alamance (1771), but they exposed the growing divide between eastern elites and western settlers.

The Regulators' uprising advanced individual liberty by challenging corruption and arbitrary power, demanding fair taxation and equal representation, mobilizing ordinary citizens to assert their rights, and anticipating the revolutionary principle of government by consent.

Though ultimately suppressed, the movement fed directly into the political climate that led to the American Revolution, demonstrating that liberty sometimes requires open resistance to unjust authority.

In colonial America, the cause of individual liberty was advanced through religious tolerance, written legal protections, and the development of self-government. Rebellions and resistance movements reflected a determination to challenge arbitrary power, while local assemblies nurtured traditions of representative governance. Together, these experiences laid the foundation for Revolutionary principles such as consent of the governed, equality before the law, and the protection of natural rights.

7.7 The American Revolution

The colonists sought a return to the traditional governance that had once supported their economic independence. However, as the British Parliament and the King increasingly imposed taxes and regulations, discontent steadily grew.

Antagonism developed between the colonies and the mother country. Here, we begin to see the colonists appealing to some of the very ideas we have developed and discussed in this book, including frequent reference to individual liberty, personal property, and natural rights.

As the movement toward independence progressed, the colonists created a framework to safeguard individual liberty by dividing governmental power into smaller, distinct sections. This highlights another essential element of individual liberty: the fragmentation of power. By ensuring that power was distributed among numerous smaller units, the revolution laid the foundation for states' rights, local self-governance, and a limited central government.

1765, The Stamp Act

The British Parliament imposed the Stamp Act on the American colonies. This was a tax requiring all colonial residents to purchase and use specially stamped paper for legal documents, newspapers, playing cards, and other printed materials. It was part of Britain's effort to raise revenue to pay off debts from the Seven Years' War and to finance the ongoing defense of the colonies.

This tax sparked widespread protests. The Stamp Act Congress, held in New York City, summoned representatives from the various colonies to approve a joint statement of grievances to be issued to the British government. These were the first significant organized colonial objections to British taxation.

Colonists protested that their traditional, chartered rights were being violated, and they contended their own colonial legislatures were the only ones who could legitimately tax them. John Adams, among others, condemned the Stamp Act as unconstitutional. In support of his position, he referred to the grand and fundamental principle of the British constitution that no freeman should be subject to any tax to which he has not given his own consent in person or by proxy—an idea you will recall from previous chapters.

1766, The Declaratory Act

Because of colonial resistance and economic pressure from British merchants affected by colonial boycotts, the Stamp Act was repealed. However, it was accompanied by the Declaratory Act, asserting Parliament's authority to legislate for the colonies "in all cases whatsoever."

This marked a direct confrontation between Parliament and the local colonial governments, channeling the colonists' discontent into a movement for local representation and self-governance.

1767, The Townshend Acts

Britain imposed the Townshend Acts: taxes on common goods such as tea, glass, paper, and paint. Colonists responded with boycotts and protests. Tensions over these acts led to the presence of British troops in Boston.

Though taxation was broadly unpopular, the new taxes once again drew the colonists' attention to the deeper issue: being governed by a distant Parliament rather than local representation.

1768, Dickinson and "Letters from a Farmer in Pennsylvania"

In response to the Townshend Acts, John Dickinson published a series of twelve letters, known collectively as "Letters from a Farmer in Pennsylvania." In the final installment, he emphasized the essential role of private property rights:

> Let these truths be indelibly impressed on our minds—that we cannot be HAPPY, without being FREE—that we cannot be free, without being secure in our property—that we cannot be secure in our property, if, without our consent, others may, as by right, take it away.[81]

In recognition of his contributions to independence, John Dickinson earned the nickname "Penman of the Revolution." He took the position that the road to happiness is built on individual liberty, which in turn is built on private property rights.

1770, The Boston Massacre

Tensions had been escalating between British soldiers stationed in Boston and local colonists, who were frustrated with British-imposed taxes and the presence of troops in the city. On the evening of March 5, 1770, a group of colonists confronted a lone British sentry, taunting and throwing objects at him.

The situation escalated as more British soldiers arrived and a larger crowd of colonists gathered, hurling insults and snowballs. Amid the chaos, one of the soldiers fired into the crowd, prompting others to do the same. In the end, five colonists were killed, including Crispus Attucks, who is often remembered as one of the first casualties of the American Revolution.

The incident, referred to as the Boston Massacre, fueled anti-British sentiment throughout the colonies, as it was widely publicized and used as propaganda by leaders like Samuel Adams and Paul Revere to illustrate British oppression.

The eight soldiers involved were later tried for murder, with John Adams, a future U.S. president, serving as their defense attorney. Six were acquitted of all charges, as the jury found they acted in self-defense under provocation from the mob, which had thrown objects like snowballs, ice, and clubs. Two soldiers, Hugh Montgomery and Matthew Kilroy, were convicted of the lesser charge of manslaughter rather than murder.

This event became a powerful symbol of colonial resistance, fueling the growing desire for independence from British rule. Events were spiraling beyond the control of both the British and the colonists. Open acts of violence signaled the end of peaceful negotiation.

By continuing to violate colonial property rights through regulation, taxation, and now violence, the King and Parliament made it clear they would not honor individual liberty. For the colonists, the point of no return was drawing ever closer.

1773, The Boston Tea Party

The Tea Act allowed the British East India Company to sell tea directly to the colonies at a reduced rate, effectively granting it a monopoly. In protest, on December 16, 1773, members of the Sons of Liberty, disguised as Native Americans, boarded British ships in Boston Harbor and dumped 342 chests of tea into the water. This event, known as the Boston Tea Party, was a direct act of defiance against British control.

Did the Sons of Liberty violate the non-aggression principle by destroying the tea? Under this principle, aggression is only justified in cases of self-defense or the defense of others. One could argue that the British government initiated aggression by granting and enforcing a monopoly on the tea trade, effectively infringing on the property rights of the colonists. If so, the colonists' actions could be viewed as a form of self-defense, and therefore consistent with the non-aggression principle.

The Boston Tea Party advanced the cause of individual liberty by rejecting taxation imposed by the British Parliament, opposing government-granted monopolies, and inspiring the colonists to assert their natural rights. It turned widespread grievances into organized resistance and accelerated the push for independence, reinforcing the principle that free people must resist arbitrary power.

1774, The Coercive Acts and The First Continental Congress

In response to the Boston Tea Party, Britain enacted the Coercive Acts, known to the colonists as the "Intolerable Acts." These measures closed Boston Harbor, curtailed Massachusetts' self-governance, permitted British officials to face trial in Britain, and expanded the Quartering Act to force colonists to house British soldiers. The acts galvanized colonial opposition. The Virginia House of Burgesses called for an inter-colonial congress to plan collective action, a proposal swiftly endorsed by other colonies, ultimately leading to the formation of the First Continental Congress.

The First Continental Congress convened from September 5 to October 26, 1774, in Philadelphia. Fifty-six delegates from twelve of the thirteen colonies (all except Georgia) gathered to discuss a unified approach to these punitive laws and to address colonial grievances against British rule.[x]

Notable delegates included Richard Henry Lee, George Washington, and Patrick Henry (Virginia); John Adams and Samuel Adams (Massachusetts); John Jay (New York); and Christopher Gadsden (South Carolina). Thomas Jefferson was chosen as a delegate from Virginia, but he fell ill and could not travel to Philadelphia for the Congress.

The First Continental Congress passed the Declaration and Resolves, asserting the colonies' rights to self-governance and protest-ing British actions, especially those that interfered with colonial

---

[x]   Georgia did not participate in the First Continental Congress primarily because it was heavily reliant on British support to address conflicts with neighboring Native American tribes. Additionally, the colony's leadership was divided, with many loyalists opposing revolutionary sentiment. As a result, Georgia chose to abstain from the Congress.

autonomy (such as taxation imposed by the British Parliament) and overrode local representation.[82] Included in this document is this declaration of individual rights:

> That the inhabitants of the English Colonies in North America, by the immutable laws of nature, the principles of the English constitution, and the several charters or compacts, have the following Rights:
>
> 1. That they are entitled to life, liberty, and property, and they have never ceded to any sovereign power whatever, a right to dispose of either without their consent.

The Congress implemented a unified boycott of British goods, known as the Continental Association, to exert economic pressure on Britain. The agreement called for a halt in the importation of British goods and, eventually, the cessation of exports to Britain if demands were not met.

Furthermore, the Congress urged the colonies to form local committees that would enforce the boycott and coordinate efforts in case of British military action, effectively establishing a network of colonial governance.

While the Congress expressed a preference for peaceful resolution, it advised the colonies to prepare their militias for potential conflict in case negotiations failed.

The Congress adjourned with an agreement to reconvene in May 1775 if Britain did not address colonial demands. Despite its efforts at reconciliation, the British government ignored the Congress's appeals, leading to escalating tensions that soon resulted in the Battles of Lexington and Concord.

The First Continental Congress advanced the cause of individual liberty by affirming natural rights, resisting arbitrary authority, encouraging voluntary cooperation, uniting the colonies in common defense, and insisting that government be limited and accountable.

It transformed the colonists' grievances into an organized movement grounded in the protection of individual liberty.

1775, The Battles of Lexington and Concord and the Second Continental Congress

The Battles of Lexington and Concord were fought on April 19, 1775, marking the beginning of the American Revolutionary War. British troops, under orders from General Thomas Gage, were sent from Boston to seize colonial weapons stored in Concord and to arrest prominent colonial leaders Samuel Adams and John Hancock, who were suspected of inciting rebellion.

The British sustained significant casualties, with over 250 soldiers killed or wounded. The colonial forces lost fewer men, so they were understandably emboldened by their success. These battles demonstrated the colonists' willingness to take up arms in defense of their rights.

In May 1775, delegates from all thirteen colonies convened in Philadelphia in what became known as the Second Continental Congress. Initially, the Congress aimed to seek reconciliation with Britain while preparing for defense. The Congress issued the "Olive Branch Petition" to King George III, calling for a return to peace and a removal of unfavorable regulation.[83] The petition contains this passage:

> Your Majesty's Ministers, persevering in their measures, and proceeding to open hostilities for enforcing them, have compelled us to arm in our own defence, and have engaged us in a controversy so peculiarly abhorrent to the affections of your still faithful Colonists, that when we consider whom we must oppose in this contest, and if it continues, what may be the consequences, our own particular misfortunes are accounted by us only as parts of our distress. Knowing to what violent resentments and incurable animosities civil discords are apt to exasperate and inflame the contending parties, we think ourselves required by indispensable obligations to Almighty God, to your Majesty, to our fellow subjects, and to ourselves,

immediately to use all the means in our power, not incompatible with our safety, for stopping the further effusion of blood, and for averting the impending calamities that threaten the British Empire.

The reply to this petition by King George III was the "Proclamation for Suppressing Rebellion and Sedition," issued on August 23, 1775. The essence of the proclamation follows:[84]

> Whereas many of our subjects in divers parts of our colonies and plantations in North America, misled by dangerous and ill-designing men, and forgetting the allegiance which they owe to the power that has protected and supported them, after various disorderly acts committed in disturbance of the public peace, to the obstruction of lawful commerce, and to the oppression of our loyal subjects carrying on the same, have at length proceeded to an open and avowed rebellion, by arraying themselves in a hostile manner to withstand the execution of the law, and traitorously preparing, ordering, and levying war against us:

> ...by and with the advice of our Privy Council, to issue this our Royal Proclamation, hereby declaring, that not only all our officers, civil and military, are obliged to exert their utmost endeavors to suppress such rebellion, and to bring the traitors to justice, but that all our subjects of this realm and the dominions thereunto belonging are bound by law to be aiding and assisting in the suppression of such rebellion, and to disclose and make known all traitorous conspiracies and attempts against us, our crown and dignity; and we do accordingly strictly charge and command all our officers as well civil as military, and all other our obedient and loyal subjects, to use their utmost endeavors to withstand and suppress such rebellion...

In essence, King George III left no room for compromise. This response hardened the resolve of many colonists and diminished hopes for a peaceful resolution, pushing the colonies further toward declaring independence.

The King's refusal to even acknowledge the Olive Branch Petition was a turning point, illustrating that reconciliation was unlikely and that the British government viewed the colonies as rebellious subjects rather than equal members of the empire. The King's rejection of colonial self-government denied the colonists their natural rights, exposing his intent to rule through coercion and enforced submission. This realization pushed the colonies to fight for full independence, as they recognized that only through self-rule could their individual liberty be preserved. This required the Second Continental Congress to take on some of the roles of a central government: they created the Continental Army, issued paper currency, and coordinated colonial war efforts.

1776, The Declaration of Independence, etc.

The long struggle that would ultimately secure individual liberty over tyranny was about to begin. It started with small but deliberate steps taken by individuals determined to leave a legacy of freedom. Here, we explore the early writings, resolutions, and events that paved the way to the signing of the Declaration of Independence.

"Common Sense"

Thomas Paine published "Common Sense" on January 10, 1776. This pamphlet expressed Paine's passion for individual liberty and his contempt for tyranny:

> Society is produced by our wants, and government by our wickedness. …

> Could we take off the dark covering of antiquity … we should find the first [king] nothing better than the principal ruffian of some restless gang, whose savage manners or pre-eminence in subtlety obtained him the title of chief among plunderers.

Society in every state is a blessing, but government, even in its best state, is but a necessary evil; in its worst state an intolerable one: for when we suffer, or are exposed to the same miseries by a government, which we might expect in a country without government, our calamity is heightened by reflecting that we furnish the means by which we suffer.

THESE are the times that try men's souls. The summer soldier and the sunshine patriot will, in this crisis, shrink from the service of their country, but he that stands it now deserves the love and thanks of man and woman.

Tyranny, like hell, is not easily conquered; yet we have this consolation with us, that the harder the conflict, the more glorious the triumph.

What we obtain too cheap, we esteem too lightly: it is dearness only that gives everything its value. Heaven knows how to put a proper price upon its goods, and it would be strange indeed if so celestial an article as FREEDOM should not be highly rated.[85]

Resolved to be free

On June 7, 1776, Richard Henry Lee of Virginia introduced this resolution in the Second Continental Congress proposing independence for the American colonies:

Resolved: That these United Colonies are, and of right ought to be, free and independent States, that they are absolved from all allegiance to the British Crown, and that all political connection between them and the State of Great Britain is, and ought to be, totally dissolved.

That it is expedient forthwith to take the most effectual measures for forming foreign Alliances.

> That a plan of confederation be prepared and transmitted to the respective Colonies for their consideration and approbation.

Three committees

On June 11, 1776, the Congress appointed three concurrent committees in response to the Lee Resolution: the first to draft a declaration of independence, the second to draw up a plan "for forming foreign alliances," and the third to "prepare and digest the form of a confederation."

The committee appointed to draft the Declaration of Independence consisted of two New England men, John Adams of Massachusetts and Roger Sherman of Connecticut; two men from the Middle Colonies, Benjamin Franklin of Pennsylvania and Robert R. Livingston of New York; and one southerner, Thomas Jefferson of Virginia.

Thomas Jefferson (1743–1826) was the principal author of the Declaration of Independence and would go on to become the third President of the United States (1801–1809). He was also an architect, diplomat, and philosopher who was deeply influenced by Enlightenment ideals, advocating for individual liberty, economic freedom, and limited, accountable government.

He insisted that individual liberty is impossible without secure private property:

> A right to property is founded in our natural wants, in the means with which we are endowed to satisfy these wants, and the right to what we acquire by those means without violating the similar rights of other sensible beings...

Jefferson rejected envious appeals to seize wealth:

> To take from one, because it is thought his own industry and that of his fathers had acquired too much in order to spare to others who, or whose fathers have not exercised equal

industry and skill, is to violate arbitrarily the principle of association, the guarantee to everyone a free exercise of his industry and the fruits acquired by it.

He also provided a warning:

Eternal vigilance is the price of liberty.

The Declaration

The document produced by the committee, the Declaration of Independence, presented to the Congress on July 4, 1776, is an affirmation of natural law (emphasis added):

We hold these truths to be self-evident, that all men are created equal, **that they are endowed by their Creator with certain unalienable Rights, that among these are Life, Liberty and the pursuit of Happiness. —That to secure these rights, Governments are instituted among Men, deriving their just powers from the consent of the governed**, —That whenever any Form of Government becomes destructive of these ends, it is the Right of the People to alter or to abolish it, and to institute new Government, laying its foundation on such principles and organizing its powers in such form, as to them shall seem most likely to effect their Safety and Happiness.

The influence of John Locke

It is evident that John Locke's interpretation of the natural rights to life, liberty, and property shaped Jefferson's language in the Declaration. The pursuit of happiness is also described by Locke as a natural right.

Locke presents this theory in *An Essay Concerning Human Understanding* (1689):

> The necessity of pursuing happiness [is] the foundation of liberty. As therefore the highest perfection of intellectual nature lies in a careful and constant pursuit of true and solid happiness; so the care of ourselves, that we mistake not imaginary for real happiness, is the necessary foundation of our liberty. The stronger ties we have to an unalterable pursuit of happiness in general, which is our greatest good, and which, as such, our desires always follow, the more are we free from any necessary determination of our will to any particular action...[86]

Locke viewed happiness as the highest good and the ultimate aim of human life, and he aligned with the classical tradition of philosophers like Aristotle, who also regarded happiness (*eudaimonia*) as the ultimate goal of human action. In Locke's framework, happiness is achieved by living in accordance with reason and pursuing what truly benefits oneself in the long term.

Locke emphasized that the pursuit of happiness depends on individual liberty and private property, that is, allowing people to make their own choices in seeking what they perceive as good.

Thirteen independent nations

The Declaration of Independence recognized the existing colonies as independent states, each with sovereign powers (emphasis added):

> We, therefore, the Representatives of the united States of America, in General Congress, Assembled, appealing to the Supreme Judge of the world for the rectitude of our intentions, do, in the Name, and by Authority of the good People of these Colonies, solemnly publish and declare, **That these United Colonies are, and of Right ought to be Free and Independent States**; that they are Absolved from

all Allegiance to the British Crown, and that all political connection between them and the State of Great Britain, is and ought to be totally dissolved; **and that as Free and Independent States, they have full Power to levy War, conclude Peace, contract Alliances, establish Commerce, and to do all other Acts and Things which Independent States may of right do.** And for the support of this Declaration, with a firm reliance on the protection of divine Providence, we mutually pledge to each other our Lives, our Fortunes and our sacred Honor.

The British offensive war

On August 27, 1776, the British army began offensive operations in New York with the Battle of Long Island (Brooklyn Heights). This was the first major battle after the Declaration of Independence was signed. British forces, under General William Howe, decisively defeated George Washington's Continental Army and forced them to retreat to Manhattan.

After a series of maneuvers and skirmishes, the British landed at Kip's Bay (on the east side of Manhattan) on September 15 and quickly occupied New York City. Washington's forces retreated farther north.

The British completed their control of the area by taking Fort Washington on November 16, the last major American stronghold in the vicinity, resulting in heavy American losses.

On December 26, George Washington led a surprise attack on Hessian forces stationed in Trenton, New Jersey, after crossing the icy Delaware River on Christmas night. The victory significantly boosted the morale of the Continental Army and renewed hope for the American cause.

Washington later executed another bold maneuver, defeating British forces near Princeton, New Jersey, on January 3, 1777. This victory further undermined British control in New Jersey and inspired greater confidence in the revolutionary effort.

There was no turning back for the colonists—especially for those who signed the Declaration of Independence. In doing so, they had pledged to one another their lives, their fortunes, and their sacred honor. They understood the full risk, knowing they had sacrificed everything to secure individual liberty for themselves, their families, and their fellow citizens.

1777, The Articles of Confederation, etc.

The Articles of Confederation were adopted by the Second Continental Congress on November 15, 1777.[87] The intent and purpose of this Confederation were clearly stated (emphasis added):

> Article II. **Each state retains its sovereignty, freedom and independence, and every Power, Jurisdiction and right,** which is not by this confederation expressly delegated to the United States, in Congress assembled.

> Article III. **The said States hereby severally enter into a firm league of friendship with each other**…

> Article V. In determining questions in the United States, in Congress assembled, **each state shall have one vote.**

> Article XIII. …nor shall any alteration at any time hereafter be made in any of them, unless such alteration be agreed to in a congress of the united states, **and be afterwards confirmed by the legislatures of every state.**

Under the Articles of Confederation, the only governing body was the "The United States in Congress Assembled," commonly referred to as "The Confederation Congress." There was no President, Senate, or federal court system.

The Articles created a "league of friendship" for the thirteen sovereign and independent states. The confederation was not in any sense a single nation; the state was not one but thirteen.

Battles, French support, and military victory

In October of 1777, the American victory at the Battle of Saratoga proved pivotal. It convinced France to ally formally with the colonies, bringing essential military support, resources, and naval power, which shifted the balance of the war against Britain.

With French support, the war expanded beyond North America as Spain and the Netherlands entered the conflict against Britain. French troops and naval forces, working with American forces, put Britain on the defensive. Despite this, Britain redirected its efforts to the Southern colonies, capturing Charleston in 1780.

The British faced unexpected resistance in the South, where American forces used guerrilla tactics and local militia to challenge British advances. Key battles, including Kings Mountain and Cowpens in 1780 and 1781, weakened British forces.

In the fall of 1781, Washington's army, with French support under General Rochambeau and naval assistance from Admiral de Grasse, surrounded British General Cornwallis's forces at Yorktown, Virginia. Cornwallis surrendered on October 19, 1781, effectively ending the major fighting.

Soon after, peace negotiations between the United States and Britain began in Paris.

1783, The Treaty of Paris

The Treaty of Paris was signed on September 3, 1783. Negotiations involved complex diplomacy among multiple parties, including the United States, Great Britain, France, and Spain.[88] The American negotiating team—comprising John Adams, Benjamin Franklin, and John Jay—secured favorable terms for the United States.

The Treaty of Paris references each of the thirteen colonies individually (emphasis added):

Article 1st:

His Brittanic Majesty acknowledges the said United States, viz., New Hampshire, Massachusetts Bay, Rhode Island and Providence Plantations, Connecticut, New York, New Jersey, Pennsylvania, Delaware, Maryland, Virginia, North Carolina, South Carolina and Georgia, to be free sovereign and Independent States; that he treats with them as such, and for himself his Heirs & Successors, relinquishes all claims to the Government, Propriety, and Territorial Rights of the same and every Part thereof.

Article 1 of the Treaty uses the term "States" to mean independent nations like France and Spain, rather than regional administrations like Iowa and Missouri. This wording intentionally affirms each state's sovereignty, reflecting the principles of the Articles of Confederation.

The Treaty also established U.S. borders from the Atlantic to the Mississippi River and required Britain to cede Florida to Spain, another U.S. ally.

1784, Thirteen New Nations

The Second Continental Congress ratified the Treaty of Paris on January 14, 1784, officially ending the Revolutionary War and establishing thirteen new nations.

The new nations now had the freedom to govern themselves without interference from the King or Parliament. It was up to their citizens to design and manage local governments that would protect natural rights and promote individual liberty.

1786 – 1787, Shays' Rebellion and the Convention of Delegates

Still, there was unrest. Shays' Rebellion in Springfield, Massachusetts, was led by Daniel Shays, a Revolutionary War veteran, and was primarily composed of farmers from rural Massachusetts. The rebellion was a response to years of poor harvests, depressed commodity prices, and high taxes that had left these farmers facing the loss of their farms or even imprisonment.

The most serious acts of the rebellion occurred in Springfield, where the rebels attempted to seize the federal arsenal in January 1787. However, they were intercepted and defeated by a private army raised by Massachusetts's governor, James Bowdoin.

The rebellion was ultimately suppressed, but it sparked debates about the limitations of the Articles of Confederation. These debates resulted in an agreement to amend that document.

In *Our Enemy, the State* (1935), Albert Jay Nock examined the debate over amending the Articles of Confederation and the separation of powers it established. He argued that advocates of expanded central power used deceitful tactics, concluding with this statement:

> It is quite certain that dissatisfaction with the existing arrangement was not general, for when the redistribution took place in 1789, it was effected with great difficulty and only through a coup d'état, organized by methods which if employed in any other field than that of politics, would be put down at once as not only daring, but unscrupulous and dishonourable.[89]

On February 21, 1787, the Confederation Congress passed the following resolution (emphasis added):

> Resolved That in the opinion of Congress it is expedient that on the second Monday in May next a Convention of delegates who shall have been appointed by the several States be held at Philadelphia **for the sole and express purpose of revising the Articles of Confederation** and reporting to Congress and the several Legislatures such alterations and provisions therein as shall, when agreed to in Congress and confirmed by the States, render the federal Constitution

adequate to the exigencies of Government and the preservation of the Union.

The Convention of Delegates

The Convention of Delegates was held in Philadelphia from May 25 to September 17, 1787. While the stated goal was to amend the Articles of Confederation, many proponents aimed from the start to create an entirely new system of government. Thomas Jefferson was absent, as he was in Paris at the time, and Rhode Island chose not to send any delegates.

The Convention of Delegates arose from special interests dissatisfied with their inability to pass favorable legislation through the Confederation Congress. Speculators in federal and state debt sought higher taxes to fund discounted debts they had purchased. Bankers pushed for a federally chartered central bank to enable credit expansion. Northern shippers and manufacturers advocated protective tariffs and regulations; shippers targeted rival shipbuilders while manufacturers focused on tariffs. Merchants sought a stronger Midwest military and a Caribbean navy to enforce trade agreements. However, these policies faced opposition from the states under the Articles of Confederation.

The special interests used Shays' Rebellion as an excuse to "amend" the Articles of Confederation. Their true desire was to create an entirely new federal government that was much more powerful than the states. It was, in a sense, as Albert Jay Nock observed, a coup d'état. These special interests referred to themselves as Federalists, implying a desire for a balance of power between the federal government and the states. In reality, the Federalists sought to significantly increase the power of the federal government over the states.

Prominent Federalists included Alexander Hamilton (New York), James Madison (Virginia), John Adams (Massachusetts), George Washington (Virginia), John Jay (New York), John Marshall (Virginia), James Wilson (Pennsylvania), Gouverneur Morris (Pennsylvania), Rufus King (Massachusetts), and John Dickinson (Delaware).

The Federalists established a strong federal government designed to appear limited. Power was distributed among the executive, legislative, and judicial branches (the balance of powers), with the federal government expressly granted only seventeen enumerated powers.

History shows that the balance of powers can be defeated when the executive, legislative, and judicial branches collaborate to consolidate and expand their collective power. There is also the potential for the expansion of enumerated powers through vague clauses, such as the Necessary and Proper Clause, the General Welfare Clause, and the Interstate Commerce Clause. While these clauses don't explicitly authorize specific actions, they can be interpreted broadly, effectively enabling the federal government to justify almost any action. This flexibility has often been used to support various special interest policies.

The Constitution and ratification

The draft of the Constitution was signed on September 17, 1787, but it still required ratification by nine of the thirteen states to become effective. The ratification process sparked intense debate between Federalists, who supported the new Constitution, and Anti-Federalists, who feared it gave too much power to the central government and lacked specific protections for individual rights.

The Federalists had created a process in which only nine out of thirteen states needed to ratify the new Constitution. Under the Articles of Confederation, any amendment to the Articles required unanimous ratification by each state legislature. Under the Federalist-devised ratification process, nine states would ratify this constitution not through the state legislatures but through special state conventions.

The ratification process became a source of great controversy, as the selection of delegates to the conventions in many states favored the Federalists. Federalists were often well-organized and influential; they used their political and social influence to rally support, sometimes exerting pressure to ensure that delegates favorable to the Constitution were elected. In some states, Federalists controlled the convention rules and procedures, which further increased tensions and fed suspicions that the process was manipulated to favor ratification.

In states where Anti-Federalist sentiment was strong, opponents of the Constitution sometimes tried to delay the convention process, hoping to sway public opinion or force amendments. They argued that the quick pace of ratification pushed by Federalists limited debate and the public's opportunity to understand the full implications of the Constitution.

In some states, economic and regional interests influenced delegate selection. Wealthier commercial coastal regions tended to support the Constitution, while rural agrarian areas often harbored more Anti-Federalist sentiment. These divisions sometimes led to accusations that the conventions were biased toward commercial elites who would benefit from a stronger federal government.

During the ratification debates, many Anti-Federalists were wary of a strong central government and expressed concerns that the new federal system could threaten state sovereignty. They worried that the federal government would impose laws that might conflict with state interests and rights. Some delegates argued that states retained inherent sovereignty and thus could resist federal laws they deemed unconstitutional. But the Anti-Federalists voiced concerns that the Constitution lacked sufficient safeguards against federal encroachment on states' rights. They feared that without explicit limits on federal power, states might need to act independently to protect their rights.

Delaware was the first to ratify on December 7, 1787, with subsequent states following. Several states provided conditional ratifications.

Virginia's ratification statement affirmed the right to alter or abolish the government if it became destructive to the liberties of the people. It declared that powers not explicitly delegated to the federal government remained with the states.

New York's ratification document expressed similar reservations, asserting that the powers granted to the federal government were limited and that any powers not explicitly given were reserved to the states. This foreshadowed the principle later formalized in the Tenth Amendment. Their ratification statements emphasized that they reserved the right to reassess the union if the federal government exceeded its constitutional authority.

Massachusetts strongly debated the Constitution, particularly over fears of excessive federal authority. It ratified the Constitution in 1788 with a formal proposal for amendments, including protections for individual liberties and limitations on federal power. These proposals heavily influenced the Bill of Rights.

South Carolina included language asserting that powers not explicitly delegated to the federal government were reserved to the states. Though not explicitly conditional, South Carolina's ratification reflected an apprehensive approach to federal power.

Many states ratified the Constitution with the expectation that a Bill of Rights would be added to address concerns about individual liberties and states' rights. The addition of the Tenth Amendment, which reserved powers not delegated to the federal government for the states or the people, was seen as a crucial safeguard against federal overreach and a potential way to avert conflicts that could lead to drastic measures.

New Hampshire became the ninth state to ratify on June 21, 1788, officially bringing the Constitution into effect. Virginia and New York ratified shortly after, despite significant opposition.

In 1788, North Carolina refused to ratify the Constitution, citing the absence of a Bill of Rights as a major concern. For nearly a year and a half, beginning in July 1788, the state remained independent rather than accepting the Constitution. After the Constitution took effect, North Carolina operated as a de facto independent republic for nearly nine months, even appointing Hugh Williamson as a foreign diplomat to the United States. His mission was to advocate for amendments that aligned with North Carolina's interests. The state ultimately ratified the Constitution in 1789 after the Bill of Rights was promised and was in the process of being drafted.

Rhode Island refused to ratify the Constitution even after George Washington's presidency began in 1789. In response, the new U.S. Congress threatened to treat Rhode Island as a foreign entity, imposing trade restrictions and tariffs that would have crippled its economy. This appalled an opposing senator from Pennsylvania, William Maclay, who considered the practice the method of a tyrant "meant to be used the same way that a robber does a dagger or a highwayman a pistol." Even under the threat of economic sanctions, Rhode Island only ratified the Constitution by two votes, 34 to 32, on May 29, 1790.[90]

Henry Marchant made the following observation during the Rhode Island ratification convention: "The power to guarantee quickly becomes the power to control."[91]

Under the Articles of Confederation and the Treaty of Paris, the States were superior to the meager Federal Government. With the Constitution, the Federalists overturned this relationship and provided the Federal Government with new powers appropriated from the States.

Thomas Jefferson's opinion

On November 13, 1787, Thomas Jefferson wrote the Tree of Liberty letter while he was in Paris. This letter presented Jefferson's opinion of the Constitution:

> I will now add what I do not like. First the omission of a
> Bill of Rights providing clearly and without the aid of soph-
> isms for freedom of religion, freedom of the press, protec-
> tion against standing armies, restriction of monopolies, the
> eternal and unremitting force of the Habeas Corpus laws,
> and trials by jury in all matters of fact triable by the laws
> of the land and not by the laws of nations. To say, as Mr.
> Wilson does, that a bill of rights was not necessary because
> all is reserved in the case of the general government which
> is not given, while in the particular ones, all is given which
> is not reserved, might do for the audience to whom it was
> addressed; but it is surely a gratis dictum, opposed by strong

inferences from the body of the instrument as well as from the omission of the clause of our present confederation which had made the reservation in express terms.

What country can preserve its liberties if their rulers are not warned from time to time that their people preserve the spirit of resistance? Let them take arms. The remedy is to set them right as to facts, pardon and pacify them. What signify a few lives lost in a century or two? The tree of liberty must be refreshed from time to time with the blood of patriots and tyrants. It is its natural manure. Our Convention has been too much impressed by the insurrection of Massachusetts: and on the spur of the moment they are setting up a kite to keep the hen yard in order. I hope in God, this article will be rectified before the new constitution is accepted.[92]

In this letter, Jefferson laments that the Second Continental Congress rushed to rewrite the U.S. foundational document based on the events of Shays' Rebellion. His use of the term "kite" is likely a reference to a bird of prey, specifically the red kite, known for its predatory behavior and its ability to hover menacingly over smaller animals. Jefferson was concerned that the proposed Federal Government would be a bigger threat to individual liberty than the abstract problem it was intended to solve.

Jefferson was critical of the Federalist position promoted by James Wilson, that a Bill of Rights was unnecessary. Wilson's reasoning was that the federal government was only granted specific, enumerated powers by the Constitution; therefore, any power not expressly given to the federal government remained with the states or the people. In other words, he believed that there was no need to list rights the government could not infringe upon because the government had no authority to infringe on them in the first place.

It's implied in Jefferson's letter that Wilson's argument might be persuasive for certain audiences but lacks substance. He suggests that Wilson's claim is more rhetorical than factual: It might convince those who trust the good intentions of government, but it does not hold up under closer scrutiny. Jefferson calls Wilson's statement a "gratis dictum," meaning it is an unproven or unsupported assertion. He argued that Wilson's statement rests on an assumption—that the government would strictly adhere to only those powers explicitly given to it—without adequate proof or guarantees to back up this assumption.

Jefferson pointed out that the Articles of Confederation, the current governing document, included a clear statement that any powers not specifically given to the federal government were reserved to the states. The Constitution, however, did not contain such an explicit reservation clause at the time of drafting. Jefferson saw this as a significant omission, weakening Wilson's argument that powers were automatically reserved to the states. Jefferson felt that the absence of an explicit reservation of rights and powers in the Constitution was a flaw that could open the door to federal overreach.

He argued that, without a Bill of Rights, Wilson's reasoning was insufficient to prevent potential government encroachment. He believed that certain fundamental rights should be explicitly protected in the Constitution to ensure they were beyond the reach of federal power. His concerns and those of others eventually led to the addition of the Bill of Rights, including the Tenth Amendment, which expressly reserves to the states or the people any powers not delegated to the federal government.

Under the Articles of Confederation, the thirteen states managed to defeat the world's most powerful army by forming a Continental Army, coordinating militias, and forging strategic alliances with foreign powers. Despite the absence of centralized authority, the states successfully raised revenue, managed borders, facilitated interstate and international trade, and protected the life, liberty, and property of their citizens.

With the ratification of the Constitution, the thirteen states were brought together under a much stronger federal government. This marked a significant shift from the first fourteen years of the United States, during which there was no centralized federal government—no president, senate, federal court system, or standing army.

1777, Hume and *Essays: Moral, Political, and Literary*

While world-shaping events were occurring in America, Enlightenment philosophers were still hard at work researching and writing. One of these was the Scottish philosopher, historian, economist, and author David Hume.

His book *Essays: Moral, Political, and Literary* was published posthumously. In this book, Hume observed that submission forms the basis of tyranny:

> Nothing appears more surprising to those who consider human affairs with a philosophical eye, than the easiness with which the many are governed by the few; and the implicit submission, with which men resign their own sentiments and passions to those of their rulers. When we enquire by what means this wonder is effected, we shall find, that, as Force is always on the side of the governed, the governors have nothing to support them but opinion. It is therefore, on opinion only that government is founded; and this maxim extends to the most despotic and military governments, as well as to the most free and most popular.[93]

Hume's observation provides confirmation of the ideas in Étienne de La Boétie's 1552 book *Discourse on Voluntary Servitude*, which we discussed earlier. La Boétie concluded that the few rule over the many only because the many consent to their own subjugation.

1798, The Federalists and Democratic-Republicans

After the ratification of the Constitution, the U.S. government shifted from a new framework on paper to a functioning national authority. Federal institutions were established, executive power grew under Washington and Adams, partisan politics emerged, and federal authority expanded through taxation, law enforcement, and controversial measures like the Alien and Sedition Acts—raising debates over liberty, federal power, and states' rights.

Two major political parties had formed in the United States: the Federalists and the Democratic-Republicans. The Federalist Party favored a strong central government with a focus on manufacturing and trade, while the Democratic-Republicans emphasized states' rights, agricultural interests, and a more limited federal government. Prominent members of the Federalist Party included Alexander Hamilton, John Adams, and Timothy Pickering. Prominent members of the Democratic-Republican Party included Thomas Jefferson, James Madison, James Monroe, and Aaron Burr.

On July 6, 1798, President John Adams signed into law the four measures collectively known as the Alien and Sedition Acts. Passed by the Federalist-controlled Congress during heightened tensions with France, these laws aimed to bolster national security but faced widespread criticism for suppressing dissent and infringing on constitutional rights. The following is a summary of the four acts:

Naturalization Act

Extended the residency requirement for immigrants to become U.S. citizens from five to fourteen years.

Aimed to reduce the influence of immigrant voters, who often supported the Democratic-Republicans.

Alien Friends Act

Allowed the president to deport any non-citizen deemed "dangerous to the peace and safety of the United States," even during peacetime.

Alien Enemies Act

Authorized the president to detain or deport citizens of hostile nations during times of war.

(This law remains in force and was used in 2025 by President Trump to deport foreign-born gang members.)

<u>Sedition Act</u>

Made it a crime to publish "false, scandalous, and malicious" statements against the government, Congress, or the president.

This act targeted Democratic-Republican Party–leaning newspapers and critics of the Federalist administration.

The Alien and Sedition Acts became a flash point in the struggle over individual liberty. Many Democratic-Republicans rejected what they saw as a presidential usurpation of power, and their fight to restore individual liberty gave rise to the States' Rights movement.

1798, The Kentucky Resolutions and Virginia Resolutions

In November of 1798, the Kentucky Resolutions were drafted by Thomas Jefferson (then Vice President of the United States) and introduced into the Kentucky legislature by John Breckinridge.[94] The resolutions were a protest against the Alien and Sedition Acts and articulated the principles of states' rights, constitutional limits on federal power, and the doctrine of nullification. The Kentucky legislature passed the resolutions on November 10.

The resolutions argued that the federal government was a creation of the states, and its powers were limited to those explicitly delegated by the Constitution. The Constitution was viewed as a compact among the states, and any powers not granted to the federal government remained with the states. If the federal government enacted laws that exceeded its constitutional authority, states had the right to declare those laws null and void within their borders. On this basis, they declared the Alien and Sedition Acts unconstitutional, claiming they infringed on First Amendment rights and exceeded federal authority.

With these resolutions, Jefferson portrayed the Union as voluntarily entered by the states; the states were "not united on the principle of unlimited submission to their general government."

The Union was created by the ratification of the Constitution, which served as a "compact" by which the states "delegate … certain definite powers" to the Federal Government.

The Federal Government's exercise of powers not expressly granted to it by the Constitution was thus illegitimate. For Jefferson, the Constitution both defined and limited the Union's nature and essence.

To keep a Federal Government of limited and expressly delegated powers, Jefferson warned that it should not be "the exclusive or final judge of the extent of the powers delegated to itself," because in that case, it would consistently grant itself ever more power.

Jefferson advocated state legislatures' right to judge the constitutionality of federal actions. As parties to the constitutional compact, the states had no impartial judge, since the Supreme Court was itself a component of the federal government. Therefore, each state should have an equal right to determine for itself both the existence of infractions and the appropriate means of redress when the federal government enacted unconstitutional legislation.

Later in the year, the Virginia Resolutions were drafted by James Madison as a protest against the Alien and Sedition Acts.[95] The resolutions were adopted by the Virginia General Assembly on December 24.

Similar to the Kentucky Resolutions, the Virginia Resolutions argued that the Constitution was a compact among the states and that the federal government was limited to the powers explicitly delegated to it by the states.

The Alien and Sedition Acts were declared unconstitutional by these resolutions because of their violation of the First Amendment (freedom of speech and press) and the Tenth Amendment (the federal government could not exercise a power it had not been delegated).

The resolutions asserted Virginia's strong commitment to the U.S. Constitution and the Union, pledging to defend both. However, they emphasized that the Constitution grants only specific, limited powers to the federal government, with all remaining powers reserved to the states.

Virginia argued that the states had the right and duty to "interpose" when the federal government exercised powers not granted by the Constitution. The resolutions expressed concern that, without this check, federal overreach could endanger the liberties and rights of the states and the people.

Virginia called on other states to join in opposition to the Alien and Sedition Acts, arguing that a collective stance would help preserve the "authorities, rights, and liberties" that belonged to the states and the people.

1799, Another Kentucky Resolution

Thomas Jefferson authored another resolution in the Kentucky legislature that expanded upon the earlier 1798 Resolutions, reinforcing the principles of states' rights and nullification.[96] This resolution was passed by the Kentucky General Assembly on November 22, 1799.

This resolution explicitly asserted that states had the authority to nullify federal laws they deemed unconstitutional. This expanded on the doctrine introduced in the 1798 Resolutions, even including the word "nullification."

The federal government was declared to be a creation of the states, with powers strictly limited to those explicitly granted by the Constitution. States retained the right to judge the constitutionality of federal actions and to take appropriate measures to protect their citizens from unconstitutional laws.

The Kentucky and Virginia Resolutions of 1798/99 were attempts by these states to formally protest the Alien and Sedition Acts, which they believed violated the Constitution. However, the resolutions did not lead to the immediate repeal of the Alien and Sedition Acts. Congress did not overturn the acts, but the Sedition Act expired in

1801, and the Alien Friends Act was allowed to fade out without further enforcement.

The resolutions introduced the idea of nullification, the notion that states could declare federal laws unconstitutional and nullify them within their borders. This principle influenced future states' rights arguments, particularly during the Nullification Crisis in the 1830s, when South Carolina attempted to nullify federal tariffs. Despite their lack of immediate success, the resolutions did set a precedent for states' rights advocacy.

The backlash against the Alien and Sedition Acts and the associated federal overreach contributed to public support for the Democratic-Republican Party, which was led by Thomas Jefferson and James Madison. This shift in public sentiment helped lead to Jefferson's election as president in 1800, often called the "Revolution of 1800" because it marked a peaceful transfer of power from the Federalists to the Democratic-Republicans.

The ideas in the Kentucky and Virginia Resolutions laid the groundwork for ongoing debates about the balance between federal and state power. The Tenth Amendment, which reserves to the states or the people any powers not delegated to the federal government, became a rallying point for states' rights advocates. Among them, the phrase "the Principles of '98" emerged as a common way to express the belief that the federal Constitution was limited in scope and that individual states, the fundamental components of the Union, retained the right to resist federal overreach.

The American Revolution stands as one of the most pivotal events in human history. For the first time, individuals united to overthrow a tyrannical government and establish a society founded on the principles of natural law and individual liberty.

7.8 The Modern Era

During this era, the Enlightenment's ideas were put into practical application, profoundly influencing Western civilization and fostering advancements in economics and political philosophy. These developments fostered individual liberty and personal responsibility, creating a climate of laissez-faire capitalism and economic prosperity.

1791, The First Bank

The First Bank of the United States was proposed by Alexander Hamilton, the first Secretary of the Treasury, as part of his plan to build a strong federal government. He argued that the Necessary and Proper Clause (Article I, Section 8, Clause 18) of the U.S. Constitution permitted a central bank. His argument was that the bank was "necessary and proper" to carry out the federal government's enumerated powers, such as taxing, borrowing money, regulating commerce, and providing for "the general welfare."

Jefferson, Madison, and many other Anti-Federalists opposed the bank, arguing that a reasonable interpretation of the Constitution granted no authority for a central bank. They rejected Hamilton's use of the Necessary and Proper Clause, which they viewed as a case of overreach of federal authority.

President George Washington sided with Hamilton and signed the bank into law with a charter for a term of twenty years. This decision ushered in a new era of government involvement in money and banking, disrupting private transactions and infringing on economic freedom.

1801 – 1850, Bastiat and *The Law*

In the history of individual liberty, a Frenchman you likely will never have heard of—and with whom even most French people are likely unfamiliar—played an essential role in articulating and spreading important ideas for the cause of freedom.

His name was Frédéric Bastiat, and he was an economist, statesman, and author. His father, Pierre Bastiat, was a prominent businessman. His mother died in 1808. Pierre himself died in 1810, leaving Frédéric an orphan to be raised by his paternal grandfather and his unmarried aunt, Justine Bastiat.

At age seventeen, Frédéric left school at Sorèze to work for his uncle in his family's export business, the same firm where his father had been a partner. When Bastiat was twenty-four, his grandfather died and left him the family estate, thereby providing him with the means to further his studies. Bastiat became politically active; he was elected justice of the peace of Mugron in 1831 and to the Council General (county-level assembly) of Landes in 1832. He was elected to the national legislative assembly after the Revolution of 1848.

As France slid into socialism, Bastiat wrote *The Law* (1850). In this book, he examined the purpose and impact of law. The only legitimate purpose of law, said Bastiat, is to protect life, liberty, and property:

> Life, faculties, production—in other words, individuality, liberty, property—this is man. And in spite of the cunning of artful political leaders, these three gifts from God precede all human legislation and are superior to it. Life, liberty, and property do not exist because men have made laws. On the contrary, it was the fact that life, liberty, and property existed beforehand that caused men to make laws in the first place.

Bastiat argued that force is only justified in defending life, liberty, and property. If individuals have the right of self-defense, they may unite for mutual defense. However, since no one has the right to initiate aggression, a group formed for mutual defense does not have the right to collectively initiate aggression against others. An individual cannot confer upon another person or group a right they do not themselves possess:

Each of us has a natural right—from God—to defend his person, his liberty, and his property. These are the three basic requirements of life, and the preservation of any one of them is completely dependent upon the preservation of the other two. For what are our faculties but the extension of our individuality? And what is property but an extension of our faculties? If every person has the right to defend—even by force—his person, his liberty, and his property, then it follows that a group of men have the right to organize and support a common force to protect these rights constantly. Thus, the principle of collective right—its reason for existing, its lawfulness—is based on individual right. And the common force that protects this collective right cannot logically have any other purpose or any other mission than that for which it acts as a substitute. Thus, since an individual cannot lawfully use force against the person, liberty, or property of another individual, then the common force—for the same reason— cannot lawfully be used to destroy the person, liberty, or property of individuals or groups.

Collective action can have harmful consequences when driven by aggression. Bastiat recognized that a group may distort the law for its own gain, using it to violate the life, liberty, and property of others:

But, unfortunately, law by no means confines itself to its proper functions. And when it has exceeded its proper functions, it has not done so merely in some inconsequential and debatable matters. The law has gone further than this; it has acted in direct opposition to its own purpose. The law has been used to destroy its own objective: It has been applied to annihilating the justice that it was supposed to maintain; to limiting and destroying rights which its real purpose was to respect. The law has placed the collective force at the disposal of the unscrupulous who wish, without risk, to exploit the person, liberty, and property of others. It has converted plunder into a right in order to protect plunder. And it has converted lawful defense into a crime in order to punish lawful defense.

A precise definition of theft is essential for recognizing violations of property rights. Bastiat defined plunder in this short paragraph:

> When a portion of wealth is transferred from the person who owns it—without his consent and without compensation, and whether by force or by fraud—to anyone who does not own it, then I say that property is violated, that an act of plunder is committed.

The public, Bastiat feared, had grown accustomed to what he called "legal plunder," in which governments use their powers of coercion to take from some and give to others. Everyone recognizes the moral horror of such forced transfers of property from one person to another when they take the form of a common thief robbing an innocent person. But when governments do the same thing in the name of "social welfare," it is easy to miss that the same principle is at work:

> I say that this act is exactly what the law is supposed to suppress, always and everywhere. When the law itself commits this act that it is supposed to suppress, I say that plunder is still committed, and I add that from the point of view of society and welfare, this aggression against rights is even worse. In this case of legal plunder, however, the person who receives the benefits is not responsible for the act of plundering. The responsibility for this legal plunder rests with the law, the legislator, and society itself. Therein lies the political danger.

> But how is this legal plunder to be identified? Quite simply. See if the law takes from some persons what belongs to them and gives it to other persons to whom it does not belong. See if the law benefits one citizen at the expense of another by doing what the citizen himself cannot do without committing a crime.

When addressing social problems, regardless of the type, Bastiat was convinced that the solution always lies in individual liberty:

I believe that my theory is correct; for whatever be the question upon which I am arguing, whether it be religious, philosophical, political, or economical; whether it affects well-being, morality, equality, right, justice, progress, responsibility, property, labor, exchange, capital, wages, taxes, population, credit, or Government; at whatever point of the scientific horizon I start from, I invariably come to the same thing—the solution of the social problem is in liberty.

Away, then, with quacks and organizers! … Away with their artificial methods! Away with their social laboratories, their governmental whims, their centralization, their tariffs, their universities, their state religions, their inflationary or monopolizing banks, their limitations, their restrictions, their moralizations, and their equalization by taxation! And now, after having vainly inflicted upon the social body so many systems, let them end where they ought to have begun—reject all systems and try liberty—liberty, which is an act of faith in God and in His work.[97]

In Bastiat's famous essay "That Which Is Seen, and That Which Is Not Seen" (1850), he introduced the "broken window fallacy." He used the analogy of a shopkeeper whose window is broken by a careless boy. In the immediate aftermath, people observe the shopkeeper having to pay a glazier to replace the window. Some argue that this is beneficial, as it creates work for the glazier, who will spend his earnings elsewhere, thus stimulating the economy. These are the consequences that are "seen."

Bastiat challenged this view by highlighting the "unseen" consequences of the broken window. In this essay, he points out that the shopkeeper, rather than spending money on new investments or other goods, where he might have spent his money otherwise, must instead pay to replace the broken window. This diverted spending represents a lost opportunity to create additional economic value: He would have had a window plus something else; now, he has only the window

This example illustrates that destruction does not create net economic gain. Those who would say society benefits from the broken window overlook the costs and lost opportunities incurred. Real wealth comes from production and investment, not from repairing damage.

The broken window fallacy warns against viewing only the immediate effects of economic actions while ignoring their unseen—and often more significant—impacts. According to Bastiat, a good economist evaluates the economic effects of a particular event on all individuals and groups, not just the one group that is most visible to us:

> In the economic sphere an act, a habit, an institution, a law produces not only one effect but a series of effects. Of these effects, the first alone is immediate; it appears simultaneously with its cause; it is seen. The other effects emerge only subsequently; they are not seen; we are fortunate if we foresee them.
>
> There is only one difference between a bad economist and a good one: the bad economist confines himself to the visible effect; the good economist takes into account both the effect that can be seen and those effects that must be foreseen.[98]

Bastiat skillfully employed satire to criticize protectionism in his 1847 essay "The Candlemakers' Petition," framed as an open letter to the French Parliament. His fictional petition from candlemakers and related industries requests that the government mandate covering all windows to block out sunlight, because in so doing, it will increase the demand for candles. The candlestick makers argue that by eliminating competition from the sun, they will sell more candles, lamps, and oil, thereby creating jobs and stimulating the economy.

This absurd scenario is intended to highlight the flawed logic of protectionism, which seeks to boost certain industries artificially by shielding them from competition. By protecting domestic industries from foreign competition (or, in this case, "natural competition" from sunlight), society ultimately suffers, as it must pay more for goods and services. Bastiat argued that such policies hinder economic growth and reduce wealth by forcing people to support inefficient industries rather than allowing resources to flow to more productive uses.

In essence, the petition mocks the idea that economic prosperity can be achieved by restricting competition, showing that such policies ultimately harm consumers and the broader economy.

Bastiat's insights unite moral philosophy, legal principle, and economic reality into a compelling defense of individual liberty. He argued that true justice requires safeguarding life, liberty, and property. By blending timeless moral reasoning with practical economic analysis, Bastiat presented one of the clearest and most eloquent, enduring, and accessible portrayals of individual liberty to date.

1803, Say and *A Treatise on Political Economy*

In 1803, Jean-Baptiste Say, who belonged to the same economic school of thought as Bastiat, published *A Treatise on Political Economy*. In this book, he developed "the law of markets," also known as "Say's Law":

> A product is no sooner created, than it, from that instant, affords a market for other products to the full extent of its own value. ... As each of us can only purchase the productions of others with his own productions—as the value we can buy is equal to the value we can produce—the more men can produce, the more they will purchase.[99]

Say's insight has been intentionally misrepresented as "supply creates its own demand." Since that statement sounds absurd, some people have unjustly dismissed Say's Law altogether. What Say's Law really means, however, is that for consumers to exist, there must first be producers—you must produce before you can consume. Say's insights remind us that production is not just a means to satisfy demand—it's what makes demand possible in the first place.

Your ability to buy things in the market depends on you first having the means to do so. To acquire these means, you must work, create, and produce something of value for others, earning a payment that enables you to make purchases. Money is a receipt for your contribution to the value created in society.

Widespread understanding and acceptance of Say's Law could have prevented the disastrous economic policies of the twentieth century that focused attention on demand rather than supply. We are often told that consumer spending drives the economy and that stimulating demand is the key to economic recovery. Say saw this logic as backward: Real wealth comes from human productivity, not consumption. Allowing government officials to "stimulate" spending is like inviting the vampire into your house. They "stimulate" only by taxing, borrowing, or inflating the currency—methods that seize our property and divert it to political purposes. In the end, they create no prosperity; they merely drain the lifeblood of genuine production and destroy individual liberty.

1808 – 1887, Spooner, Government Monopolies, and the Constitution

Lysander Spooner was born on a farm in Athol, Massachusetts, on January 19, 1808. Over the course of his life, he developed into an abolitionist, attorney, entrepreneur, and author. He founded the American Letter Mail Company in 1844 as a challenge to the U.S. government's monopoly on mail delivery. At that time, federal law granted the U.S. Postal Service exclusive rights to deliver mail, with high postage rates that Spooner believed were unjust and burdensome to individuals and businesses.

Spooner's company operated between major cities, including Boston, New York, Philadelphia, and Baltimore, delivering letters at a significantly lower rate than the government—sometimes as low as six cents per letter, compared to the government's rate of eighteen to twenty-five cents. While the government's mail service at the time delivered letters only to local post offices, where recipients had to collect them, Spooner's company offered home deliveries in some areas as part of its operations. This service undercut the government monopoly by not only lowering costs but also improving convenience. His initiative aimed not only to provide cheaper mail delivery but also to demonstrate the inefficiency of government monopolies and advocate for free-market alternatives.

The American Letter Mail Company was popular with the public, especially among merchants, because of its lower costs and faster service. However, the federal government quickly came to view Spooner's business as a threat. In response, they pursued legal action and tightened postal regulations to shut down private competition. By 1845, new federal laws and enforcement efforts effectively forced Spooner out of business.

Though the company's operations were short-lived, Spooner's challenge left a legacy. His efforts helped pave the way for future discussions about monopoly restrictions and inspired calls for postal reform. Some historians regard the American Letter Mail Company as an early example of civil disobedience and a pro-market critique of state power.

In 1870, Spooner published *No Treason. No. VI. The Constitution of No Authority*. Spooner believed that supporters of "constitutional government," however well-meaning, had been duped into believing absurdities:

> The ostensible supporters of the Constitution, like the ostensible supporters of most other governments, are made up of three classes, viz.:
>
> 1. Knaves, a numerous and active class, who see in the government an instrument which they can use for their own aggrandizement or wealth.
>
> 2. Dupes – a large class, no doubt – each of whom, because he is allowed one voice out of millions in deciding what he may do with his own person and his own property, and because he is permitted to have the same voice in robbing, enslaving, and murdering others, that others have in robbing, enslaving, and murdering himself, is stupid enough to imagine that he is a "free man," a "sovereign"; that this is a "free government"; "a government of equal rights," "the best government on earth," and such like absurdities.

3.   A class who have some appreciation of the evils of government, but either do not see how to get rid of them, or do not choose to so far sacrifice their private interests as to give themselves seriously and earnestly to the work of making a change.

In the appendix to this book, Spooner unleashed his opinion of the effectiveness of the U.S. Constitution as a mechanism for limiting the U.S. government:

> But whether the Constitution really be one thing, or another, this much is certain—that it has either authorized such a government as we have had, or has been powerless to prevent it. In either case, it is unfit to exist.[100]

Spooner's views may seem shocking, as we've been taught to revere the Constitution, but he was not alone in sounding the alarm. During the drafting and ratification of the Constitution, Federalists defended provisions such as the General Welfare Clause, the Interstate Commerce Clause, and the Necessary and Proper Clause as practical tools for an effective government. Anti-Federalists, however, strongly objected to these phrases, warning that their vague wording would be stretched to justify powers far beyond what was originally intended. They feared such clauses would erode state authority and individual liberty—a prediction that later constitutional interpretations would confirm.

The Anti-Federalists and Lysander Spooner were correct in their predictions and apprehension about the Constitution. Today, the U.S. federal government stands as the largest, most costly, and most powerful in history—a reality that starkly betrays the Founders' vision. The Declaration of Independence proclaimed: "We hold these truths to be self-evident, that all men are created equal, that they are endowed by their Creator with certain unalienable Rights, that among these are Life, Liberty and the pursuit of Happiness. —That to secure these rights, Governments are instituted among Men, deriving their just powers from the consent of the governed." What was meant to be a limited government, established solely to protect individual liberty, has instead grown into an institution that often overshadows—and even destroys—the very individual liberty it was created to defend.

1816, The Second Bank

When the First Bank of the United States' charter expired in 1811, it was not renewed. In 1816, the Second Bank of the United States was chartered with a twenty-year term by Congress under the "Act to Incorporate the Subscribers to the Bank of the United States" and signed into law by President James Madison.

The stated purpose of the Second Bank was to regulate state banks, stabilize the currency, and provide loans to the government. It was headquartered in Philadelphia, was privately managed under federal oversight, and had branches across the United States.

The bank was criticized as an elitist institution favoring wealthy urban interests over farmers and workers. President Andrew Jackson, who became a staunch opponent of the bank, argued that it concentrated too much power in a private institution. Jackson vetoed the renewal of its charter in 1832, framing the issue as a battle for democracy against entrenched privilege.

The Second Bank's charter expired in 1836, at which point it became a state-chartered bank in Pennsylvania. It ultimately collapsed in 1841 due to mismanagement and financial difficulties.

1820 – 1903, Spencer and Social Theory

Herbert Spencer was a British philosopher, sociologist, and political theorist known for his contributions to social theory and his advocacy of liberal individualism. A major figure of the Victorian era, Spencer's work was influential across various disciplines, from politics to biology.

He presented his philosophy of individual liberty in his book *Social Statics* (1851):

> Wherefore we arrive at the general proposition, that every man may claim the fullest liberty to exercise his faculties compatible with the possession of like liberty by every other man.[101]

In works like *The Principles of Sociology* (1876), Spencer applied the idea of evolution not only to biology but also to human societies. He argued that societies progress from simple, homogenous structures to complex, differentiated ones.

Spencer was a strong advocate for minimal government intervention in personal and economic affairs. His book *The Man Versus the State* (1884) warned of the dangers of expanding state control and championed individual liberty and free-market principles.

He believed that education and moral development were essential to personal growth and societal progress, and he laid out these ideas in *Education: Intellectual, Moral, and Physical* (1861).

In his essay "The Sins of Legislators," Spencer summarized the origin of government:

> Be it or be it not true that Man is shapen in iniquity and conceived in sin, it is unquestionably true that Government is begotten of aggression, and by aggression.[102]

Herbert Spencer advanced the cause of individual liberty by grounding it in a universal principle: Each person may exercise their faculties freely, so long as they respect the equal liberty of others. He warned that government, born of aggression, tends to expand, which restricts freedom—making vigilance against state overreach essential. By championing minimal government, free markets, and the role of moral and intellectual development, Spencer highlighted that true social progress arises not from coercion but from voluntary cooperation and individual responsibility.

1835, De Tocqueville and *Democracy in America*

The French political philosopher and historian Alexis de Tocqueville traveled across the United States to examine its society. He recorded his observations in the two-volume work *Democracy in America*. Tocqueville was particularly struck by Americans' independence and their capacity to collaborate without government assistance:

> The European sees himself as an isolated individual, and he is lost if he does not perceive the hand of the government stretched out to come to his aid. The American relies on himself and upon his associates...

> ...Americans of all ages, all stations in life, and all types of dispositions are forever forming associations. They have not only commercial and manufacturing companies, in which all take part, but associations of a thousand other kinds—religious, moral, serious, futile, general or restricted, enormous or diminutive. The Americans make associations to give entertainments, to found seminaries, to build inns, to construct churches, to distribute books, to send missionaries to the antipodes; in this manner, they found hospitals, prisons, and schools.

In contrast to their constituents, Tocqueville found American politicians no more impressive than their French counterparts. He expressed his disdain for politicians in general:

> The pursuit of wealth generally diverts men of great talents and of great passions from the pursuit of power, and it very frequently happens that a man does not undertake to direct the fortune of the State until he has discovered his incompetence to conduct his own affairs.[103]

Alexis de Tocqueville showed that in America, individual liberty thrived not through reliance on government but through habits of self-reliance and voluntary association. By working together freely to build institutions, solve problems, and improve their communities,

Americans demonstrated that individual liberty is best preserved when citizens trust themselves and each other rather than politicians or the state. His observations highlight that the strength of a free society lies in voluntary cooperation, not political authority.

1834 – 1902, The Quotations of Lord Acton

Lord Acton (John Emerich Edward Dalberg-Acton), in correspondence with Mandell Creighton, composed this unforgettable quotation, written on April 5, 1887:

> I cannot accept your canon that we are to judge Pope and King unlike other men, with a favorable presumption that they did no wrong. If there is any presumption, it is the other way against holders of power, increasing as power increases. Historic responsibility has to make up for the want of legal responsibility. Power tends to corrupt, and absolute power corrupts absolutely.

In a lecture delivered in 1877, Lord Acton uttered another of his well-known quotations (which, in fact, forms the epigraph of this book):

> "Liberty is not a means to a higher political end. It is itself the highest political end."

Here are a few more noteworthy quotations attributed to Lord Acton:

> "Individual liberty is the moral standard by which governments must be judged."

> "Liberty occupies the final summit. … It is almost, if not altogether, the sign, and the prize, and the motive in the onward and upward advance of the race."

> "A people averse to the institution of private property is without the first element of freedom."

Acton understood that individual liberty is not just a tool or a means to achieve other political goals, such as prosperity, security, or stability. Instead, he realized that individual liberty is the ultimate goal, the highest value in political life.

By stating that liberty is the highest political end, he was asserting that individual liberty has intrinsic worth. It should be pursued for its own sake, not merely for the benefits it might bring.

This view aligns with a philosophical perspective that prioritizes individual liberty and autonomy as the foundation of a just society. It suggests that a political system should be judged primarily on how well it preserves and promotes individual liberty.

Notably, Acton's statements contrast with utilitarian approaches. While the latter justify limitations on individual liberty if they lead to greater overall happiness or other societal benefits, Acton argued that liberty should not be compromised for the sake of other political or social ends.

1851, Calhoun and *A Disquisition on Government*

John C. Calhoun served as Vice President of the United States under both John Quincy Adams and Andrew Jackson. His treatise, *A Disquisition on Government,* explored the nature of government, human society, and the importance of constitutional mechanisms to protect minority interests. Calhoun's work presented his theory of the "concurrent majority," which he argued was necessary to protect the rights of minority groups, especially in a diverse society like the United States.

Calhoun stated that government is an inevitable part of human society, required to manage conflict and maintain order because humans are driven by self-interest, which can lead to clashes. He also argued that government, by its very nature, tends to expand its power over time, often at the expense of written constitutional limits. The party in power will always construe its constitutional powers as widely as it possibly can, while the party threatened by government power will construe the limitations on that power as strictly as possible, leading to subversion of the constitution. If there are no structural mechanisms to balance these conflicting interpretations, the dominant side (whichever it may be) can steadily reshape constitutional meaning to its advantage.

He contended that power tends to be abused when it is unchecked, leading to tyranny, especially by the majority over the minority. To guard against this, Calhoun proposed a system that requires the consent of all significant interests within society—what he called the "concurrent majority." In practice, this means that key decisions should require agreement from various groups within society rather than a simple numerical majority.

Calhoun saw the U.S. Constitution as an example of an attempt to create this balance through federalism and states' rights, allowing different regions and interests to coexist. He argued that without such protections, majoritarian democracy would inevitably oppress minority groups, reducing individual liberty for all.

1883, Sumner and "The Forgotten Man"

William Graham Sumner's lecture, delivered in Brooklyn and entitled "The Forgotten Man" (published posthumously in 1918), offers a powerful critique of social reform efforts that impose burdens on ordinary, hardworking citizens. Sumner described the "Forgotten Man" as the typical law-abiding individual who quietly works, pays taxes, and takes care of his responsibilities, yet is overlooked by reformers and policymakers. This man is "forgotten" because social programs and charity policies are frequently designed to help others at his expense, forcing him to support causes or people he may not directly benefit from or agree with.

Sumner argued that well-intentioned reformers frequently advocate policies that take resources from the Forgotten Man to support various causes, failing to recognize the impact this has on his livelihood and freedom. The Forgotten Man is the one who must bear the costs of "helping" others through government intervention, taxes, or forced charity, even though he himself may receive no aid. Sumner described this process as follows:

> A and B put their heads together to decide what C shall be made to do for D.[104]

Sumner's lecture emphasizes individual responsibility and the unintended consequences of social reform. His concept of the Forgotten Man serves as a call for a focus on self-reliance and minimal interference in individual lives.

1840 – 1921, Menger and the "Marginalist Revolution"

Carl Menger was born in Neu-Sandez (now Nowy Sącz in Poland), then part of the Austro-Hungarian Empire.

He studied at the Universities of Prague and Vienna and achieved his doctoral degree in law. Menger started his career as a journalist, writing economic analyses. He observed discrepancies in the classical cost-of-production theories while reporting on market prices and economic issues, which spurred his interest in the subjective theory of value.

Menger is credited as the founder of the Austrian School of Economics. He is best known for his role in the "Marginalist Revolution," a key intellectual shift in the nineteenth century that transformed economics by introducing the concept of marginal utility.

In his book *Principles of Economics* (1871), Menger challenged the classical labor theory of value—dominant in the works of economists like Adam Smith and David Ricardo—which posited that the value of goods is determined by the labor required to produce them. Instead, Menger argued that value is subjective, rooted in individuals' preferences and the additional satisfaction (or utility) gained from consuming one more unit of a good.

This insight about marginal utility was simultaneously discovered by two other economists—William Stanley Jevons in England and

Léon Walras in Switzerland—marking the birth of the Marginalist Revolution. Their ideas collectively moved economics away from aggregate labor theories and toward a framework that emphasized the roles of individual decision-making, scarcity, and personal valuation in determining prices.

Menger showed that economic value is not dictated by labor or authority but by the subjective choices of individuals. His theory of marginal utility emphasized that people freely determine what goods and services are worth to them, making the market a reflection of countless personal decisions rather than of central control. By grounding economics in individual preference and voluntary exchange, Menger laid the intellectual foundation for the Austrian School's defense of free markets, entrepreneurship, and spontaneous order—all essential to protecting individual liberty from coercive interference.

1849, De Molinari and *The Production of Security*

Gustav de Molinari, a Belgian economist and political philosopher, was a strong advocate of free markets and individual liberty. He argued that even core government functions, such as security and defense, could be privatized. In *The Production of Security,* he laid the groundwork for abolishing monopolies in the provision of security, where most people assume a monopoly is necessary:

> If there is one well-established truth in political economy, it is this: That in all cases, for all commodities that serve to provide for the tangible or intangible needs of the consumer, it is in the consumer's best interest that labor and trade remain free, because the freedom of labor and of trade have as their necessary and permanent result the maximum reduction of price. And this: That the interests of the consumer of any commodity whatsoever should always prevail over the interests of the producer. Now, in pursuing these principles, one arrives at this rigorous conclusion: That the production of security should, in the interests of the consumers of this intangible commodity, remain subject to the law of free competition.

> Whence it follows: That no government should have the right
> to prevent another government from going into competition
> with it, or to require consumers of security to come exclu-
> sively to it for this commodity.[105]

De Molinari extended the logic of free markets to the very heart of government by arguing that security and defense, like all other goods, should be open to competition. By treating security as a service subject to consumer choice rather than a state monopoly, he challenged the assumption that government coercion is necessary to protect individual liberty. His insight highlights a radical but consistent principle: Individual liberty is best preserved when even essential services are provided through voluntary exchange, where consumers—not rulers—decide what meets their needs.

1851 – 1914, Von Böhm-Bawerk and *Capital and Interest*

Eugen von Böhm-Bawerk was an economist and a central figure in the Austrian School of Economics. His work laid the foundation for modern economic theory, particularly in areas of capital theory, interest, and value.

Born in Brno (then part of the Austro-Hungarian Empire), Böhm-Bawerk studied law and economics at the University of Vienna. He was deeply influenced by the earlier work of Carl Menger, the founder of the Austrian School. After completing his studies, he became a professor of political economy at the University of Innsbruck.

He is best known for his three-volume work *Capital and Interest* (1884), in which he analyzed the role of time in economic processes. He argued that interest arises because people value present goods more than future goods—a concept known as "time preference." To persuade someone to wait (i.e., forego present consumption) and lend resources for a future return, the borrower offers compensation (interest) that reflects the lender's time preference. The higher someone's time preference, the stronger their preference for consuming now, and thus the higher the interest rate they will require to postpone that consumption.

Böhm-Bawerk is also remembered for his systematic critique of the labor theory of value. He challenged the idea that labor alone determines value, emphasizing instead the subjective nature of value and the role of time and capital.

He introduced the concept of "roundaboutness" in production (sometimes referred to as the length of the production process), explaining how capital-intensive processes can lead to greater productivity over time. He realized that by investing in new equipment or processes, an increase in production could be achieved.

Böhm-Bawerk served as Austria's Minister of Finance on three occasions. His tenure was marked by a commitment to fiscal discipline and a rejection of inflationary policies, earning him a reputation as a principled and competent policymaker. Despite his theoretical focus, his policy work reflected his belief in free markets and sound monetary principles.

1885, Herbert and *The Right and Wrong of Compulsion by the State*

Auberon Herbert was a British political philosopher and writer, as well as an outspoken advocate of individual liberty and voluntaryism. A member of the English aristocracy and a former Member of Parliament, Herbert rejected his early conservative political leanings and embraced a radical philosophy of individualism, influenced by thinkers such as Herbert Spencer and John Stuart Mill. He is best known for developing and promoting the concept of voluntaryism: the idea that all forms of human interaction, including governance, should be based on voluntary cooperation rather than coercion.

The Right and Wrong of Compulsion by the State (1885) is a critique of state-enforced compulsion. Herbert argued that all forms of compulsion by the state—whether for taxation, regulation, or enforcement of moral codes—are fundamentally unjust and contrary to individual liberty. He contrasted the morality of voluntary action with the immorality of coercion, insisting that individuals should be free to manage their own lives, property, and associations without interference, provided they do not harm others.

Herbert's central thesis in the book is that compulsion undermines human dignity and creativity by stripping individuals of their ability to make independent choices. He condemned both collectivist and authoritarian systems, believing that individual liberty and personal responsibility are essential for social harmony and progress. While recognizing the need for some form of governance, Herbert advocated for a "voluntary state" funded and supported by those who choose to participate, rather than through compulsory taxation or force.

Herbert believed that accountability for one's actions is essential to human interaction:

> ...you will not make people wiser and better by taking liberty of action from them. A man can only learn when he is free to act. It is the consequences of his own actions, and the consequences of these same actions as he sees them in other persons, that teach him.

He was unconvinced that majority rule is the just method to organize society:

> You tell me a majority has a right to decide as they like for their fellow-men. What majority? 21 to 20? 20 to 5? 20 to 1? But why any majority? What is there in numbers that can possibly make any opinion or decision better or more valid, or which can transfer the body and mind of one man into the keeping of another man? ...

> There cannot possibly be two supreme laws. Either the will of the majority or the rights of the individual are the highest law of our existence; one, whichever one it is to be, must yield in presence of the other....

> By what right do men exercise power over each other?

Herbert asked this fundamental question:

> Whatever party names we may give ourselves, this is the question always waiting for an answer: Do you believe in force and authority, or do you believe in liberty?[106]

Herbert advanced individual liberty by insisting that all human relations—even governance—should rest on voluntary cooperation rather than coercion. He argued that compulsion by the state, whether through taxation, regulation, or majority rule, robs people of dignity, responsibility, and the ability to learn from their choices. By defending voluntaryism and questioning the legitimacy of state power, Herbert reminded us that individual liberty means not just limiting government but rejecting the idea that force can ever be the foundation of justice or progress.

During the Modern Era, the study of economics blossomed, transforming the way people understood society and government. By incorporating economic analysis into political discussions, philosophers revealed that prosperity and social order arise not from central control but from the voluntary actions of individuals in the marketplace. This shift exposed the unseen costs of government intervention—such as taxation, regulation, and protectionism—and highlighted how free exchange, private property, and entrepreneurship create wealth and expand opportunity.

Economic reasoning provided a powerful tool to defend individual liberty, showing that when individuals are left free to make choices, society as a whole benefits. In this way, the fusion of economics with political thought advanced individual liberty by offering rational, evidence-based arguments against coercion and in favor of the natural harmony of voluntary cooperation.

7.9 The Twentieth Century

The gains in individual liberty made before and during the Enlightenment suffered great setbacks during the twentieth century.

Large nation states expanded the apparatus of government and waged devastating wars.

It became fashionable to believe that government had to be more "positive" and active in providing social safety nets for the masses against the uncertainties of life. Hence, the "progressives" in England, France, and especially the United States soon were referring to their ideas as a newer and more-enlightened "liberalism," which would create a truer and more complete "freedom" from want and worry.

The concept of liberalism, especially in the United States, was changing from a political and economic philosophy of individual liberty and free enterprise under the rule of law and limited government to a notion of political paternalism with an increasingly intrusive hand of government in the social and commercial affairs of its citizens.

Both the communists and the fascists rejected the ideas and the institutions of classical liberalism. Constitutional government, the rule of law, civil liberties, and economic freedom were declared by both these variations on the collectivist theme as reactionary hindrances to the success of the worker's state in Soviet Russia and national greatness in Fascist Italy. Both communism and fascism insisted that the individual needed to be "re-educated" and made to conform to the wider socialist or nationalist good. The individual was to be reduced to a cog in the machinery of the all-powerful and all-planning state.

1908, Oppenheimer and *The State*

In 1908, Franz Oppenheimer's book *The State* was published. His work offered a useful way of distinguishing between two different ways of obtaining material goods (one peaceful, the other coercive):

> There are two fundamentally opposed means whereby man, requiring sustenance, is impelled to obtain the necessary means for satisfying his desires. These are work and robbery, one's own labor and the forcible appropriation of the labor of others. ... I propose in the following discussion to call one's

own labor and the equivalent exchange of one's own labor for the labor of others the "economic means" for the satisfaction of needs, while the unrequited appropriation of the labor of others will be called the "political means".

He also argued that the state's origins are not peaceful or rational but rooted in violence (his explanation is systematic and comprehensive, so instead of summarizing it, I'll present it in full, followed by a discussion of its significance):

In the genesis of the state, from the subjection of a peasant folk by a tribe of herdsmen or by sea nomads, six stages may be distinguished. In the following discussion, it should not be assumed that the actual historical development must, in each particular case, climb the entire scale step by step.

The first stage comprises robbery and killing in border fights, endless combats broken neither by peace nor by armistice. It is marked by killing of men, carrying away of children and women, looting of herds, and burning of dwellings. Even if the offenders are defeated at first, they return in stronger and stronger bodies, impelled by the duty of blood feud. Sometimes, the peasant group may assemble, may organize its militia, and perhaps temporarily defeat the nimble enemy, but mobilization is too slow and supplies to be brought into the desert too costly for the peasants. The peasants' militia does not, as does the enemy, carry its stock of food—its herds—with it into the field. In the case of primitive levies, this difficulty is increased by the narrow spirit of the peasant, who considers only his own neighborhood, and by the fact that while the war is going on, the lands are uncultivated. Therefore, in such cases, in the long run, the small but compact and easily mobilized body constantly defeats the greater disjointed mass, as the panther triumphs over the buffalo.

This is the first stage in the formation of states. The state may remain stationary at this point for centuries, for a thousand years.

Gradually, from this first stage, there develops the second, in which the peasant, through thousands of unsuccessful attempts at revolt, has accepted his fate and has ceased every resistance. About this time, it begins to dawn on the consciousness of the wild herdsman that a murdered peasant can no longer plow and that a fruit tree hacked down will no longer bear. In his own interest, then, wherever it is possible, he lets the peasant live and the tree stand. The expedition of the herdsmen comes just as before, every member bristling with arms but no longer intending nor expecting war and violent appropriation. The raiders burn and kill only so far as is necessary to enforce a wholesome respect or to break an isolated resistance. But in general, principally in accordance with a developing customary right—the first germ of the development of all public law—the herdsman now appropriates only the surplus of the peasant. That is to say, he leaves the peasant his house, his gear, and his provisions up to the next crop. The herdsman in the first stage is like the bear, who, for the purpose of robbing the beehive, destroys it. In the second stage, he is like the beekeeper who leaves the bees enough honey to carry them through the winter.

The third stage arrives when the "surplus" obtained by the peasantry is brought by them regularly to the tents of the herdsmen as "tribute," a regulation which affords to both parties self-evident and considerable advantages. By this means, the peasantry is relieved entirely from the little irregularities connected with the former method of taxation, such as a few men knocked on the head, women violated, or farmhouses burned down. The herdsmen, on the other hand, need no longer apply to this "business" any "expense" and labor, to use a mercantile expression, and they devote the time and energy thus set free toward an "extension of the works," in other words, to subjugating other peasants.

The fourth stage, once more, is of very great importance since it adds the decisive factor in the development of the state as we are accustomed to see it, namely, the union on one strip of land of both ethnic groups. (It is well known that no jural definition of a state can be arrived at without the concept of state territory.) From now on, the relation of the two groups, which was originally international, gradually becomes more and more intra-national.

The logic of events presses quickly from the fourth to the fifth stage and fashions almost completely the full state. Quarrels arise between neighboring villages or clans, which the lords no longer permit to be fought out, since by this the capacity of the peasants for service would be impaired. The lords assume the right to arbitrate and, in case of need, to enforce their judgment. In the end, it happens that at each "court" of the village king or chief of the clan, there is an official deputy who exercises the power, while the chiefs are permitted to retain the appearance of authority.

The necessity of keeping the subjects in order and at the same time of maintaining them at their full capacity for labor leads step by step from the fifth to the sixth stage, in which the state, by acquiring full intra-nationality and by the evolution of "Nationality," is developed in every sense. The need becomes more and more frequent to interfere, to allay difficulties, to punish, or to coerce obedience; and thus develop the habit of rule and the usages of government. The two groups, separated to begin with, and then united on one territory, are at first merely laid alongside one another, then are scattered through one another like a mechanical mixture, as the term is used in chemistry, until gradually they become more and more of a "chemical combination." They intermingle, unite, amalgamate to unity in customs and habits, in speech and worship. Soon, the bonds of relationship unite the upper and the lower strata. In nearly all cases, the master class picks the handsomest virgins from the subject races for its concubines. A race of bastards thus develops, sometimes taken into the ruling class, sometimes rejected, and then, because of the blood of the masters in their veins, becoming the born leaders of the subject race. In form and in content, the primitive state is completed.[107]

Oppenheimer's model presents the state not as a voluntary social contract but as the institutionalization of conquest and exploitation. What begins as violent robbery evolves into systematic tribute, territorial control, judicial authority, and ultimately, a stable political order maintained by coercion and cultural assimilation.

This is a very important thesis that is fundamental to understanding the essence of government; therefore, I will present a summary:

- **First Stage**: Robbery and killing dominate border conflicts—men are slain, women and children abducted, herds looted, and dwellings burned.

- **Second Stage**: Conquerors realize that dead peasants cannot plow and ruined orchards bear no fruit. In their own interest, they begin to spare peasants and property, taking only surplus. As Oppenheimer puts it, the herdsman shifts from acting like a bear that destroys the hive to a beekeeper who harvests honey but leaves enough for the bees to survive.

- **Third Stage**: Surplus is no longer seized by raids but delivered regularly as tribute. Violence is minimized; exploitation is systematized.

- **Fourth Stage**: Conquerors and conquered settle on the same land. Territory becomes essential, transforming their relationship from external conflict to an internal political order.

- **Fifth Stage**: Lords assume judicial authority, forbidding private feuds and enforcing their judgments. Local chiefs retain symbolic authority while real power is exercised by the conquerors' deputies.

- **Sixth Stage**: The two groups gradually intermingle, merging customs, language, and worship. Intermarriage binds the upper and lower strata, and the state reaches its "primitive" yet complete form.

Oppenheimer argued that the State did not emerge from social cooperation but from conquest—the institutionalization of one group living off the labor of another. Its origins are not rooted in a social contract. Recognizing this dispels political illusions, highlights the moral contrast between voluntary exchange (the economic means) and coercion (the political means), and encourages the pursuit of social order through individual liberty and voluntary cooperation rather than force and violence.

1863 – 1952, The Quotations of Santayana

George Santayana was a Spanish-American philosopher, essayist, poet, and novelist. As a philosopher, he is recognized for his notable sayings:

Those who cannot remember the past are condemned to repeat it. (*The Life of Reason: The Phases of Human Progress*)

Only the dead have seen the end of war. (*Soliloquies in England and Later Soliloquies*)

He is additionally noted for stating the following:

Unless all those concerned keep a vigilant eye on the course of public business and frequently pronounce on its conduct, they will before long awake to the fact that they have been ignored and enslaved.

By presenting individual liberty as something that must be actively preserved rather than passively enjoyed, Santayana emphasized that a free society relies on continuous participation, collective memory, and vigilance from its citizens.

1864 – 1920, Weber and *The Protestant Ethic and the Spirit of Capitalism*

Maximilian Karl Emil Weber, known as Max Weber, was a prominent German sociologist and philosopher. Widely regarded as one of the founding figures of sociology, Weber made groundbreaking contributions that shaped modern social science, particularly through his work on the nature of authority, bureaucracy, and the role of culture in economic development.

Weber's scholarship crossed diverse fields, including law, history, and philosophy, but he was best known for his analysis of social organization and the concept of "rationalization" in modern societies. His book *The Protestant Ethic and the Spirit of Capitalism* (1905) explored the relationship between Protestant ethics and the development of Western capitalism, arguing that cultural beliefs and values profoundly influence economic behavior.

In "Politics as a Vocation," a lecture on January 28, 1919, to the Free (i.e., Non-incorporated) Students Union of Bavaria, Weber explained the origin of the State—and he found violence there, too:

> "Every state is founded on force," said Trotsky at Brest-Litovsk. That is indeed right. If no social institutions existed which knew the use of violence, then the concept of "state" would be eliminated, and a condition would emerge that could be designated as "anarchy" in the specific sense of this word. Of course, force is certainly not the normal or the only means of the state—nobody says that—but force is a means specific to the state. Today, the relation between the state and violence is an especially intimate one. In the past, the most varied institutions—beginning with the sib[xi]—have known the use of physical force as quite normal. Today, however, we have to say that a state is a human community that (successfully) claims the monopoly of the legitimate use of physical force

---

[xi]   Sib: Sibling, a blood relation.

within a given territory. Note that "territory" is one of the characteristics of the state. Specifically, at the present time, the right to use physical force is ascribed to other institutions or to individuals only to the extent to which the state permits it. The state is considered the sole source of the "right" to use violence. Hence, "politics" for us means striving to share power or striving to influence the distribution of power, either among states or among groups within a state.[108]

Weber's definition strips away illusions: The state is not the guardian of individual liberty or justice; it is simply the institution that claims a monopoly on violence.

1870 – 1945, Nock and *Our Enemy, the State*

Albert Jay Nock was an influential American libertarian author, educator, and social critic, renowned for his advocacy of individualism and his skeptical view of state power. Nock's writings often emphasized the importance of self-reliance, personal freedom, and a minimal role for government in the lives of individuals. He is best known for his books *Our Enemy, the State* (1935) and *Memoirs of a Superfluous Man* (1943), which outline his philosophy of limited government and his critique of centralized authority.

His disdain for tyranny is evident in this passage from *Our Enemy, the State*:

> The State claims and exercises the monopoly of crime. ... It forbids private murder, but itself organizes murder on a colossal scale. It punishes private theft, but itself lays unscrupulous hands on anything it wants.[109]

Throughout his career, Nock challenged prevailing political and economic doctrines, arguing that the expansion of state power inevitably leads to the erosion of personal liberties. He drew from classical liberal and libertarian traditions, stressing the value of education, culture, and individual character as the foundations of a free society. His work significantly influenced later libertarian thinkers and remains a standard for those advocating a restrained and decentralized approach to governance.

1880 – 1956, Mencken, the "Sage of Baltimore"

Henry Louis Mencken, often known as H.L. Mencken, was an American journalist, essayist, satirist, and cultural critic who gained fame for his wit, intellectual boldness, and sometimes controversial perspectives. Known as the "Sage of Baltimore," he was a defining voice in American literature and social commentary during the early twentieth century. Mencken's work encompassed a wide range of topics, from politics and religion to American life, journalism, and linguistics.

One of Mencken's best-known contributions was his role in cofounding and editing *The American Mercury*, a prominent literary magazine where he published critical essays and introduced emerging writers. His bold opinions and often scathing critiques of American democracy, Puritanism, and conventional values positioned him as a critical yet popular figure, known for his humor and irreverence.

Mencken was particularly famous for his coverage of the 1925 Scopes Trial, in which he used his sharp writing style to satirize the prosecution of John T. Scopes for teaching evolution in Tennessee. Among Mencken's works is also *The American Language*, an influential study of American English that showcased his interest in linguistics and the nuances of the American vernacular.

A few of his memorable quotations include the following:

> Democracy is the theory that the common people know what they want, and deserve to get it good and hard.

> Faith may be defined briefly as an illogical belief in the occurrence of the improbable.

Every normal man must be tempted, at times, to spit on his hands, hoist the black flag, and begin slitting throats.

A good politician is quite as unthinkable as an honest burglar.

The average man does not want to be free. He simply wants to be safe.

Love is the triumph of imagination over intelligence.

In his collection of essays *Notes on Democracy* (1926), he criticized the exalted and dehumanized view of government:

What keeps such notions in full credit, and safeguards them against destructive analysis, is chiefly the survival into our enlightened age of a concept hatched in the black days of absolutism—the concept, to wit, that government is something that is superior to and quite distinct from all other human institutions—that it is, in its essence, not a mere organization of ordinary men, like the Ku Klux Klan, the United States Steel Corporation or Columbia University, but a transcendental organism composed of aloof and impersonal powers, devoid wholly of self-interest and not to be measured by merely human standards. One hears it spoken of, not uncommonly, as one hears the law of gravitation and the grace of God spoken of—as if its acts had no human motive in them and stood clearly above human fallibility. This concept, I need not argue, is full of error. The government at Washington is no more impersonal than the cloak and suit business is impersonal. It is operated by precisely the same sort of men, and to almost the same ends. When we say that it has decided to do this or that, that it proposes or aspires to do this or that— usually to the great cost and inconvenience of nine-tenths of us—we simply say that a definite man or group of men has decided to do it, or proposes or aspires to do it; and when we examine this group of men realistically we almost invariably find that it is composed of individuals who are not only not superior to the general, but plainly and depressingly inferior, both in common sense and in common decency—that the act of government we are called upon to ratify and submit to is, in its essence, no more than an act of self-interest by men who, if no mythical authority stood behind them, would have a hard time of it surviving in the struggle for existence.[110]

Although controversial, Mencken's impact on American literature and thought was profound, marking him as one of the twentieth century's foremost commentators on society and culture. He advanced individual liberty not through policy or political activism but through his cultural influence; he demystified government, defended free expression, mocked conformity, and emboldened Americans to view power skeptically. His work helped cultivate a society more resistant to political illusions and more tolerant of free thought and individuality.

1878 – 1954, Garrett and *The People's Pottage*

Garet Garrett was an influential American writer, journalist, and economist, known for his deeply critical stance on government intervention in the economy and his support of individual liberty. His career began in journalism, where he worked for leading publications, including *The New York Times* and *The Wall Street Journal*. He eventually became an editorial writer and later the editor-in-chief of *The Saturday Evening Post*. Garrett's sharp economic insights and eloquent writing style distinguished him as one of the era's prominent voices against the expansion of federal powers.

Garrett's economic philosophy is often associated with the Old Right, a group of intellectuals who opposed New Deal policies and, later, U.S. involvement in World War II. His notable works, such as *The People's Pottage* (1953), criticized government overreach and the shift toward collectivist policies, which he believed undermined individual liberty and fiscal responsibility.

The following is a selection of some of his popular quotes:

The New Deal was not an election, it was a revolution.

> Between government in the republican meaning, that is, limited by certain unalienable rights of the individual, and government in the paternal sense, that is, unlimited, the difference is as wide as that which separated the old monarchy from the new democracy.
>
> There are those who have never forgiven me for having been right while they were wrong.

Garrett's writings combined economic analysis with a narrative style that drew readers into his arguments, particularly in his opposition to what he saw as the dangers of an expanding state.

1882 – 1964, Flynn and *The Roosevelt Myth*

John T. Flynn was an American journalist, author, and outspoken critic of both the New Deal and U.S. interventionist policies during World War II. Initially supporting progressive causes, Flynn became a key figure in the isolationist and non-interventionist movements of the 1930s and 1940s. His shift in political views reflected a broader skepticism of government expansion, especially under Franklin D. Roosevelt's administration, which Flynn criticized as overly authoritarian and economically unsustainable.

Flynn was a vocal member of the America First Committee, which opposed U.S. involvement in WWII, and his writings often focused on government overreach and civil liberties. His books, such as *The Roosevelt Myth* (which hit number two on the *New York Times* bestseller list in 1948), provided a critical perspective on FDR's legacy, depicting him as a manipulator of public opinion and power. Later in life, Flynn continued to critique the growth of the military-industrial complex, which he believed endangered both economic stability and individual liberty.

1886 – 1961, Paterson and *The God of the Machine*

Isabel Paterson was an influential American writer, critic, and philosopher and is often considered one of the founding figures of American libertarian thought. Born in rural Canada, she emigrated to the United States after World War I, where she would become a significant voice advocating for individual liberty, limited government, and free-market principles. Her most famous work, *The God of the Machine* (1943), presents a compelling case for economic and political freedom, drawing a unique analogy between energy flow in mechanical systems and the importance of unimpeded human creativity and productivity in society.

Paterson was a prominent literary critic, writing a widely read column in the *New York Herald Tribune*, where she not only reviewed books but also infused her commentary with ideas on philosophy, history, and politics. She was known for her sharp intellect, independence of thought, and close associations with other major figures of the libertarian movement—including Ayn Rand and Rose Wilder Lane, with whom she formed an informal intellectual trio sometimes referred to as the "Three Furies" of libertarianism.

Her work challenged the rising tide of collectivism in the twentieth century, arguing that true progress and human flourishing could only occur in a society where individuals were free to innovate and pursue their own paths without excessive government interference.

1886 – 1968, Lane and *The Discovery of Freedom: Man's Struggle Against Authority*

Rose Wilder Lane was an influential American writer, journalist, and political theorist. She is widely regarded as one of the founders of American libertarianism, alongside contemporaries such as Ayn Rand and Isabel Paterson. Lane was the daughter of Laura Ingalls Wilder, author of the *Little House on the Prairie* series, and she played a significant role in editing and shaping these books, which brought her mother international acclaim.

Throughout her life, Lane championed the ideals of individual liberty, self-reliance, and limited government. Her 1943 work, *The Discovery of Freedom: Man's Struggle Against Authority,* articulated her belief in personal autonomy and the importance of freedom from coercion. This book became a foundational text for the modern libertarian movement, advocating for the rights of individuals to govern their own lives without undue interference from centralized authority.

Lane initially embraced communist ideologies, influenced in her youth by socialist thinkers like Eugene Debs. However, her political philosophy underwent a significant transformation during her extensive travels through Eastern Europe, the Middle East, and the Soviet Union during the 1920s and 1930s, where she witnessed the oppressive conditions under totalitarian regimes. These experiences solidified her belief in the potential and necessity of individual liberty.

1881 – 1973, Mises and the Theory of Praxeology

When I speak of standing on the shoulders of giants, Ludwig von Mises stands among the tallest. He built upon the insights of earlier economists and political philosophers, extending their work and, more importantly, introducing several groundbreaking ideas of his own.

He was born in Lemberg (now Lviv, Ukraine), then part of the Austro-Hungarian Empire. In high school, he selected a verse from *Aeneid* by Virgil to be his motto: *"Tu ne cede malis sed contra audentior ito"* ("Do not give in to evil but proceed ever more boldly against it"). He attended the University of Vienna, where he was influenced by the work of Carl Menger, and he earned his doctorate in law and economics in 1906.

After graduation, Mises worked as an economic advisor to the Austrian government and private institutions. He also attended lectures given by Austrian economist Eugen von Böhm-Bawerk.

During World War I, Mises served as a frontline officer in the Austro-Hungarian artillery, which led to partial hearing impairment that affected him for the rest of his life. He also served as an economic advisor to the War Department.

In 1934, Mises left Austria for Geneva, Switzerland, where he worked as a professor at the Graduate Institute of International Studies. While in Switzerland, Mises married Margit Herzfeld Serény. He told Margit that he would write a lot about money but would never have very much of it.

On the day the German Army entered Vienna, soldiers stormed Mises's apartment, seemingly searching for him. They confiscated his library and papers, as his Jewish heritage and staunch opposition to authoritarianism made him a target. Mises was in Geneva, Switzerland, at the time, but in 1940, when the German invasion of France was about to leave Switzerland completely surrounded by Fascist- and Nazi-controlled territory, Mises and Margit fled through France, dodging German troops on their way to Spain and Portugal, where they managed to leave Europe for the United States.

Upon his arrival in the United States, Mises faced significant challenges in securing an academic position. At the time, the academic environment in the U.S. was dominated by Keynesian economics, which emphasized government intervention and macroeconomic management. The Austrian School's emphasis on free markets and methodological individualism was seen as less relevant and even out of step with prevailing trends. Mises's radical critiques of socialism and interventionist economics positioned him outside the mainstream, making universities hesitant to offer him positions.

In 1945, Mises began teaching at New York University (NYU), though his position was unique. He held the title of visiting professor in the Graduate School of Business Administration, but his salary was not paid by the university. Instead, it was funded by private supporters, including businessmen and foundations sympathetic to his ideas, such as the William Volker Fund. Mises remained at NYU until 1969, where he influenced economists such as F.A. Hayek, Murray Rothbard, Israel Kirzner, and Hans Sennholz.

Mises made the following contributions to the field of economics:

- **Praxeology (Methodology)**: Mises defined economics as the study of human action, based on the observation that individuals act purposefully. He developed praxeology as a deductive, logical approach to understanding behavior. Unlike the natural sciences, economics cannot rely on experiments; it must proceed from self-evident truths about human action.

- **Theory of Money (Regression Theorem)**: To explain the origin of money's value, Mises developed the regression theorem, showing that money must have originally derived its value from being a commodity with direct utility. This traced the purchasing power of money back to its non-monetary use.

- **Austrian Business Cycle Theory (ABCT)**: Mises contended that credit expansion and artificially low interest rates—typically driven by fractional reserve banking and central banks—distort price signals, mislead entrepreneurs, and create unsustainable booms that inevitably lead to busts.

- **Critique of Socialism (Economic Calculation Problem)**: Mises argued that rational economic calculation is impossible under socialism. Without private property and market prices for capital goods, planners lack the information necessary to allocate resources efficiently.

- **Defense of Free Markets**: Mises emphasized that only voluntary exchange and freely determined market prices can effectively coordinate complex economic activity.

- **Economic Freedom and Individual Liberty**: Mises connected economics with political philosophy, arguing that economic freedom is essential to individual liberty. Without efficient free markets, personal and political freedoms erode.

Each of these six contributions deserves further exploration. A brief overview of each is provided below.

Praxeology

Mises's theory of praxeology is one of his most significant contributions to economic thought. It represents a distinctive methodological approach to understanding human behavior.

Praxeology, from the Greek words *praxis* (action) and *logos* (study), is the science of human action. Mises developed this framework to analyze economic and social phenomena by focusing on the purposeful choices individuals make to achieve their desired ends.

Mises defined action as behavior directed toward achieving specific goals. Unlike reflexive or involuntary movements, human action is always intentional and aimed at addressing perceived needs or improving one's state of being.

In Mises's praxeological framework, humans cannot truly "not act" while conscious, as action is defined as purposeful behavior aimed at achieving a desired goal. Even inaction, such as choosing to remain still or abstaining from physical activity, is itself an intentional decision and, therefore, qualifies as action. This focus on intentionality sets praxeology apart from other approaches that treat human behavior as driven purely by external stimuli or inevitable forces.

Mises argued that praxeology is an a priori science, meaning its principles are derived from logical reasoning rather than empirical observation. For example, the statement "human beings act to achieve goals" is self-evident and does not require experimental validation. This deductive approach contrasts sharply with the empirical methods of mainstream economics, which rely heavily on numerical data and economic statistics.

Mises emphasized that value is subjective and varies from person to person. Individuals assign value to goods and services based on how well they believe those items will help them achieve their goals. This principle underpins the theory of marginal utility developed earlier by Carl Menger, which explains how individuals make decisions about resource allocation.

Mises recognized that scarcity (i.e., limited resources) forces individuals to prioritize their goals. Praxeology examines how people allocate scarce resources to satisfy competing wants.

He also highlighted the importance of time in human action. Mises elaborated on Eugen von Böhm-Bawerk's concept of time preference, the idea that individuals prefer present satisfaction over future satisfaction. This principle is crucial for understanding interest rates and capital investment. As Mises pointed out, human action takes place in a world of uncertainty. Entrepreneurs play a critical role in praxeology, as they take risks and allocate resources in anticipation of future demands in an uncertain world.

Praxeology underscores the importance of individual liberty, as it views human action as inherently subjective and purposeful. Economic systems that respect personal choice and voluntary exchange are, therefore, more consistent with human nature.

Theory of Money

Mises published *The Theory of Money and Credit* in 1912. Here, he traced the origins of money to the evolution of barter systems, explaining how money emerged as the most marketable good, as it simplified trade and enabled economic calculation. He refined Carl Menger's theory of the origin of money, emphasizing its emergence through spontaneous order rather than as a creation of the state.

In his work, Mises included the effects of credit in the study of money's effects. By showing how both money and credit function in human action, Mises revealed that government manipulation of currency undermines stability, prosperity, and individual liberty. Sound, market-based money protects property and voluntary exchange, making it essential to individual liberty.

Mises distinguished between two types of credit:

> **Commodity Credit**: This is credit backed by real savings, which contributes to productive investment.

> **Circulation Credit**: This is credit created by banks without corresponding savings, which leads to distortions in the economy. This occurs when banks lend more money than they have on deposit, a system known as "fractional reserve banking."[xii, 111]

In his 1943 essay "Cyclical Changes in Business Conditions, The Sequel of Credit Expansion," Mises explained the damage caused by circulation credit:

> Credit expansion cannot increase the supply of real goods. It merely brings about a rearrangement. It diverts capital investment away from the course prescribed by the state of economic wealth and market conditions. It causes production to pursue paths which it would not follow unless the economy were to acquire an increase in material goods. As a result, the upswing lacks a solid base. It is not real prosperity. It is illusory prosperity. It did not develop from an increase in economic wealth. Rather, it arose because the credit expansion created the illusion of such an increase. Sooner or later, it must become apparent that this economic situation is built on sand.[112]

[xii] A banking system in which banks hold only a fraction of their customers' deposits as reserves, either in cash or at a central bank, and lend out the remaining portion. This system allows banks to create credit and expand the money supply, but it also relies on the assumption that not all depositors will withdraw their funds simultaneously.

Austrian Business Cycle Theory

Mises described inflation as an increase in the money supply that reduces the purchasing power of money, distorting prices and economic signals. He critiqued inflationary monetary policies, warning that they create temporary booms followed by inevitable busts. This insight laid the foundation for the Austrian Business Cycle Theory (ABCT), which was later expanded by F.A. Hayek. Mises argued that artificially low interest rates, resulting from credit expansion by fractional reserve banking and the printing of money by a central bank, lead to malinvestment in unsustainable projects. These distortions eventually cause economic downturns when the malinvestment and unsustainable projects fail and are liquidated. In his book *Human Action: A Treatise on Economics* (1949), he summarized ABCT:

The wavelike movement affecting the economic system, the recurrence of periods of boom which are followed by periods of depression, is the unavoidable outcome of the attempts, repeated again and again, to lower the gross market rate of interest by means of credit expansion. There is no means of avoiding the final collapse of a boom brought about by credit expansion. The alternative is only whether the crisis should come sooner as the result of a voluntary abandonment of further credit expansion, or later as a final and total catastrophe of the currency system involved.[113]

Critique of Socialism

In 1920, Mises published the essay "Economic Calculation in the Socialist Commonwealth." In this most devastating critique of socialism, he illuminated its central flaw: By monopolizing ownership of key factors of production—such as factories, raw materials, and land—a socialist government eliminates genuine market prices for these inputs. Therefore, even after the fact, it would be impossible for the socialist central planners to tell whether or not their commands made economic sense. They would see the benefits of their production plans—so many cars, diapers, apple pies, and so on—but they would have no way of judging the efficiency of their commands because they cannot calculate profit or loss (as they lack the prices necessary to conduct such calculations).

Without prices for key factors of production—land, natural resources, and essential commodities (lumber, steel, rubber, plastic, etc.)—efficient allocation becomes impossible. For instance, should a factory use rubber or plastic as a crucial component? Similarly, without clear pricing, other critical decisions, such as whether to build a shoe factory closer to raw material sources or to retail markets, cannot be made effectively.

Defense of Free Markets

Mises followed that essay with the book *Socialism: An Economic and Sociological Analysis* (1922). This work is celebrated for the penetrating economic calculation argument discussed above. However, the book contains much more. In it, Mises not only demonstrated the impossibility of socialism but also defended capitalism against the primary arguments socialists and other critics have raised against it. A centrally planned system cannot substitute some other form of economic calculation for market prices because no such alternative exists. Capitalism is true economic democracy.

Socialism addresses the contemporary issues of economic inequality and argues that wealth can exist for long periods only to the extent that wealthy producers succeed in satisfying the consumers. Mises also showed that there is no tendency toward monopoly in a free-market system.

He additionally analyzed utilitarian measures such as social security and labor legislation, which in fact impede the efforts of the capitalist system to satisfy the demand for goods and services from individuals.

It became fashionable in the twentieth century to advocate a "middle of the road" system between socialism and capitalism. In his 1927 book *Liberalism: In the Classical Tradition*, Mises dismissed that idea:

> There is simply no other choice than this: either to abstain
> from interference in the free play of the market or to delegate
> the entire management of production and distribution to the
> government. Either capitalism or socialism: there exists no
> middle way.[114]

In his 1944 book *Bureaucracy*, Mises unmasked the essence of bureaucracy: "The ultimate basis of an all-around bureaucratic system is violence." As for the bureaucrats making the rules, Mises observed, "He who is unfit to serve his fellow citizens wants to rule them."

Economic Freedom and Individual Liberty

In his 1951 essay "Profit and Loss," Mises examines the roles of capital and entrepreneurship. In economic analysis, capital refers to all man-made goods used in wealth production: machinery, tools, equipment, buildings, transportation, communication systems, and raw materials. Karl Marx referred to these capital goods as "the means of production." Mises challenged Marx's misconception that capital alone generates profit, arguing instead that profit stems from the entrepreneur's foresight and decision-making, not merely from owning capital:

> But it is not the capital employed that creates profits and
> losses. Capital does not "beget profit" as Marx thought. The
> capital goods as such are dead things that in themselves do
> not accomplish anything. If they are utilized according to a
> good idea, profit results. If they are utilized according to a
> mistaken idea, no profit or losses result. It is the entrepre-
> neurial decision that creates either profit or loss. It is mental
> acts, the mind of the entrepreneur, from which profits ulti-
> mately originate. Profit is a product of the mind, of success in
> anticipating the future state of the market. It is a spiritual and
> intellectual phenomenon.[115]

In his 1958 speech to the Mont Pelerin Society, later published as "Liberty and Property," Mises reached this conclusion:

Government is essentially the negation of liberty.[116]

With that single sentence, he makes it clear that government can never advance individual liberty. As you well know by now, individual liberty requires freedom from coercion—the ability to choose, exchange voluntarily, and enjoy the fruits of one's labor. Government, however, is by its nature an institution of coercion. Every action it takes—whether through taxation, regulation, or restrictions on personal choice—replaces voluntary action with coercion. Though some form of government might sometimes be necessary to protect life and property, its essence is coercion, and every expansion of its role inevitably diminishes individual liberty.

1894 – 1993, Hazlitt and *Economics in One Lesson*

Henry Hazlitt was an influential American economist, journalist, and author, renowned for his clear, accessible writing on economic principles and free-market ideas. Born in Philadelphia and raised in Brooklyn, Hazlitt grew up in poverty, his father having died when Hazlitt was an infant. He attended New York City College but left after only a short time to support his twice-widowed mother.

His career spanned multiple high-profile roles, including as an editor at *The Wall Street Journal*, *The New York Times*, and *Newsweek*, where he wrote columns on economic theory, policy, and philosophical insights. Working in the tradition of philosophers such as Frédéric Bastiat and economists like Ludwig von Mises, Hazlitt was a vocal critic of Keynesian economics, arguing instead for the power of the free market and warning against the unintended consequences of government intervention.

Throughout his life, Hazlitt engaged with other intellectuals and made significant contributions to the modern libertarian movement. His writings remain a significant source of economic education and are often cited by economists and policymakers interested in market-based solutions and individual liberty.

His most famous work, *Economics in One Lesson* (1946), simplifies complex economic concepts into clear, accessible lessons, stressing the importance of considering long-term consequences over immediate effects. It modernizes the ideas explored in Bastiat's 1850 essay, "That Which Is Seen, and That Which Is Not Seen." Widely regarded as a foundational text, Hazlitt's book continues to influence advocates of economic freedom and individual liberty to this day.

Hazlitt's insights are still relevant to present-day policy disputes and controversies, especially during inflationary periods. Thus, Hazlitt once wrote,

> Inflation tears apart the whole fabric of stable economic relationships. It drives men toward desperate remedies. It leads men to demand totalitarian controls. It ends invariably in bitter disillusion and collapse.[117]

Monetary inflation, a topic of great importance to Hazlitt, has indeed been the inspiration for unwise and oppressive policies—once the inflation of the money supply generates its negative effects (high prices), the public is more easily persuaded to adopt measures like wage and price controls or to demonize private business as a way of solving the very problem caused by increasing the money supply in the first place.

1899 – 1992, Hayek and Equality

Friedrich August von Hayek, commonly known as F.A. Hayek, began his career in Austria, studying law and economics at the University of Vienna. At the University, he became associated with the Austrian School of Economics, led by his mentor Ludwig von Mises. Hayek's early work focused on capital theory, money, and economic cycles, leading to his prominent role in debates on business cycles during the Great Depression. In 1931, he joined the London School of Economics, where he famously debated John Maynard Keynes on economic policy.

Hayek argued against Keynes's interventionist approach, warning of the dangers of inflation and government interference.

In *The Road to Serfdom* (1944), Hayek argued that any shift from a free market to government planning undermines human freedom and pushes society toward dictatorship—a principle he applied universally. He maintained that all forms of collectivism oppose individual liberty, and he discussed the shared collectivist and authoritarian roots of Communism, Fascism, and Nazism. According to Hayek, these regimes were built on the same fundamental philosophy that the collective is superior to the individual. He also refuted claims that government control could improve social well-being, asserting instead that such planning leads to a harsher, more oppressive, and less livable society.

In his 1949 essay "The Intellectuals and Socialism," Hayek explored why intellectuals consistently advocate for socialism. He observed that in every country that had moved toward socialism, the transition had been preceded by years of intellectuals shaping public thought with socialist ideals.

Hayek used the term "intellectuals" broadly—to refer not just to professors or informed laypeople but to a wider group he called "second-hand dealers in ideas." This includes journalists, teachers, columnists, writers, publicists, politicians, and others whose primary work involves spreading ideas rather than generating them.

According to Hayek, intellectuals serve as intermediaries, translating complex or technical theories into language the public can understand. Regardless of where ideas originate, intellectuals play a key role in shaping public opinion.

He observed that many intellectuals view socialism as morally superior, highlighting its emphasis on equality, fairness, and social justice—values that strongly appeal to those concerned with addressing inequality.

However, Hayek argued that because intellectuals often lack deep knowledge of economics, they are prone to embrace simplified, idealistic solutions. These may seem humane in theory, but they always fail in practice due to unforeseen consequences and economic misunderstandings.

One of Hayek's key contributions to economics was his concept of spontaneous order, which suggested that social order and economic efficiency arise naturally when individuals make independent decisions. In his 1945 article "The Use of Knowledge in Society," Hayek argued that prices in a free-market economy efficiently convey information about scarcity and demand, guiding resource allocation better than any central authority could. This insight is foundational to modern economics, showing how decentralized markets can organize society more effectively than planned economies.

In *The Constitution of Liberty* (1960), Hayek argued that a free society depends not only on democratic elections but also on institutional checks, the rule of law, and a culture of personal responsibility.

For Hayek, individual liberty requires that people take responsibility for their actions. When individuals are accountable, society remains open, adaptable, and capable of self-correction. As he put it, "Individual responsibility—facing the consequences of one's actions—is a prerequisite for a free society."

He warned that democracy, if left unchecked, can slip into the tyranny of the majority or evolve into a cult of personality, where citizens willingly cede power to authoritarian rulers. Simply having the right to vote is not enough to guarantee freedom; liberty depends on constitutional limits and a citizenry committed to personal responsibility. As Hayek observed,

> Perhaps the fact that we have seen millions voting themselves into complete dependence on a tyrant has made our generation understand that to choose one's government is not necessarily to secure freedom.[118]

In 1974, Hayek was awarded the Nobel Prize in Economic Sciences for his work on the theory of money and economic fluctuations—the Austrian Business Cycle Theory discussed earlier. In addition to Hayek, many economists from the Austrian School, most notably Ludwig von Mises, were instrumental in developing this theory. As mentioned before, it explains how economic booms and busts are driven by government intervention, particularly through the manipulation of interest rates by central banks and by private banks under the protection of the central bank through fractional reserve banking.

When interest rates are driven below their natural market level, businesses and individuals borrow and invest more than they otherwise would, leading to overinvestment in long-term projects. These investments are often unsustainable because they are based on artificially low borrowing costs rather than real savings. Resources get allocated toward projects that look profitable in the short term because of cheap credit, but lack sustainable consumer demand in the long term.

Initially, this manipulation of interest rates leads to economic growth (the boom phase): More projects are undertaken, which creates jobs and increases spending. However, because this boom is driven by distorted interest rates rather than actual consumer preferences, it is unsustainable.

Eventually, reality sets in as these unprofitable projects fail to produce the expected returns or cannot even be completed, leading to business failures, job losses, and economic contraction (the bust phase). The economy then undergoes a painful readjustment, in which resources are reallocated to more sustainable uses.

ABCT emphasizes that these cycles are not inherent to a free market but are caused by distortions introduced by central banks and fractional reserve banking. Austrian economists argue that avoiding such cycles requires minimizing government intervention and allowing interest rates to be determined by the market.

Hayek was influential in both economics and political philosophy, as reflected in his philosophical definition of law from his 1979 book *Law, Legislation, and Liberty*. Hayek argued that law should be understood as a set of abstract, general rules that emerge and evolve spontaneously (often described as "cosmos," or natural order). By contrast, legislation is the deliberate creation of new, targeted rules (often described as "taxis," or constructed order) by governing bodies. Relying too heavily on legislative centralized rule-making, in Hayek's view, risks politicizing everyday life and undermining the genuine rule of law.

Hayek included this provocative statement as a warning of the effects of excessive legislation in daily life:

> A claim for equality of material position can be met only by a government with totalitarian powers.[119]

He refined this concept by sharply distinguishing between equality before the law and equality of outcome. Hayek advocated for a system where all individuals are treated equally under general, abstract rules—without special privileges or penalties for particular groups. In contrast, he argued that striving to equalize outcomes such as income, wealth, or status inevitably requires centralized and coercive control. He maintained that moral worth and economic reward rarely align in reality, and efforts to force such alignment through legislation come at the cost of individual liberty. True individual liberty, he contended, enables individuals to pursue their own goals, naturally leading to unequal outcomes because of differences in talent, effort, and luck. Enforcing uniform outcomes, therefore, demands restricting the very freedom that produces those differences.

Hayek's book *The Fatal Conceit: The Errors of Socialism,* published in 1988, defined the "fatal conceit" as the mistaken belief that society can be successfully organized according to a centralized, rational plan. He argued that this conceit arises from overconfidence in human reason and ignorance of the complex processes that underpin social order.

He emphasized that human societies and institutions are products of cultural evolution rather than deliberate design. Practices like private property, free exchange, and markets emerged because they were effective at promoting cooperation and survival, not because they were consciously devised. He condemned socialism for assuming that planners can gather and process all the information necessary to allocate resources effectively, a task that markets accomplish through decentralized decision-making.

Hayek highlighted the limits of human reason, warning against hubris in trying to control or redesign complex systems. He argued that humility is necessary to appreciate the benefits of spontaneous order and to resist the allure of utopian schemes.

When considering a brilliant new theory, economists would be wise to follow Hayek's advice:

> The curious task of economics is to demonstrate to men how little they really know about what they imagine they can design.[120]

Hayek advanced the cause of individual liberty by demonstrating that freedom is essential to knowledge, prosperity, and progress; warning against the dangers of central planning and collectivism; defending the rule of law; and inspiring an intellectual movement committed to preserving and expanding human freedom.

1911 – 2004, Ronald Reagan

Ronald Reagan served as Governor of California from 1967 to 1975 and as President of the United States from 1981 to 1989. His political career took off with his "A Time for Choosing" speech during the 1964 presidential election, which established him as a prominent conservative leader.

Although Reagan championed individual liberty, his administration failed to shrink the size of the government, managing only to slow its growth. Federal spending and deficits rose during his presidency. However, increased U.S. military spending pressured the Soviet Union into a costly arms race that ultimately contributed to its economic collapse.

Reagan, known as "The Great Communicator," left behind many memorable quotes, including these two:

> Freedom is never more than one generation away from extinction. We didn't pass it to our children in the bloodstream. It must be fought for, protected, and handed on for them to do the same. (An address to the Phoenix Chamber of Commerce, 1961)

> Government is not the solution to our problem; government is the problem. (From his first inaugural address, 1981)

Reagan consistently linked America's political freedom to its economic freedom, arguing that liberty in one sphere cannot exist without the other. He championed free expression, religious liberty, and individual dignity in opposition to collectivist ideologies. Reagan played a key role in the collapse of the Soviet Union, symbolized by his famous challenge to "tear down this wall" in Berlin. He revived public enthusiasm for classical liberalism and free-market principles, helping to spark a broader movement for limited government, entrepreneurship, and self-reliance.

1913, The Fed

The Federal Reserve System (commonly known as the Fed), the third central bank of the United States, was established through the Federal Reserve Act.

According to the official narrative, the Fed was established to

- enable the monetary system to expand or contract as needed to meet the demands of the economy, reducing the frequency of financial panics and ensuring liquidity during crises.

- create a decentralized system of Federal Reserve Banks to oversee and regulate member banks, ensuring sound banking practices and reducing systemic risks.

- provide emergency liquidity to banks and financial institutions during economic crises to prevent widespread bank failures and financial collapses (a lender of last resort).

- improve the efficiency and reliability of the national payments system, particularly by standardizing check clearing and currency distribution.

- ensure that the financial system supports economic growth by maintaining stable credit conditions and fostering an environment conducive to investment and expansion.

Today, the Fed operates under a dual mandate introduced by the 1978 Humphrey-Hawkins Act:

Price Stability: Controlling consumer and producer price inflation

Maximum Employment: Supporting conditions that achieve full employment

Further details on the origins of the Fed can be found in *The Creature from Jekyll Island: A Second Look at the Federal Reserve* by G. Edward Griffin (1994).

Griffin's research reveals that the blueprint for the Federal Reserve was crafted during a secret meeting on Jekyll Island, Georgia, in 1910. Three senior U.S. politicians and three influential bankers attended the meeting, all traveling incognito under the cover story of a duck hunting trip.[xiii] Ultimately, the Fed was conceived to centralize monetary authority, prioritizing private interests over public accountability.

[xiii] The meeting was organized by Nelson Aldrich, a U.S. Senator from Rhode Island. Attendees included Arthur Shelton, Aldrich's secretary and aide to the National Monetary Commission; A. Piatt Andrew, Assistant Secretary of the Treasury; Henry P. Davison, partner at J.P. Morgan & Co.; Frank A. Vanderlip, president of the National City Bank of New York (later Citibank) and former Treasury official; and Paul M. Warburg, partner at Kuhn, Loeb & Co.

If you have trouble believing Griffin's account of these events, you can read the exact details directly from the Federal Reserve's website under Federal Reserve History. Look for the article titled "The Meeting at Jekyll Island," and don't overlook the second section, subtitled "The Duck Hunt." The following paragraphs from the Federal Reserve's own website confirm that Griffin was neither fabricating nor exaggerating his account:

> By the fall of 1910, Aldrich was persuaded of the necessity of a central bank for the United States. With Congress ready to begin meeting in just a few weeks, Aldrich—most likely at Davison's suggestion—decided to convene a small group to help him synthesize all he had learned and write down a proposal to establish a central bank.

> The group included Aldrich; his private secretary Arthur Shelton; Davison; Andrew (who by 1910 had been appointed assistant Treasury secretary); Frank Vanderlip, president of National City Bank and a former Treasury official; and Warburg.

> A member of the exclusive Jekyll Island Club, most likely J.P. Morgan, arranged for the group to use the club's facilities. Founded in 1886, the club's membership boasted elites such as Morgan, Marshall Field, and William Kissam Vanderbilt I, whose mansion-sized "cottages" dotted the island. Munsey's Magazine described it in 1904 as "the richest, the most exclusive, the most inaccessible" club in the world.

> Aldrich and Davison chose the attendees for their expertise, but Aldrich knew their ties to Wall Street could arouse suspicion about their motives and threaten the bill's political passage. So he went to great lengths to keep the meeting secret, adopting the ruse of a duck hunting trip and instructing the men to come one at a time to a train terminal in New Jersey, where they could board his private train car. Once aboard, the men used only first names—Nelson, Harry, Frank, Paul, Piatt, and Arthur—to prevent the staff

from learning their identities. For decades after, the group referred to themselves as the "First Name Club."[121]

In essence, the Fed is a cartel that benefits major banks and financial elites at the expense of ordinary citizens. It was designed to limit competition, maximize profits for member banks, and consolidate economic power.

Twenty years after the Fed was established, the Roosevelt administration abandoned the gold standard in favor of fiat currency. This shift devalued the dollar, fueled price inflation, and led to economic instability, while also contributing to rising national debt and recurring financial crises.

The Fed encourages fractional reserve banking, which enriches banks while grinding the middle class into dust under the millstone of devalued currency and price inflation.

As an institution, the Fed is part of a larger push toward global governance and economic control. It can be linked to organizations like the International Monetary Fund and the World Bank, playing a major role in the "New World Order" agenda.

Finally, Griffin explored how the abolition of the Fed and a return to a monetary system based on tangible assets, like gold or silver, would restore transparency and justice in economic policy.

1918, Bourne and "War is the Health of the State"

In 1918, the political essayist Randolph Bourne died during the Spanish flu pandemic. He left behind the unfinished essay "The State"—the first part of which, titled "War is the Health of the State," was published posthumously and is largely considered his most influential work. In this essay, he made no excuses for wartime authoritarianism:

> Wartime brings the ideal of the State out into very clear relief
> and reveals attitudes and tendencies that were hidden. In

times of peace, the sense of the State flags in a republic that is not militarized. For war is essentially the health of the State. The ideal of the State is that within its territory its power and influence should be universal....

War is the health of the State. It automatically sets in motion throughout society those irresistible forces for uniformity, for passionate cooperation with the Government in coercing into obedience the minority groups and individuals which lack the larger herd sense....

All of which goes to show that the State represents all the autocratic, arbitrary, coercive, belligerent forces within a social group, it is a sort of complexus of everything most distasteful to the modern free creative spirit, the feeling for life, liberty, and the pursuit of happiness. War is the health of the State. Only when the State is at war does the modern society function with that unity of sentiment, simple uncritical patriotic devotion, cooperation of services, which have always been the ideal of the State lover.[122]

Bourne explained that war fuels the expansion of state power at the expense of individual liberty. His essay stands as a powerful defense of peace, voluntary cooperation, and resistance to state coercion.

1945, De Jouvenel and *On Power: The Natural History of Its Growth*

In 1945, Bertrand de Jouvenel published *On Power: The Natural History of Its Growth*. This work explores the inherent characteristics of political power, emphasizing its tendency to grow and consolidate. De Jouvenel argued that power seeks to expand its reach, often using crises and wars as justifications for increased control. One of the book's central themes is the tension between power and individual liberty.

De Jouvenel explored the idea that true liberty lies in individuals' sovereignty over their own lives. He critiqued the modern state's inclination to centralize authority and regulate various aspects of society, and he highlighted the implications this has for democracy. He warned of the dangers posed by a powerful bureaucratic state, arguing that as political power expands, it inevitably infringes upon personal freedoms and undermines individual autonomy.

The book examines the concept of consent in the legitimacy of power. De Jouvenel argued that power often masks its coercive nature by seeking consent from the governed. He scrutinized the processes through which consent is manufactured and the impact this has on genuine democratic governance.

He discussed the relationship between power and war, arguing that war is often used as a pretext to expand and solidify power. Another theme explored in his work is how governments leverage wartime conditions to impose controls and increase their authority. The book addresses the societal consequences of growing political power, including the erosion of social structures and community bonds. Ultimately, De Jouvenel warned of the dangers of a society increasingly dominated by centralized power, which can lead to alienation and loss of individual agency.

1947, The Mont Pelerin Society

The Mont Pelerin Society was established in 1947 as a response to the growing influence of socialism, collectivism, and government intervention in the economy. It is an international organization of scholars, economists, and intellectuals dedicated to advancing classical liberalism, free market policies, and limited government.

The founding members were Friedrich A. Hayek, Ludwig von Mises, Milton Friedman, Karl Popper, Frank Knight, George Stigler, Lionel Robbins, Michael Polanyi, Wilhelm Röpke, Walter Eucken, and Bertrand de Jouvenel.

The mission statement of the Mont Pelerin Society includes the following:

> The group does not aspire to conduct propaganda. It seeks to establish no meticulous and hampering orthodoxy. It aligns itself with no particular party. Its object is solely, by facilitating the exchange of views among minds inspired by certain ideals and broad conceptions held in common, to contribute to the preservation and improvement of the free society.

The Mont Pelerin Society advances individual liberty by preserving classical liberal ideas, fostering an international community of scholars, shaping reforms that expand freedom, and sustaining the intellectual defense of free societies against collectivism.

1905 – 1982, Rand and the Power of Human Reason

Ayn Rand, born Alisa Zinovyevna Rosenbaum in St. Petersburg in 1905, grew up during the chaotic years of the Russian Revolution. The Bolshevik regime's collectivist policies profoundly shaped her disdain for socialism and her advocacy for individual liberty.

In 1926, she emigrated to the United States, determined to pursue a career in writing. She initially stayed with relatives in Chicago. During her time there, Rand took steps to learn English, develop her writing skills, and immerse herself in American culture.

She departed Chicago to seek work as a screenwriter in Hollywood. Starting out with work as an extra on movie sets, she found a full-time job working in the wardrobe department at RKO Studios, eventually becoming head of the department by 1932.

Rand left Hollywood and moved to New York when she sold a screenplay, "Red Pawn," to Universal Pictures. Her first real breakthrough came with a play—variously entitled "Night of January 16," "Penthouse Legend," and "Woman on Trial"—which ran first in Hollywood and then for seven months on Broadway in New York.

She was then able to dedicate her time to writing novels that reflected her philosophy, advocating for individual liberty grounded in rational judgment. The central role of human reason in her work is evident in the following attributions:

> As human beings, our basic means of living—our basic means of identifying and pursuing our life-serving values—is our rational judgment.

> When and to the extent physical force (coercion) is used against a person, it stops him from acting in accordance with his judgment.

> If people are to act in accordance with their basic means of living, then they must be left free from the initiation of physical force (including fraud and extortion).

Rand's 1938 novel *Anthem* describes a dystopian future society where equality has become the fundamental principle. The main character is forced to conform to the rigid rules of equality. The nightly ritual is depicted thus:

> Before we removed our garments, we stood in the great sleeping hall, and we raised our right arms, and we said all together with the three Teachers at the head:

> We are nothing. Mankind is all. By the grace of our brothers are we allowed our lives. We exist through, by, and for our brothers who are the State. Amen.

Upon escaping from his dystopian captivity and discovering the ideals of individual achievement and liberty, the protagonist is overcome with emotion, expressing his newfound vision with passion:

> These are the things before me. And as I stand here at the door of glory, I look behind me for the last time. I look upon the history of men, which I have learned from the books, and I wonder. It was a long story, and the spirit which moved it was

the spirit of man's freedom. But what is freedom? Freedom from what? There is nothing to take a man's freedom away from him, save other men. To be free, a man must be free of his brothers. That is freedom. That and nothing else.

At first, man was enslaved by the gods. But he broke their chains. Then, he was enslaved by the kings. But he broke their chains. He was enslaved by his birth, by his kin, by his race. But he broke their chains. He declared to all his brothers that a man has rights which neither God nor king nor other men can take away from him, no matter what their number, for his is the right of man, and there is no right on earth above this right. And he stood on the threshold of the freedom for which the blood of the centuries behind him had been spilled.[123]

In her 1957 novel *Atlas Shrugged,* Rand included a speech by the hero of the story, John Galt, which builds to this dramatic conclusion:

Do not let the hero in your soul perish, in lonely frustration for the life you deserved, but have never been able to reach. Check your road and the nature of your battle. The world you desired can be won, it exists, it is real, it is possible, it's yours.

But to win it requires your total dedication and a total break with the world of your past, with the doctrine that man is a sacrificial animal who exists for the pleasure of others. Fight for the value of your person. Fight for the virtue of your pride. Fight for the essence of that which is man: for his sovereign rational mind. Fight with the radiant certainty and the absolute rectitude of knowing that yours is the Morality of Life and that yours is the battle for any achievement, any value, any grandeur, any goodness, any joy that has ever existed on this earth.

You will win when you are ready to pronounce the oath I have taken at the start of my battle—and for those who wish to know the day of my return, I shall now repeat it to the hearing of the world:

I swear—by my life and my love of it—that I will never live for the sake of another man, nor ask another man to live for mine.[124]

She also revealed an undeniable truth in her 1966 book *Capitalism: The Unknown Ideal*:

The smallest minority on earth is the individual. Those who deny individual rights cannot claim to be defenders of minorities.[125]

Rand's philosophy emphasized the preeminence of the individual:

Man—every man—is an end in himself, not a means to the ends of others; he must live for his own sake, neither sacrificing himself to others nor sacrificing others to himself; he must work for his rational self-interest, with the achievement of his own happiness as the highest moral purpose of his life.[126]

Rand provided a moral and philosophical defense of capitalism, exposing the dangers of collectivism, dramatizing the heroism of independent individuals, and popularizing the idea that individual liberty is both a moral necessity and the precondition for human flourishing.

1956, De-Stalinization

A political reform known as de-Stalinization was launched in the Soviet Union at the 20th Party Congress on February 25, 1956, by Soviet Communist Party First Secretary Nikita Khrushchev. This reformation condemned the cult of personality and the crimes committed by his predecessor, Joseph Stalin. These disclosures destroyed Stalin's image as an infallible leader and promised a return to so-called "socialist legality" and Leninist principles of party rule. This sent shockwaves through communists worldwide, who had been taught to revere Stalin. The reform severely damaged the Soviet Union's prestige, strained the international communist movement, and helped spark uprisings in Poland and Hungary.

The Polish uprising, also known as the Poznań June, was a major protest against the communist government of Poland and Soviet influence. It began on June 28, 1956, in the city of Poznań, where workers at the Cegielski factories organized a strike to demand better wages, improved working conditions, and more political freedom. The protests quickly escalated, with around 100,000 people taking to the streets to call for an end to the oppressive policies of the government and Soviet control.

The Polish government, under the leadership of Boleslaw Bierut, initially responded with force, deploying soldiers and tanks to quell the demonstrations. Over fifty people were killed, and hundreds were wounded.

In the aftermath, the Polish United Workers' Party sought to address the people's grievances by electing a new leader, Władysław Gomułka, who was perceived as more moderate and sympathetic to Polish nationalism. Gomułka negotiated with Soviet Premier Nikita Khrushchev and managed to secure some concessions, including reduced Soviet interference in Polish domestic affairs.

Later, also in 1956, a similar rebellion occurred in Hungary. This was a spontaneous revolt against the Soviet-backed communist government, lasting from October 23 to November 10. Sparked by widespread dissatisfaction with political repression, economic hardship, and Soviet domination, it began as a student-led demonstration in Budapest that called for democratic reforms, freedom of speech, and the withdrawal of Soviet troops.

As protests grew, Hungarian citizens joined the movement, and within days, demonstrations escalated into a full-blown revolution. Hungarian workers, students, and soldiers took up arms, dismantling Stalinist symbols and forming militias.

The leader of the Hungarian freedom fighters during the 1956 uprising was Imre Nagy. Nagy was a reform-minded communist politician who had served as Prime Minister of Hungary before being marginalized by the Soviet-backed government due to his more liberal policies. As the uprising began, the people called for his return, and on October 24, he was reappointed as Prime Minister. These events forced the ruling Hungarian Communist Party to promise reforms, and on October 28, the government declared an intention to withdraw from the Warsaw Pact.

However, on November 4, the Soviet Union launched a massive military intervention to crush the uprising. Thousands of tanks entered Budapest and other cities, leading to intense fighting that resulted in significant casualties.

Imre Nagy made several radio addresses during the uprising, and one of his messages began with the plea "This is Hungary calling." In these broadcasts, Nagy spoke directly to both the Hungarian people and the international community, urgently appealing for help as Soviet forces invaded.

His most famous radio address was made on November 4, 1956, just as Soviet tanks entered Budapest. In this speech, he announced the Soviet invasion, declaring, "Our troops are fighting ... the government is in its place." He called on the United Nations and the world to support Hungary's struggle for independence, affirming Hungary's desire to live as a free nation.

The international community did not respond with support, and ultimately, approximately 2,500 Hungarians and 700 Soviet troops were killed. Over 200,000 Hungarians fled as refugees (two percent of the population), with most crossing by foot into Austria. The revolt was ultimately suppressed, and a pro-Soviet government was reinstated under János Kádár.

The Eisenhower administration was criticized for its inaction during these movements; despite encouraging citizens in communist countries to rise up and overthrow their leaders, the United States did nothing to support the freedom fighters in Poland and Hungary. When questioned about this lack of support, members of the Eisenhower administration characterized their Eastern European strategy as part of a broader policy of "keeping the pot boiling, without letting it boil over."

One U.S. celebrity felt compelled to help the people of Hungary. Elvis Presley, at the close of his last appearance on the Ed Sullivan Show on January 6, 1957, made an appeal for donations to an audience of 54.6 million people. By the end of 1957, the Geneva-based International Red Cross had received $6 million in donations for Hungary—the equivalent of over $71 million in 2025.

Although the 1956 Hungarian rebellion was brutally crushed by Soviet tanks—leaving thousands dead and forcing hundreds of thousands to flee into exile—the spirit of resistance did not die. The uprising revealed the Hungarian people's yearning for freedom and their refusal to fully submit to Soviet domination. Even under the decades of repression that followed, Hungary remained restless, keeping alive the memory of defiance and demonstrating that the human desire for individual liberty cannot be permanently extinguished by force.

1898 – 1983, Read and the Foundation for Economic Education

Leonard E. Read was born on a family farm in Hubbardston, Michigan. His father died when he was eleven years old. He helped his mother sell the farm and establish the first boarding house in town. To supplement the family income, he worked long hours as a farmhand and in the village store.

When the United States entered World War I, Read enlisted in the Army and served in the Aviation Section of the U.S. Signal Corps. After being discharged in 1919, he pursued various careers to save enough money for college and medical school. Read married and soon became a father to two sons. He started the Ann Arbor Produce Company, which sold produce from local farmers; the business thrived until supermarkets began to dominate the grocery business. Eventually, Read closed the Ann Arbor Produce Company and moved his family to California.

Over the next eighteen years, he worked in the Chamber of Commerce; he managed branches in four locations and ultimately served as General Manager of the Los Angeles Chamber. In this role, he oversaw a staff of 150 supporting 18,000 members.

During his time with the Chamber of Commerce, Read attended a meeting with William C. Mullendore, the executive vice president of Southern California Edison. During that meeting, Read became fully convinced of the inefficiency and moral bankruptcy of the New Deal. Thereafter, his views grew increasingly libertarian: His exploration of political philosophy and economics would be profoundly shaped by Albert Jay Nock and later enriched by the ideas of Ludwig von Mises, Ayn Rand, and Henry Hazlitt.

In 1945, Read became Executive Vice President of the National Industrial Conference Board in New York, where he looked forward to launching a nationwide educational program for the restoration of individual liberty and economic freedom. However, he left this position after several months, disillusioned with the methods being used to promote individual liberty.

In 1946, during a meeting with David Goodrich, Chairman of B.F. Goodrich Company, Read was offered the opportunity to establish his own organization dedicated to promoting education in economics and the philosophy of individual liberty. This meeting led to the creation of the Foundation for Economic Education.[127]

In 1958, Read published his essay "I, Pencil," a first-person account of a pencil's creation from raw materials sourced worldwide. The essay illustrates the miraculous coordination enabled by free markets and the impossibility of central economic planning. It also masterfully explains the concepts of division of labor and spontaneous order.

As Milton Friedman put it,

> I know of no other piece of literature that so succinctly, persuasively, and effectively illustrates the meaning of both Adam Smith's invisible hand—the possibility of cooperation without coercion—and Friedrich Hayek's emphasis on the importance of dispersed knowledge and the role of the price system in communicating information that will make the individuals do the desirable things without anyone having to tell them what to do.

Economics professor Donald J. Boudreaux added,

> For its sheer power to display in just a few pages the astounding fact that free markets successfully coordinate the actions of literally millions of people from around the world into a productive whole, nothing else written in economics compares to Leonard Read's celebrated essay, "I, Pencil."

Personally, "I, Pencil" is one of my favorite essays, and I recommend it to everyone. At first, the concepts of the division of labor and spontaneous order may seem miraculous, yet it eventually becomes evident how they form the foundation of economic freedom and prosperity. Through clear and memorable writing, Leonard E. Read popularized free-market ideas, emphasized personal responsibility, and inspired a movement that continues to educate and advocate for freedom today.

1961, Cowperthwaite and Hong Kong

In 1961, Hong Kong's Financial Secretary John Cowperthwaite began implementing laissez-faire economic policies, which would transform a small, sparsely populated, inconsequential trading port into a global financial powerhouse.

The economic model adopted in Hong Kong was characterized by low taxes, minimal government intervention, and free trade, encouraging entrepreneurship and attracting foreign investment.

Hong Kong established a strong rule of law, transparent governance, and robust property rights under British colonial administration, which fostered investor confidence. A flexible labor market and minimal bureaucratic barriers encouraged innovation and efficiency, creating a society where voluntary exchange, entrepreneurship, and property rights—not government control—determined economic life. It showed that when individuals are free to act, prosperity and human flourishing follow.

Within a generation, Hong Kong transformed from a struggling trading port into one of the world's leading financial centers, lifting millions out of poverty in the process. Its success became a real-world demonstration of the power of economic freedom.

1965, Yew and Singapore

Singapore gained independence from Malaysia on August 7, 1965. Under the leadership of Prime Minister Lee Kuan Yew, Singapore embarked on an ambitious economic development strategy focused on attracting foreign investment, industrializing, and building a skilled workforce, prioritizing meritocracy and efficiency.

Singapore fostered a highly favorable environment for businesses with its low taxes, minimal corruption, and streamlined regulations. It actively attracted foreign direct investment by offering incentives to multinational corporations and creating free trade agreements.

Despite its small size and lack of natural resources, Singapore has become a global leader in trade, finance, and innovation.

Singapore's economic policies unmistakably expanded individual liberty and economic freedom by showing how open markets, meritocracy, and the rule of law can transform a struggling society into a thriving, prosperous one.

1912 – 2006, Friedman and *Capitalism and Freedom*

Milton Friedman was born in Brooklyn, New York City, on July 31, 1912, to working-class immigrants from Beregszász, Hungary (now Berehove, Ukraine). Shortly after Friedman's birth, his family moved to Rahway, New Jersey. During his senior year of high school, Friedman's father passed away, leaving him and his two older sisters to support their mother.

Friedman graduated from Rahway High School in 1928, just shy of his sixteenth birthday. He earned a competitive scholarship to Rutgers

University, from which he graduated in 1932. Offered scholarships for graduate studies in both mathematics at Brown University and economics at the University of Chicago, he chose the latter; he earned his Master of Arts degree in 1933, and in 1946, he was awarded a PhD from Columbia University. Friedman returned to the University of Chicago to teach, where he spent the next thirty years shaping the field of economics.

He was awarded the Nobel Memorial Prize in Economic Sciences, the sole recipient for 1976, "for his achievements in the fields of consumption analysis, monetary history and theory, and for his demonstration of the complexity of stabilization policy."

Friedman retired from teaching at the University of Chicago in 1977. He and his wife, Rose, relocated to San Francisco, where he became a contributing scholar at the Hoover Institution at Stanford University.

His book *Capitalism and Freedom* was published in 1962 and identifies fourteen government activities that could not be justified under principles of individual liberty:

1. Parity price support programs for agriculture.

2. Tariffs on imports or restrictions on exports, such as current oil import quotas, sugar quotas, etc.

3. Governmental control of output, such as through the farm program, or through prorationing of oil as is done by the Texas Railroad Commission.

4. Rent control, such as is still practiced in New York, or more general price and wage controls such as were imposed during and just after World War II.

5. Legal minimum wage rates, or legal maximum prices, such as the legal maximum of zero on the rate of interest that can be paid on demand deposits by commercial banks, or the legally

fixed maximum rates that can be paid on savings and time deposits.

6. Detailed regulation of industries, such as the regulation of transportation by the Interstate Commerce Commission. This had some justification on technical monopoly grounds when initially introduced for railroads; it has none now for any means of transport. Another example is detailed regulation of banking.

7. A similar example, but one which deserves special mention because of its implicit censorship and violation of free speech, is the control of radio and television by the Federal Communications Commission.

8. Present social security programs, especially the old-age and retirement programs compelling people in effect (a) to spend a specified fraction of their income on the purchase of retirement annuity, (b) to buy the annuity from a publicly operated enterprise.

9. Licensure provisions in various cities and states which restrict particular enterprises or occupations or professions to people who have a license, where the license is more than a receipt for a tax which anyone who wishes to enter the activity may pay.

10. So-called "public-housing" and the host of other subsidy programs directed at fostering residential construction such as F.H.A. and V.A. guarantee of mortgage, and the like.

11. Conscription to man the military services in peacetime. The appropriate free market arrangement is volunteer military forces; which is to say, hiring men to serve. There is no justification for not paying whatever price is necessary to attract the required number of men. Present arrangements are inequitable and arbitrary, seriously interfere with the freedom of young men to shape their lives, and probably are even more

costly than the market alternative. (Universal military training to provide a reserve for war time is a different problem
and may be justified on liberal grounds.)

12. National parks.

13. The legal prohibition on the carrying of mail for profit.

14. Publicly owned and operated toll roads.[128]

On January 27, 1973, one item was eliminated from Friedman's list:
The Selective Service Administration announced that there would be
no further draft calls. U.S. military forces would now be composed of
volunteers.

During the Congressional Gates Commission's discussions about ending the draft and moving to an all-volunteer force, Friedman famously
clashed with General William Westmoreland over the concept of conscription. Westmoreland, a career military officer, was concerned that a
volunteer army might be more costly and less effective than one formed
by conscription. He argued that requiring service from citizens was justified in times of national need.

In a memorable exchange, Friedman challenged Westmoreland's views
on the draft, framing it as a matter of freedom and individual choice.
Friedman asked Westmoreland whether he would rather command an
army of volunteers or conscripts. Westmoreland responded by saying he
did not want to lead an army of "mercenaries." Friedman replied sharply,
"General, would you rather command an army of slaves?"

In *Capitalism and Freedom,* Friedman elegantly and concisely described
his philosophy:

> The heart of the liberal philosophy is a belief in the dignity of
> the individual, in his freedom to make the most of his capac-
> ities and opportunities according to his own lights, subject
> only to the proviso that he not interfere with the freedom of
> other individuals to do the same. This implies a belief in the

equality of men in one sense; in their inequality in another. Each man has an equal right to freedom. This is an important and fundamental right precisely because men are different, because one man will want to do different things with his freedom than another, and in the process can contribute more than another to the general culture of the society in which many men live.[129]

Also in *Capitalism and Freedom,* he provided us with a purpose:

> Only a crisis, real or perceived, produces real change. When that crisis occurs, the actions that are taken depend on the ideas that are lying around. That, I believe, is our basic function: to develop alternatives to existing policies, to keep them alive and available until the politically impossible becomes politically inevitable.[130]

Friedman had a gift for distilling complex issues into clear, concise ideas. His insights on government spending from a 1980 TV interview are a brilliant example of this talent:

> Keep your eye on one thing and one thing only—how much government is spending. Because that's the true tax. Every budget is balanced. There is no such thing as an unbalanced federal budget. You're paying for it. If you're not paying for it in the form of explicit taxes, you're paying for it in the form of inflation, or in the form of borrowing.

In his book *Free to Choose* (1980), Friedman passionately promoted the benefits of individual liberty:

> A society that puts equality—in the sense of equality of outcome—ahead of freedom will end up with neither equality nor freedom. The use of force to achieve equality will destroy freedom, and the force, introduced for good purposes, will end up in the hands of people who use it to promote their own interests.

On the other hand, a society that puts freedom first will, as a happy by-product, end up with both greater freedom and greater equality. Though a by-product of freedom, greater equality is not an accident. A free society releases the energies and abilities of people to pursue their own objectives. It prevents some people from arbitrarily suppressing others. It does not prevent some people from achieving positions of privilege, but so long as freedom is maintained, it prevents those positions of privilege from becoming institutionalized; they are subject to continued attack by other able, ambitious people. Freedom means diversity but also mobility. It preserves the opportunity for today's disadvantaged to become tomorrow's privileged and, in the process, enables almost everyone, from top to bottom, to enjoy a fuller and richer life.[131]

Throughout his career, Friedman championed free markets as essential to political freedom, exposed the failures of government intervention, advocated sound money, pioneered school choice, and brought the principles of individual liberty to a global audience.

1968, The Prague Spring

The Prague Spring was a period of political liberalization and reform in Czechoslovakia in 1968, led by Alexander Dubček, the new leader of the Communist Party of Czechoslovakia. Starting in January, Dubček introduced reforms aimed at creating "socialism with a human face," seeking to reduce censorship, increase freedom of speech and the press, decentralize the economy, and give more autonomy to Czechoslovakia's two regions: the Czech Republic and Slovakia.

The reforms sparked widespread enthusiasm among Czechoslovak citizens, who supported Dubček's vision for a more open and democratic socialist society. Intellectuals, students, and workers held rallies and discussions, expressing ideas freely for the first time in decades. This movement inspired hope across Eastern Europe, as people saw it as a potential model for a more democratic socialism within the Soviet sphere.

However, the Soviet Union and other Warsaw Pact countries saw the Prague Spring as a threat to their control over the Eastern Bloc. They feared that Czechoslovakia's liberalization could lead to similar demands in neighboring countries and weaken Soviet influence. On August 20 and 21,1968, Soviet-led Warsaw Pact forces invaded Czechoslovakia, effectively ending the Prague Spring. Despite some resistance, Dubček was arrested, and the reforms were rolled back.

The following months saw the beginning of a period known as "normalization," in which the Soviet Union reinstated strict authoritarian rule, silencing dissent and reinforcing centralized control. Dubček was replaced, and many reformers were removed from power. Even so, the Prague Spring became a powerful symbol of resistance to Soviet oppression and an inspiration for later democratic movements.

The Prague Spring briefly expanded freedoms in Czechoslovakia, inspiring resistance to authoritarianism and keeping alive the vision of a freer society, which would resurface in the revolutions of 1989.

1926 – 1995, Rothbard, "Enemy of the State"

Murray Rothbard was born in the Bronx, New York City, to immigrant parents. His father, a chemist, moved the family to Manhattan's Upper West Side, where Rothbard attended the Birch Wathen School; he later said he much preferred Birch Wathen to the "debasing and egalitarian public school system" he had attended in the Bronx. After graduating, he attended Columbia University, where he received a Bachelor of Arts degree in mathematics in 1945 and a PhD in economics in 1956 under Joseph Dorfman.

Rothbard attended seminars taught by Austrian economist Ludwig von Mises in the 1950s. Inspired, he began studying—and became a vocal advocate for—Austrian economics.

Throughout his career, Rothbard published frequently, building an unambiguous case that government is the enemy of individual liberty. A foundational figure in modern libertarianism, he combined Austrian economics with a steadfast defense of individual rights grounded in natural law. His influence extended beyond scholarship to activism: He played a key role in founding organizations like the Cato Institute and the Ludwig von Mises Institute.

Rothbard extended Mises's praxeological framework in his landmark book *Man, Economy, and State* (1962), a comprehensive exposition of Austrian economics.

He believed that the very existence of the state—the entity with a monopoly privilege to invade private property—is contrary to the ethics of liberty. By contrast, a society without a state is not only viable; it is the only one consistent with natural rights. Rothbard championed the idea of anarcho-capitalism, arguing that private institutions could provide even services like law, security, and dispute resolution more effectively than the state.

He provided the following definition in the *Libertarian Forum* (1969):

> I define an anarchist society as one where there is no legal possibility for coercive aggression against the person or property of any individual. Anarchists oppose the State because it has its very being in such aggression, namely, the expropriation of private property through taxation, the coercive exclusion of other providers of defense service from its territory, and all of the other depredations and coercions that are built upon these twin foci of invasions of individual rights.[132]

He proposed his definition of the State in his essay "Anatomy of the State" (1974):

> Briefly, the State is that organization in society which attempts to maintain a monopoly of the use of force and violence in a given territorial area; in particular, it is the only organization in society that obtains its revenue not by voluntary contribution or payment for services rendered but by coercion.

While other individuals or institutions obtain their income by production of goods and services and by the peaceful and voluntary sale of these goods and services to others, the State obtains its revenue by the use of compulsion; that is, by the use and the threat of the jailhouse and the bayonet.[133]

From 1975 to 1979, Rothbard published *Conceived in Liberty*, a history of the United States, in four volumes. In the preface, he describes the contest between liberty and power as the central drama in the story of man:

My own basic perspective on the history of man, and a fortiori on the history of the United States, is to place central importance on the great conflict which is eternally waged between Liberty and Power, a conflict, by the way, which was seen with crystal clarity by the American revolutionaries of the eighteenth century. I see the liberty of the individual not only as a great moral good in itself (or, with Lord Acton, as the highest political good), but also as the necessary condition for the flowering of all the other goods that mankind cherishes: moral virtue, civilization, the arts and sciences, economic prosperity. Out of liberty, then, stem the glories of civilized life. But liberty has always been threatened by the encroachments of power, power which seeks to suppress, control, cripple, tax, and exploit the fruits of liberty and production. Power, then, the enemy of liberty, is consequently the enemy of all the other goods and fruits of civilization that mankind holds dear. And power is almost always centered in and focused on that central repository of power and violence: the state. With Albert Jay Nock, the twentieth century American political philosopher, I see history as centrally a race and conflict between "social power"—the productive consequence of voluntary interactions among men—and state power. In those eras of history when liberty—social power—has managed to race ahead of state power and control, the country and even mankind have flourished. In those eras when state power has managed to catch up with or surpass social power, mankind suffers and declines.[134]

In 1973, Rothbard presented his vision for a free society in *For a New Liberty: The Libertarian Manifesto*, in which he challenged conventional views on government with sharp criticism:

> ...The great non sequitur committed by defenders of the State, is to leap from the necessity of society to the necessity of the State.

> ...The man who puts all the guns and all the decision-making power into the hands of the central government and then says, "Limit yourself"; it is he who is truly the impractical utopian.

> ...If we look around, then, at the crucial problem areas of our society—the areas of crisis and failure—we find in each and every case a red thread marking and uniting them all: the thread of government. In every one of these cases, government either has totally run or heavily influenced the activity.[135]

The Ethics of Liberty, published in 1982, applies his insistence on individual self-ownership to the resolution of difficult ethical questions and concludes by challenging readers to take action to achieve individual liberty:

> If liberty should be the highest political end, then what is the grounding for that goal? It should be clear from this work that, first and foremost, liberty is a moral principle, grounded in the nature of man. In particular, it is a principle of justice, of the abolition of aggressive violence in the affairs of men. Hence, to be grounded and pursued adequately, the libertarian goal must be sought in the spirit of an overriding devotion to justice. But to possess such devotion on what may well be a long and rocky road, the libertarian must be possessed of a passion for justice, an emotion derived from and channeled by his rational insight into what natural justice

requires. Justice, not the weak reed of mere utility, must be the motivating force if liberty is to be attained.

If liberty is to be the highest political end, then this implies that liberty is to be pursued by the most efficacious means, i.e., those means which will most speedily and thoroughly arrive at the goal. This means that the libertarian must be an "abolitionist," i.e., he must wish to achieve the goal of liberty as rapidly as possible. If he balks at abolitionism, then he is no longer holding liberty as the highest political end. The libertarian, then, should be an abolitionist who would, if he could, abolish instantaneously all invasions of liberty.[136]

Rothbard earned his reputation as "Enemy of the State" with this devastating statement that he applied universally:

Taxation is theft, purely and simply even though it is theft on a grand and colossal scale which no acknowledged criminals could hope to match. It is a compulsory seizure of the property of the State's inhabitants, or subjects.[137]

Rothbard's vision of a society completely free of coercion, based on voluntary cooperation in all activities and transactions, might seem like an unrealistic goal in the real world. When discussing this vision, you will likely be asked if any society has ever functioned on these principles. You can answer yes: We discussed one such society in Chapter 7.2, the early Gaelic civilizations of Ireland, known as *túath*. This was a society that functioned completely free of coercion and was based on voluntary cooperation. The result was a peaceful and prosperous society that flourished for nearly 2,000 years.

1971, Sowell and *Economics: Analysis and Issues*

Thomas Sowell, an economist, social theorist, and senior fellow at Stanford University's Hoover Institution, began his prolific writing career with the publication of his first book, *Economics: Analysis and Issues*, in 1971.

Born in North Carolina in 1930 and raised in Harlem, Sowell served in the U.S. Marine Corps during the Korean War before pursuing higher education. He earned a bachelor's degree from Harvard University, a master's from Columbia University, and a doctorate in economics from the University of Chicago, where he studied under Nobel Prize–winning economist Milton Friedman. Over his career, he taught at such institutions as Cornell, UCLA, and Amherst College.

In his youth, particularly during his college years, Sowell identified as a Marxist. When asked how he maintained this perspective while studying under Milton Friedman, he quipped, "I was stubborn." However, his Marxist views were short-lived; Sowell credits his time as an intern at the U.S. Department of Labor with prompting him to question and ultimately reject Marxism.

Sowell has expressed his opinions on economics, society, and politics with no apologies:

> The most basic question is not what is best, but who shall decide what is best. (*Knowledge and Decisions*, 1980)[138]

> In economics, there are no solutions, only trade-offs. (*A Conflict of Visions*, 1987)[139]

> The first lesson of economics is scarcity: There is never enough of anything to satisfy all those who want it. The first lesson of politics is to disregard the first lesson of economics. (*Is Reality Optional? And Other Essays*, 1993)[140]

> I have never understood why it is "greed" to want to keep the money you have earned but not greed to want to take somebody else's money. (*Barbarians Inside the Gates and Other Controversial Essays*, 1999)[141]

> It is hard to imagine a more stupid or more dangerous way of making decisions than by putting those decisions in the hands of people who pay no price for being wrong. (*Wake Up, Parents!*, 2000)[142]

The real goal should be reduced government spending, rather than balanced budgets achieved by ever rising tax rates to cover ever rising spending. (From an interview with John Hawkins, 2012)

When people get used to preferential treatment, equal treatment seems like discrimination. (Attributed to Thomas Sowell)

Through scholarship and public commentary, Sowell has made a powerful case that individual liberty thrives when government power is restrained, property rights are respected, and people are free to make choices guided by their own knowledge and responsibility.

1974, Nozick and *Anarchy, State, and Utopia*

In his 1974 book *Anarchy, State, and Utopia*, Robert Nozick argued in favor of a minimal state, "limited to the narrow functions of protection against force, theft, fraud, enforcement of contracts, and so on." When a state takes on more responsibilities than these, Nozick contended, rights will be violated.

To support the idea of the minimal state, Nozick argued that the minimalist state (which confines itself to the protection of person and property) arises naturally from anarchy, but that any expansion of state power past this minimalist threshold is unjustified.

While considering the expansion of state power, Nozick presented the following scenario:

Consider the following sequence of cases, which we shall call "The Tale of the Slave," and imagine it is about you.

1. There is a slave completely at the mercy of his brutal master's whims. He is often cruelly beaten, called out in the middle of the night, and so on.

2. The master is kindlier and beats the slave only for stated infractions of his rules (not fulfilling the work quota, and so on). He gives the slave some free time.

3. The master has a group of slaves, and he decides how things are to be allocated among them on nice grounds, taking into account their needs, merit, and so on.

4. The master allows his slaves four days on their own and requires them to work only three days a week on his land. The rest of the time is their own.

5. The master allows his slaves to go off and work in the city (or anywhere they wish) for wages. He requires only that they send back to him three-sevenths of their wages. He also retains the power to recall them to the plantation if some emergency threatens his land; and to raise or lower the three-sevenths amount required to be turned over to him. He further retains the right to restrict the slaves from participating in certain dangerous activities that threaten his financial return, for example, mountain climbing, cigarette smoking.

6. The master allows all of his 10,000 slaves, except you, to vote, and the joint decision is made by all of them. There is open discussion, and so forth, among them, and they have the power to determine to what uses to put whatever percentage of your (and their) earnings they decide to take; what activities legitimately may be forbidden to you, and so on.

Let us pause in this sequence of cases to take stock. If the master contracts this transfer of power so that he cannot withdraw it, you have a change of master. You now have 10,000 masters instead of just one; rather you have one 10,000-headed master. Perhaps the 10,000 will be kindlier than the benevolent master in case 2. Still, they are your master. However, still more can be done. A kindly single master (as in case 2) might allow his slave(s) to speak up and try to persuade him to make a certain decision. The 10,000-headed master can do this also.

7. Though still not having the vote, you are at liberty (and are given the right) to enter into the discussions of the 10,000, to try to persuade them to adopt various policies and to treat you and themselves in a certain way. They then go off to vote to decide upon policies covering the vast range of their powers.

8. In appreciation of your useful contributions to discussion, the 10,000 allow you to vote if they are deadlocked; they commit themselves to this procedure. After the discussion you mark your vote on a slip of paper, and they go off and vote. In the eventuality that they divide evenly on some issue, 5,000 for and 5,000 against, they look at your ballot and count it in. This has never yet happened; they have never yet had occasion to open your ballot. (A single master also might commit himself to letting his slave decide any issue concerning him about which he, the master, was absolutely indifferent.)

9. They throw your vote in with theirs. If they are exactly tied your vote carries the issue. Otherwise it makes no difference to the electoral outcome.

The question is: which transition from case 1 to case 9 made it no longer the tale of a slave?

Nozick chooses the details of this tale carefully. In case 5, the master demands three-sevenths of wages—about 43%—a figure comparable to the total tax burden many workers face today, considering all federal, state, and local taxes paid. In addition to collecting the tax, the master retains the authority to conscript[xiv] and regulate personal conduct. In case 8, you are allowed to vote, but your vote will only be opened and

---

[xiv] When Robert Nozick wrote this book, the United States still had conscription and an active military draft.

counted if the other votes submitted result in a tie. Note that this is precisely the situation we have in our current system of voting: Your vote only changes the outcome of an election if all other votes counted result in a tie.

As the tale progresses, the narrative shifts. What begins as a simple story of a slave evolves into a broader critique of modern taxation, conscription, regulation, and democratic participation.

Nozick's well-designed thought experiment deserves your careful consideration. Can you find a transition that makes it no longer the tale of a slave?

1976, Block and *Defending the Undefendable*

In his 1976 book *Defending the Undefendable*, Walter Block applied a strict interpretation of libertarian ethics, arguing that no act should be criminalized unless it involves aggression against another person's body or property. He contended that individuals engaged in "victimless" or socially disapproved activities—such as prostitution, blackmail, drug dealing, or usury—do not violate anyone's rights and, therefore, should not face state punishment. He simplified this concept with a brief quote: "No activity is criminal if it involves no force or fraud."

The following are some examples of "undefendable" professions and individuals that Block defends in the book:

> **The Prostitute**: Block contends that prostitution is a consensual exchange between adults and that government prohibition is unjustified. He argues, "Prostitution is merely selling a service; banning it is paternalistic meddling," and insists, "When consenting adults make exchanges, the state should step aside."

> **The Pimp**: Block presents the pimp as a facilitator who provides economic and, at times, physical protection for sex workers.

The Drug Dealer: Since the exchange of drugs is voluntary between seller and buyer, Block contends it should not be treated as a criminal act.

The Blackmailer: Although widely condemned, Block likens blackmail to selling information. If the threat involves disclosing truthful information and no force is used, he argues it should be a civil issue, not a criminal one. In his opinion, "Blackmail is simply the legitimate sale of silence—no crime is committed."

The Slumlord: Despite their negative image, Block maintains that slumlords offer housing that is often the only affordable option for low-income tenants—thereby fulfilling a real need.

Block has emphasized the role of markets in coordinating willing buyers and sellers—even in industries often viewed as disreputable. He has argued that regardless of how objectionable a transaction may seem to outsiders, free choice and competition are more effective regulators than government prohibition.

He challenged the notion that regulation is necessary to serve the common good, exposing it as an impossible dream:

> The reasoning employed by those who want governmental regulation contains a self-contradiction. On the one hand they assert that the American people are unalterably gullible. They must be protected because, left to their own devices, they become victims. They can be made to think, for example, that if they use a certain brand of aftershave lotion, they will end up with the girl in the ad. On the other hand, the argument assumes that the boobs are smart enough to pick political leaders capable of regulating these sirens. This is impossible.[143]

Block's narrative illustrates the idea that strict interpretation of the non-aggression principle permits no exceptions. Here, Block has extended the principle further, contending that any activity not violating the non-aggression principle should remain free from regulation or legal prohibition. In this way, he has placed the non-aggression principle at the center of legal and regulatory thought.

1980, Polish Resistance

The Polish labor resistance to communism, led primarily by the Solidarity (Solidarność) movement, played a critical role in undermining communist rule in Poland and inspiring democratic movements across Eastern Europe. The resistance began in the 1970s with widespread dissatisfaction among Polish workers due to economic hardship, poor working conditions, and political repression under the communist government.

In August 1980, a major wave of strikes erupted at the Lenin Shipyard in Gdańsk, led by an electrician named Lech Wałęsa. The workers demanded better wages, improved working conditions, and the right to form an independent trade union. The movement quickly gained support across Poland, and the government eventually agreed to many of the demands, resulting in the formation of Solidarity, the first independent labor union in a Soviet-bloc country. At its height, Solidarity had over ten million members, representing a powerful force against the communist regime.

Solidarity promoted not only labor rights but also broader social and political reforms, advocating for free elections, civil liberties, and democratic governance. Its activities were met with harsh repression from the government, which imposed martial law in December 1981, banned Solidarity, and arrested thousands of its leaders and members. However, the union continued to operate underground and maintained significant support among the Polish public.

Throughout the 1980s, Solidarity, with support from the Catholic Church and figures like Pope John Paul II, kept the spirit of resistance alive. By the late 1980s, economic crises and pressure from both Solidarity and the international community forced the government to negotiate. In 1989, the government agreed to hold elections, leading to a decisive victory for Solidarity candidates and the eventual peaceful transition to democracy.

Solidarity's success marked a major turning point in the collapse of communism in Eastern Europe, as Poland became the first Eastern Bloc country to transition away from one-party rule.

1987, Higgs and *Crisis and Leviathan*

In his 1987 study *Crisis and Leviathan: Critical Episodes in the Growth of American Government*, Robert Higgs discussed the "ratchet effect."

He theorized that most government growth occurred in response to real or imagined national crises and that after the crises passed, society and government rarely returned to their previous condition; some of the government interventions remained. Higgs examined the history of the American federal government from the 1880s to the 1980s, using this ratchet effect as a framework for analysis. He cited economic crises and wars as the primary sources for the growth of government, and he concluded that each emergency leaves the scope of government at least a little wider than before.

Thomas Jefferson's prophetic warning that "the natural progress of things is for liberty to yield and government to gain ground" is borne out in Robert Higgs's historical analysis. Higgs has shown that most expansions of government power have been justified with the claim that they are "necessary for your safety."

1989, Schoolland and *The Adventures of Jonathan Gullible: A Free Market Odyssey*

In 1989, Ken Schoolland published the first edition of *The Adventures of Jonathan Gullible: A Free Market Odyssey*. Schoolland is a member of the Mont Pelerin Society and an Associate Professor of Economics and Director of the Entrepreneurship Center at Hawaii Pacific University in Honolulu.

The book traces the journey of a boy who, after being swept away in a storm, is shipwrecked on a strange island. Coming from a relatively free society, he faces intense culture shock as he encounters the island's confusing laws, strict regulations, and rigid traditions. Viewed through his eyes, the story reveals the absurdity of these rules, the oppressive grip they have on people's lives, and their economic impact. Originally published in English, it has since been republished in over fifty languages.[144]

Schoolland created a companion video, "The Philosophy of Liberty," which presents the core principles of individual liberty in just five minutes (key ideas from this video are incorporated into the discussion of self-ownership in Chapter 4):

- Owning your life enables you to experience events and activities as they unfold through time—past, present, and future. This passage through time is reflected in your life, your liberty, and the property you create and acquire utilizing your life and liberty.

- Losing your life means losing your future. Losing your liberty means losing your present. And losing the products of your life and liberty—your property—means losing a part of your past that was invested in creating them.

1989, The End of the Cold War

The fall of the Berlin Wall marked a pivotal moment in world history, symbolizing the end of the Cold War and the collapse of Communist Party control in Eastern Europe. Built in 1961 by the German Democratic Republic (East Germany), the Berlin Wall physically and ideologically divided East and West Berlin for nearly three decades. It was intended to prevent East Germans from fleeing to freedom in West Berlin, and it became an enduring symbol of communist repression.

By the late 1980s, growing political unrest and economic hardship fueled demands for reform across Eastern Europe. In East Germany, mass protests demanding freedom, democratic rights, and the right to travel freely intensified throughout 1989. At the same time, reforms in the Soviet Union under Mikhail Gorbachev's policies of *glasnost* (openness) and *perestroika* (restructuring) weakened Soviet control over its satellite states, emboldening these movements.

On November 9, 1989, after weeks of escalating protests and pressure, the East German government held a press conference announcing new, relaxed travel regulations. In a moment of confusion, an official mistakenly stated that the borders would be open immediately rather than gradually. Thousands of East Germans flooded the checkpoints along the Berlin Wall, and the overwhelmed border guards eventually opened the gates.

As East and West Berliners crossed the border, people began dismantling sections of the wall, celebrating the long-awaited moment of unity. The fall of the Berlin Wall led to the reunification of Germany on October 3, 1990, and accelerated the dissolution of communist regimes throughout Eastern Europe.

1991, The Dissolution of the Soviet Union

The Soviet Union's reforms, introduced in the 1980s, were intended to improve economic performance and raise the standard of living, but they had significant unintended consequences. *Glasnost* allowed greater freedom of speech and media, exposing Soviet citizens to previously censored information, while *perestroika* aimed to revitalize the economy by introducing some market-like reforms. However, these policies inadvertently revealed the Soviet system's deep flaws and fostered a climate of dissent.

Meanwhile, independence movements surged within Soviet republics like Estonia, Latvia, Lithuania, Ukraine, and Georgia, where people demanded greater autonomy or complete independence. In Eastern Europe, Soviet satellite states like Poland, East Germany, and Czechoslovakia experienced a wave of revolutions in 1989, rejecting their communist governments and further weakening Soviet influence.

In 1991, communist hardliners attempted a coup to overthrow Gorbachev and restore authoritarian rule, but the coup failed, leading to further destabilization. Boris Yeltsin, then President of the Russian Republic, played a crucial role in opposing the coup and emerged as a leading figure, symbolizing a break from Soviet control.

In December 1991, the leaders of Russia, Ukraine, and Belarus signed the Belavezha Accords, formally dissolving the Soviet Union and establishing the Commonwealth of Independent States. Gorbachev resigned as the last President of the Soviet Union on December 25, 1991, marking the official end of the Union of Soviet Socialist Republics.

The dissolution of the Soviet Union led to the independence of fifteen republics and triggered a shift toward democracy and capitalism in Eastern Europe.

1992, The State Policy Network

The State Policy Network (SPN) was founded by Thomas A. Roe Jr., a businessman and philanthropist from South Carolina, along with other leaders from state-level policy organizations.[145] SPN was preceded in its mission by the Madison Group (also founded by Roe), an informal network of state-based free-market think tanks that began meeting in the late 1980s.

SPN was created to support and connect state-based policy organizations that promote individual liberty, free enterprise, and limited government. SPN's mission is to catalyze thriving, durable freedom movements in every state, anchored with high-performing independent think tanks.

The organization has since grown into an influential network of think tanks across the United States. When SPN was founded, there were twelve independent, market-oriented, state-focused think tanks. As of this writing, there are sixty-four, representing all fifty states.

You have much more influence over local and state governments than you do over the federal government. Your state policy think tank is actively developing solutions to advance individual liberty at the local level. If you are wondering how you can make a difference in the trajectory of society, consider contacting a local think tank using the directory provided by SPN.[146]

1995, Hasnas and "The Myth of the Rule of Law"

Georgetown University Law School professor John Hasnas, in his essay "The Myth of the Rule of Law," has explored the true nature of law and proposed the radical possibility of a society governed by private law—that is, a system of law not operated by government.[147]

Hasnas's essay opens with a quiz, which I am sure you will find thought-provoking. He then paints an overview of an elegant legal system that addresses order and justice:

> It is certainly true that one of the purposes of law is to ensure a stable social environment, to provide order. But not just any order will suffice. Another purpose of the law must be to do justice. The goal of the law is to provide a social environment which is both orderly and just.

Hasnas addresses the underlying opposition to modification of the existing system:

> …Most people have been raised to identify law with the state. They cannot even conceive of the idea of legal services apart from the government. The very notion of a free market in legal services conjures up the image of anarchic gang warfare or rule by organized crime.

He illustrates that there is a partition between law and order:

> …The primary reason for this is that the public has been politically indoctrinated to fail to recognize the distinction

between order and law. Order is what people need if they are to live together in peace and security. Law, on the other hand, is a particular method of producing order.

As it is presently constituted, law is the production of order by requiring all members of society to live under the same set of state-generated rules; it is order produced by centralized planning. Yet, from childhood, citizens are taught to invariably link the words "law" and "order." Political discourse conditions them to hear and use the terms as though they were synonymous and to express the desire for a safer, more peaceful society as a desire for "law and order."

The state nurtures this confusion because it is the public's inability to distinguish order from law that generates its fundamental support for the state. As long as the public identifies order with law, it will believe that an orderly society is impossible without the law the state provides. And as long as the public believes this, it will continue to support the state almost without regard to how oppressive it may become.

According to Hasnas, this fundamental misconception of linking law and order prevents the discussion of alternate systems of providing order:

The public's identification of order with law makes it impossible for the public to ask for one without asking for the other. There is clearly a public demand for an orderly society. One of human beings' most fundamental desires is for a peaceful existence secure from violence. But because the public has been conditioned to express its desire for order as one for law, all calls for a more orderly society are interpreted as calls for more law. And since under our current political system, all law is supplied by the state, all such calls are interpreted as calls for a more active and powerful state. The identification of order with law eliminates from public consciousness the very concept of the decentralized provision of order. With regard to legal services, it renders the classical liberal idea of a market-generated, spontaneous order incomprehensible.

Hasnas goes on to address the question of what an alternate system would look like:

What would a free market in legal services be like?

I am always tempted to give the honest and accurate response to this challenge, which is that to ask the question is to miss the point. If human beings had the wisdom and knowledge-generating capacity to be able to describe how a free market would work, that would be the strongest possible argument for central planning. One advocates a free market not because of some moral imprimatur written across the heavens, but because it is impossible for human beings to amass the knowledge of local conditions and the predictive capacity necessary to effectively organize economic relationships among millions of individuals....

The fact is that there is no such thing as a government of law and not people. The law is an amalgam of contradictory rules and counter-rules expressed in inherently vague language that can yield a legitimate legal argument for any desired conclusion. For this reason, as long as the law remains a state monopoly, it will always reflect the political ideology of those invested with decision-making power. Like it or not, we are faced with only two choices. We can continue the ideological power struggle for control of the law in which the group that gains dominance is empowered to impose its will on the rest of society, or we can end the monopoly.

The inability to predict the exact details of a free-market solution for legal services doesn't make the idea implausible or unreasonable. In fact, market-based dispute resolution methods, such as arbitration and mediation, are already widely used, accepted, and effective.

1996, EdChoice

The Milton and Rose D. Friedman Foundation for Educational Choice was founded in 1996. In 2016, that organization was renamed EdChoice to honor the desire of the Friedmans to separate their names from their enduring vision.

EdChoice's mission is to empower parents with control over their children's education and the freedom to choose the type of school that best fits their needs. School choice allows public education funds to follow students to the schools or services that best suit them—whether that's a public school, a private school, a charter school, homeschooling, or any other learning environment families choose.

School choice is becoming increasingly accepted across the United States. Currently, thirty-five states and the District of Columbia offer at least one school choice program. Options include vouchers, education savings accounts, tax-credit scholarships, individual tax credits and deductions, charter schools, magnet schools, open enrollment, online academies, homeschooling, microschools, and special needs scholarship programs. These programs are advancing individual liberty for children and their parents by providing a broader marketplace of education options to choose from.

Summarizing the twentieth century is a sobering task. It was the deadliest century in human history, marked by the rise of tyranny and catastrophic setbacks to human progress. Totalitarian regimes ignited two world wars, while communism spread across Europe, Asia, Africa, and South America. Postwar treaties divided nations, separating once-unified populations between systems of economic freedom and centralized control. Enforcing central planning required brutal totalitarian measures, resulting in the deaths of over 100 million people. The clear lesson from this devastation is that central planning has always and everywhere been a failure.

In the aftermath of these tragedies, a new generation of thinkers, leaders, and organizations arose to defend and advance the principles of individual liberty. Their continuing efforts will be explored in the next chapter.

7.10 The Twenty-First Century

The political trajectory of the twentieth century accelerated in the twenty-first century. Progressive political philosophy, with no clear end goal—much like the term "progress" itself—has driven the expansion of government, making it increasingly intrusive. In this framework, a focus on transferring resources to politically favored groups has taken priority over protecting individual rights. Yet, some minds still furthered the cause of individual liberty.

2001, Gatto and *Dumbing Us Down: The Hidden Curriculum of Compulsory Schooling*

John Taylor Gatto spent nearly thirty years as a public-school teacher, during which time he won several awards, including New York State Teacher of the Year. After leaving teaching behind, Gatto began writing and lecturing widely on education reform. In *Dumbing Us Down: The Hidden Curriculum of Compulsory Schooling,*[148] Gatto critiqued the compulsory schooling system, which he believed stifles creativity, individuality, and genuine learning.

Gatto identified seven lessons that he argued are implicitly taught in the public school system, lessons that are detrimental to true education and personal development:

1. Confusion:

Schools teach a fragmented and incoherent curriculum, presenting disconnected facts and concepts that lead to confusion rather than understanding. This approach prevents students from developing a clear, integrated view of the world.

2. Class Position:

Schools teach students to know their place in the social hierarchy. Gatto argued that students learn to accept their position in a predetermined social order, which discourages ambition and critical thinking about societal roles.

3. Indifference:

Schools instill a sense of indifference by making subjects seem unimportant and interchangeable. The ringing of the bell signals the end of one subject and the beginning of another, teaching students that nothing is worth sustained attention or deep engagement.

4. Emotional Dependency:

Schools create emotional dependency by rewarding conformity and punishing individuality. Gatto argued that students learn to seek approval from authority figures rather than developing self-reliance and independent thinking.

5. Intellectual Dependency:

Schools foster intellectual dependency by teaching students to rely on teachers and textbooks for knowledge rather than encouraging independent thought and inquiry. This dependency undermines the development of critical thinking skills.

6. Provisional Self-Esteem:

Schools teach that self-esteem is conditional upon external validation, such as grades and teacher approval. Gatto argued that this undermines true self-confidence and fosters a need for constant external validation.

7. One Can't Hide:

Schools teach that privacy is an illusion and that constant surveillance is the norm. Gatto suggested that this creates a sense of powerlessness and discourages students from developing a strong sense of individuality and personal boundaries.

Gatto's critique of the compulsory school system centered on the idea that its primary function is not to educate in the true sense but to indoctrinate. This indoctrination process serves to produce compliant and uncritical citizens rather than empowered, independent thinkers. He argued that the compulsory school system effectively produces individuals who are

- compliant—trained to follow rules and authority without question.

- uncritical—lacking the skills and inclination to critically analyze information and challenge established norms.

- dependent—reliant on external validation and direction rather than self-reliant and confident in their own judgments.

- passive—more likely to accept the status quo and less likely to engage in active, independent thought or civic participation.

Gatto's critique called for a re-evaluation of the purpose and methods of education. He advocated an educational system that truly empowers individuals, fosters independent thinking, and cultivates a love for learning, rather than one that merely produces obedient and uncritical members of society. Independent thinkers are less likely to fall victim to government propaganda and are more likely to oppose the onslaught of tyranny.

2001, Rowland and The Grassroot Institute of Hawaii

Richard (Dick) Rowland, at the age of 70, founded the Grassroot Institute of Hawaii (GRIH), a state policy think tank.[149] He realized that Hawaii was on the road to serfdom, moving farther away from individual liberty, and that there was no organized group trying to change that trajectory.

The mission of GRIH is to educate people about the principles of individual liberty, economic freedom, and limited, accountable government.

Rowland was a firm believer in the power of little platoons to change culture. He believed that politics is downstream from culture, and if culture changes, politics will follow.

From its humble beginnings, GRIH has grown into an influential voice in public policy and has achieved many legislative victories that have advanced individual liberty. GRIH's message and success resonate with the residents of the State of Hawaii, who are struggling to survive while being ground into dust under the millstones of government spending and regulation.

2006, Hoppe and the Property and Freedom Society

Hans-Hermann Hoppe was born on September 2, 1949, in Peine, West Germany. His parents, originally from East Germany, fled to the West to escape communism. He was educated in Germany, earning a PhD in philosophy, sociology, and economics from Goethe University Frankfurt, where he later obtained his habilitation, a postdoctoral qualification required for full professorship.

In 1986, Hoppe moved to the United States to study and teach under Murray Rothbard at the University of Nevada, Las Vegas. There, he became a professor of economics and remained a close associate of Rothbard until his passing in January 1995.

He has published fifteen books, with *Democracy: The God That Failed* (2001) being the most widely read. Other notable works of his include *A Theory of Socialism and Capitalism* (1989) and *The Economics and Ethics of Private Property* (2006).

Hoppe, a Senior Fellow at the Mises Institute, founded the Property and Freedom Society in 2006.[150] He outlined its purpose in his keynote address at the society's fifth anniversary meeting:

The goal of "limited"—or "constitutional"—government, which Friedrich Hayek, Milton Friedman, James Buchanan and other Mont Pelerin Society grandees had tried to promote and that every "free-market" think-tank today proclaims as its goal, is an impossible goal, much as it is an impossible goal to try squaring the circle. You cannot first establish a territorial monopoly of law and order and then expect that this monopolist will not make use of this awesome privilege of legislating in its own favor. Likewise, you cannot establish a territorial monopoly of paper money production and expect the monopolist not to use its power of printing up ever more money.

Limiting the power of the state, once it has been granted a territorial monopoly of legislation, is impossible, a self-contradictory goal. To believe that it is possible to limit government power—other than by subjecting it to competition, i.e., by not allowing monopoly privileges of any kind to arise in the first place—is to assume that the nature of Man changes as the result of the establishment of government (very much like the miraculous transformation of Man that socialists believe to happen with the onset of socialism).

That is the whole thing: limited government is an illusory goal. To believe it to be possible is to believe in miracles....

Based on this insight, then, the Property and Freedom Society was to have a twofold goal.

On the one hand, positively, it was to explain and elucidate the legal, economic, cognitive, and cultural requirements and features of a free, stateless natural order.

On the other hand, negatively, it was to unmask the State and showcase it for what it really is: an institution run by gangs of murderers, plunderers and thieves, surrounded by willing executioners, propagandists, sycophants, crooks, liars, clowns, charlatans, dupes and useful idiots—an institution that dirties and taints everything it touches.

Building on Murray Rothbard's vision of a society rooted in voluntary interaction, Hoppe has underscored the primacy of property rights in advancing individual liberty. He calls for a system that safeguards justly acquired private property, freedom of contract, and freedom of association, while rejecting imperialism and militarism in favor of peace.

2007, Skousen and FreedomFest

Mark Skousen was born in San Diego, California, in 1947, where his father worked as an FBI agent. His family relocated to Portland, Oregon, where he spent his childhood.

He earned his undergraduate degree in economics and a master's degree in economics from Brigham Young University. In 1977, he earned a PhD in monetary economics from George Washington University.

Skousen has taught economics and finance at Columbia Business School, Columbia University, Barnard College, Mercy College, Rollins College, and Chapman University. He was a columnist for *Forbes* magazine from 1997 to 2001 and served as president of the Foundation for Economic Education (FEE).

He is the author of twenty-five books, the most successful and well-known of which is *The Making of Modern Economics: The Lives and Ideas of the Great Thinkers* (2001). This book provides a comprehensive, engaging history of economic thought, covering figures like Adam Smith, Karl Marx, John Maynard Keynes, and Friedrich Hayek. Unlike standard economic histories, *The Making of Modern Economics* presents a market-friendly narrative, emphasizing free-market principles over interventionist ideas.

In his 1991 essay "Persuasion vs. Force," Skousen presented a striking contrast:

> Taxation is the price we pay for failing to build a civilized society. The higher the tax level, the greater the failure. A centrally planned totalitarian state is a complete failure of civilization, while a totally voluntary society is its ultimate success.[151]

In 2007, he founded FreedomFest,[152] an annual conference that brings together free-market advocates, libertarians, conservatives, investors, and thought leaders from various disciplines to discuss ideas on liberty, economics, politics, history, and personal development.

FreedomFest serves as a marketplace for ideas, fostering debate among people with varying perspectives. It's a key networking hub for those who support individual liberty, economic freedom, and limited, accountable government.

2008, Bitcoin

In 2008, a white paper titled "Bitcoin: A Peer-to-Peer Electronic Cash System" was published under the pseudonym Satoshi Nakamoto. The abstract from this paper explains the purpose of Bitcoin:

> A purely peer-to-peer version of electronic cash would allow online payments to be sent directly from one party to another without going through a financial institution. Digital signatures provide part of the solution, but the main benefits are lost if a trusted third party is still required to prevent double-spending. We propose a solution to the double-spending problem using a peer-to-peer network.

Bitcoin emerged as a currency in 2009, becoming the first digital alternative to compete with both fiat currencies and gold. Created by private individuals and maintained through a widely distributed private network, Bitcoin is capped at a maximum supply of 21 million—a defining feature that sets it apart. Unlike Bitcoin, the global supply of gold continues to grow through mining, while fiat currencies have no limit and are being debased at record rates.

As the first form of privately controlled money beyond the reach of governments and politicians, Bitcoin offers protection against currency depreciation and inflation. This represents a significant advance for individual liberty.

2008, Guido Hülsmann and *The Ethics of Money Production*

Jörg Guido Hülsmann is a professor of economics at the University of Angers, France, a member of the European Academy of Sciences and Arts, and a corresponding member of the Pontifical Academy for Life. He is also a Senior Fellow of the Mises Institute and has published eight books, including a comprehensive biography of Ludwig von Mises titled *Mises: The Last Knight of Liberalism* (2007).

In *The Ethics of Money Production* (2008),[153] Hülsmann addresses money not just as an economic tool but as a moral issue. He argues that how money is created, distributed, and controlled has profound ethical implications—affecting justice, social order, and human freedom. The book challenges conventional acceptance of state-managed fiat currency, presenting a principled case for sound money rooted in voluntary exchange and natural law.

Hülsmann presents money as a spontaneous outcome of human cooperation—emerging naturally from barter as individuals sought a common medium of exchange. Because money originates through voluntary transactions, any interference in its creation or use—such as monopolization or debasement—raises ethical concerns.

He critiques fiat money systems in which governments and central banks control money creation, claiming that these systems distort markets, erode savings, and redistribute wealth without consent (through inflation, credit expansion, and legal tender laws).

Fiat money, in Hülsmann's view, institutionalizes injustice by benefiting early recipients—such as banks and governments—at the expense of later ones, like wage earners and savers. (Do you remember reading about the Cantillon effect in Chapter 7.5?)

Hülsmann argues that inflation fosters debt, short-term thinking, and overconsumption while eroding virtues such as thrift, responsibility, and honesty. Fiat systems, he says, create an "inflationary culture" in which time horizons shrink and ethical standards decline.

In such a system, money steadily loses purchasing power. Savers are penalized, as holding cash or conservative investments leads to real losses. This dynamic encourages debt, speculation, and immediate consumption over long-term saving and capital accumulation.

Over time, cultural attitudes shift toward expecting bailouts, subsidies, and stimulus measures, as state intervention seems necessary to manage the very instability fiat money creates. This fosters dependency and weakens self-reliance.

Inflationary culture undermines intergenerational responsibility: Parents save less for children, governments borrow against future taxpayers, and businesses pursue short-term gains over sustainable growth.

As an alternative, Hülsmann advocates for money production grounded in free markets—ideally, commodity money (such as gold and silver) chosen voluntarily. In such systems, money preserves purchasing power, prevents hidden wealth transfers, and upholds property rights. Ethical money production, he argues, must arise through voluntary exchange, not coercion or government decree.

2011, Robert P. Murphy and *Chaos Theory: Two Essays on Market Anarchy*

Robert P. Murphy holds a BA in Economics from Hillsdale College (magna cum laude, 1998) and a PhD in Economics from New York University (Spring 2003). He is a Senior Fellow at the Mises Institute and currently serves as Chief Economist at infineo. He also hosts two podcasts: The Bob Murphy Show[154] and *The Human Action* podcast on the Mises Institute website.[155] Murphy is the author and coauthor of over thirty books, including the widely read *The Politically Incorrect Guide to Capitalism.*

In his book *Chaos Theory: Two Essays on Market Anarchy* (first published in 2002), Murphy confronts some of the most challenging questions that arise when envisioning a stateless society. Rather than focusing only on abstract theory, he addresses practical concerns; chief among them is how essential functions currently monopolized by government—such as law, courts, policing, and national defense—might be supplied through voluntary, competitive market arrangements. He explores whether private insurance companies, arbitration agencies, and defense firms could provide these services in ways that are more efficient, responsive, and ethically consistent with individual liberty.

Murphy's essays attempt to answer common objections: How would disputes between individuals be resolved without a government court system? What mechanisms would prevent private security firms from devolving into warlords or cartels? How could a stateless society defend itself against foreign aggression? While theoretical, his work provides a structured framework for imagining how the institutions of justice and security could evolve organically from voluntary cooperation rather than political compulsion.

Ultimately, *Chaos Theory* does not claim to present a flawless blueprint but instead challenges the assumption that government is a necessary arbiter of order. By addressing these "hard cases" with clarity and rigor, Murphy has expanded the conversation about anarcho-capitalism from abstract principle to concrete institutional possibility.

2011, Paul and the Liberty Movement

Ron Paul was born on August 20, 1935, in Pittsburgh, Pennsylvania, to Howard Caspar Paul and Margaret Paul. Howard owned a small dairy company.

Paul earned his doctor of medicine degree from Duke University School of Medicine in 1961. He completed his medical internship at Henry Ford Hospital in Detroit and his residency in obstetrics at Magee-Women's Hospital in Pittsburgh. From 1963 to 1965, he served as a flight surgeon in the United States Air Force, followed by service in the Air National Guard from 1965 to 1968. Afterward, he and his wife moved to Texas, where he established a private practice in obstetrics.

A longtime reader of Austrian economics and libertarian political philosophy, Paul decided to run for Congress as a Republican after President Richard Nixon took the United States off the gold standard in 1971. He lost his first race in 1974 but won a special election in 1976, though he narrowly lost the regular election later that year by just 300 votes. In 1978, he won again and served until 1985, and he returned to Congress from 1997 to 2013.

Paul launched his first presidential campaign as a Libertarian in 1988. Though he considered running again in 1992, he ultimately supported Pat Buchanan's challenge to President George H.W. Bush.

His 2008 Republican presidential campaign reshaped the liberty movement. No one played a greater role in advancing individual liberty in modern politics than Paul, whose candidacy energized young voters—many of whom might otherwise have supported the Democratic Party. He ignited a grassroots movement, with passionate crowds chanting (in reference to the Federal Reserve System), "End the Fed!"

Running again in the 2012 presidential campaign as a Republican, Paul remained an outsider, but by then, he had significantly raised his national profile. Throughout the Republican primary, he closely trailed front-runner Mitt Romney but ultimately fell short of the nomination.

In his 2011 book *Liberty Defined*, Paul provided a plan to build a peaceful and just society:

> To believe in liberty is not to believe in any particular social
> and economic outcome. It is to trust in the spontaneous order
> that emerges when the state does not intervene in human

volition and human cooperation. It permits people to work out their problems for themselves, build lives for themselves, take risks and accept responsibility for the results, and make their own decisions. It is the seed of America.

We must come to imagine liberty again and believe that it can be a reality. In order to do this, we do not need songs, slogans, rallies, programs, or even a political party. All we need is access to good ideas, some degree of idealism, and the courage to embrace the liberty that so many great people of the past have embraced. Liberty built civilization. It can rebuild civilization. And when the tides turn and the culture again celebrates what it means to be free, our battle will be won. It could happen in our time. It might happen after we are gone from this earth. But it will happen. Our job in this generation is to prepare the way.[156]

In the book's appendix, Paul laid out ten principles of a free society:

1. Rights belong to individuals, not groups; they derive from our nature and can neither be granted nor taken away by government.

2. All peaceful, voluntary economic and social associations are permitted; consent is the basis of the social and economic order.

3. Justly acquired property is privately owned by individuals and voluntary groups, and this ownership cannot be arbitrarily voided by governments.

4. Government may not redistribute private wealth or grant special privileges to any individual or group.

5. Individuals are responsible for their own actions; government cannot and should not protect us from ourselves.

6. Government may not claim the monopoly over a people's money, and governments must never engage in official counterfeiting, even in the name of macroeconomic stability.

7. Aggressive wars, even when called preventative and even when they pertain only to trade relations, are forbidden.

8. Jury nullification, that is, the right of jurors to judge the law as well as the facts, is a right of the people and the courtroom norm.

9. All forms of involuntary servitude are prohibited, not only slavery but also conscription, forced association, and forced welfare distribution.

10. Government must obey the law that it expects other people to obey and thereby must never use force to mold behavior, manipulate social outcomes, manage the economy, or tell other countries how to behave.

At his ninetieth birthday barbecue on August 9, 2025, Paul told all of us, "You have a moral obligation to spread the message of liberty."

His contributions to the cause of individual liberty are countless. The surge of enthusiastic young supporters drawn to his 2008 and 2012 presidential campaigns has since inspired a wide range of publications, podcasts, and organizations dedicated to advancing the principles of individual liberty.

2011, Libertas Institute

Libertas Institute, a state policy think tank, was founded by Connor Boyack in 2011. Their mission is to "change hearts, minds, and laws to build a freer society by creating and implementing innovative policy reforms and exceptional educational resources."

Boyack is the author of over fifty books, with collective sales of over six million copies worldwide. He is best known for the Tuttle Twins series, which introduces young readers to economic, political, and civic principles.

Since its founding, Libertas Institute has expanded and is now part of the Libertas Network,[157] though its broad mission remains the same. The network consists of the Libertas Institute, the Tuttle Twins book series, Libertas Press (a full-service publisher), the Children's Entrepreneur Market (a program that teaches young people about the power of entrepreneurship, innovation, and leadership through experiential learning), and Praxis (a personal and professional development program that serves as an alternative to traditional postsecondary education).

Libertas has driven key policy reforms in Utah, including the state's first-in-the-nation "regulatory sandbox" law, medical cannabis legalization, and reduced licensing barriers. It has championed school choice through education savings accounts, strengthened digital privacy protections, and backed civil asset forfeiture reforms to safeguard property rights and due process.

2012, Rockwell and The Mises Institute

Llewellyn Harrison Rockwell Jr. was born in 1944 in Boston, Massachusetts. For his twelfth birthday, his father gave him a copy of Henry Hazlitt's classic book *Economics in One Lesson*—a gift that sparked his lifelong interest in economics and philosophy.

After earning a Bachelor of Arts degree from Tufts University in 1966, Rockwell joined Arlington House Publishers, where he edited works by Henry Hazlitt and Ludwig von Mises. His later exposure to Murray Rothbard's writings and Rothbard's subsequent mentorship led him to become a passionate advocate of Austrian economics and anarcho-capitalism.

In 1979, Rockwell became Ron Paul's Chief of Staff on Capitol Hill. He left Paul's office in 1982 to establish the Ludwig von Mises Institute (now named the Mises Institute), named after the esteemed Austrian economist. What began at Rockwell's kitchen table with support from Burt Blumert, Henry Hazlitt, Mises's widow Margit, Ron Paul, and Murray Rothbard grew into the leading center for Austrian economics and libertarian scholarship.[158]

Rothbard, regarded as Mises's intellectual successor and a key figure in the modern libertarian movement, served as the Institute's Vice President for Academic Affairs from its founding until his passing in 1995.

From its modest beginnings, the Mises Institute has grown into an organization with more than 350 faculty members engaged in academic projects. It has hosted over 1,000 teaching conferences and seminars on topics ranging from monetary policy to the history of war, as well as annual events such as the International Austrian Economics Research Conference, the Libertarian Scholars Conference, Mises University, and the Rothbard Graduate Seminar.

At its campus in Auburn, Alabama, the Institute publishes works by Ludwig von Mises, as well as classic and contemporary writings by Austrian economists and historians. It maintains the complete Mises bibliography, houses the Murray N. Rothbard archives, and produces periodicals, including an academic journal and a scholarly literature review. The on-site Massey and Ward Libraries hold more than 40,000 volumes in multiple languages, including Rothbard's personal collection.

In addition to its scholarly work, the Mises Institute hosts educational events for the public. A notable example came in 2012, when it marked its thirtieth anniversary with a conference on war revisionism. War, long recognized as a primary driver of government expansion, is often described as "the health of the state." Because the full truth about wars rarely emerges immediately, later scholarship is essential to reassessing early, and often hasty, conclusions. For this reason, the Mises Institute emphasizes the importance of uncovering the true history of war as a key to understanding the growth of state power.

Rockwell defined the State in his 2008 book *The Left, the Right, and the State*:

> What is the state? It is the group within society that claims for itself the exclusive right to rule everyone under a special set of laws that permit it to do to others what everyone else is rightly prohibited from doing, namely, aggressing against person and property.[159]

Under Rockwell's leadership, the Mises Institute has remained steadfast in its commitment to educating young scholars in Austrian economics. Unapologetic in its convictions, it has never wavered in its mission to advance individual liberty and economic freedom.

2013, Woods, Taking a Flamethrower to the Official Narrative

Thomas E. Woods Jr. launched the *Tom Woods Show* podcast in 2013, and at the time of this writing, it has produced over 2,700 episodes. Woods is the author of fourteen books, two of which have achieved *New York Times* bestseller status: *The Politically Incorrect Guide to American History* (2004) and *Meltdown* (2009). His podcasts and books cover a wide variety of topics, but their central theme is advancing individual liberty.[160]

Woods earned a bachelor's degree in history from Harvard and a master's, MPhil, and PhD from Columbia University. He expanded his understanding of economics through his studies at the Mises Institute. In 2019, he received the Hayek Lifetime Achievement Award from the Austrian Economics Center in Vienna. Woods serves as a Senior Fellow at the Mises Institute.

His Liberty Classroom offers thirty-seven online courses in history, economics, and philosophy, delivered in video and audio formats. Members can stream or download the content at their convenience.[161]

The Tom Woods School of Life equips individuals with the tools to "find freedom in an unfree world." Its mission is to help people become resilient, enabling them to survive and thrive despite the challenges presented by government and its cronies. The school features online seminars led by experts across various fields and includes small accountability groups to keep members focused on their goals.[162]

When considering U.S. foreign policy, heed this warning from Woods:

> No matter who you vote for, you always wind up getting John McCain.

This is a reference to the late Arizona senator John McCain, who consistently and unquestioningly supported all U.S. military action throughout his years in Congress. During his 2007 presidential campaign, McCain drew attention when, in response to a question about U.S. policy toward Iran, he cheerfully sang, "Bomb, bomb, bomb, bomb, bomb Iran," to the tune of the Beach Boys' "Barbara Ann."

2016, DiLorenzo and *The Problem with Socialism*

In 2016, Tom DiLorenzo published *The Problem with Socialism*, in which he examined the failings of socialism throughout time and place. His conclusions cut to the core of socialism's failings (drawing in part from H.L. Mencken's wisdom and wit):

> The most dangerous man to any government is the man who is able to think things out for himself without regard to the prevailing superstitions and taboos. This is because government justifies itself by regulations, and regulations seek to impose uniformity and government control. Almost every government intervention in the economic sphere is, in reality, an attack on the natural division of labor and knowledge, the glue that holds human civilization together, in favor of a bureaucratic dictate. Every minimum wage–maximum hour law, progressive income tax, welfare state program, labor regulation, employment quota, tax on dividend income, special corporation income tax, and on and on whittles away at the societal benefits of the division of

Labor in the forever failing attempts to use governmental force to achieve the Holy Grail of material equality.

It is not inequity and unfairness that are at the root of socialist envy; it is a desire to stamp out diversity to enforce uniformity to order society and the economy on rationalist lines as designated by allegedly smarter than thou bureaucrats. The result, as history has shown, is often tyranny of an almost unimaginable ferocity.

When the implications of such a world are fully spelled out, we recognize that such a world and such attempts are profoundly anti-human. Being anti-human in the deepest sense, the egalitarian goal is, therefore, evil, and any attempts in the direction of such a goal must be considered evil as well.[163]

DiLorenzo is a past President of the Mises Institute. Throughout his career as a teacher and writer, he has worked to advance individual liberty. He is the author and coauthor of eighteen books, including *The Real Lincoln, How Capitalism Saved America, Lincoln Unmasked, Hamilton's Curse, Organized Crime: The Unvarnished Truth About Government, The Problem with Socialism,* and *The Politically Incorrect Guide to Economics.*

2016, The Libertarian Institute

The Libertarian Institute was founded by Scott Horton, Sheldon Richman, and Jared Labell. They are dedicated to promoting anti-war, pro-liberty, and anti-state perspectives through journalism, analysis, and education. The Institute publishes articles, books, and podcasts covering topics such as foreign policy, economics, and civil liberties.[164]

As of this writing, the Libertarian Institute has published fifteen books, the latest being *Provoked: How Washington Started the New Cold War with Russia and the Catastrophe in Ukraine* by Scott Horton. Their flagship podcast, *The Scott Horton Show,* has released over 5,500 episodes.

Their latest contribution is the recently launched Scott Horton Academy of Foreign Policy and Freedom, an online school focused on the study of foreign policy.[165]

2016, Free the People

Founded in 2016 by Matt and Terry Kibbe, Free the People is a non-profit that promotes individual liberty, free markets, and limited government through multimedia content, grassroots activism, and educational initiatives.[166]

Free the People produces documentaries, podcasts, books, and educational videos with the aim of reaching younger generations and those interested in classical liberal values. The organization has collaborated with various libertarian thinkers and institutions to advocate for personal responsibility, non-aggression, and voluntary cooperation in social and economic life.

Their underlying message encourages personal responsibility and community-based solutions over central planning. By spotlighting small, local victories—like local business owners navigating cumbersome regulations—they demonstrate that real-world improvements often happen at the grassroots level. The nonprofit promotes individual liberty using a simple slogan: "Don't hurt people and don't take their stuff."

2023, Barnett and "There Is No Limit to State Power, and There Never Has Been!"

Gary D. Barnett, a financial advisor and estate planner, has been writing on topics concerning freedom and individual liberty for many years. He provides a keen evaluation of natural rights in his essay "There Is No Limit to State Power, and There Never Has Been!":

> The natural rights of man are inherent; they do not come from the sky or heavens, nor any government, as each and every one of us as a unique individual is born with a right to live, a right to life. All other rights spring from this clear

assumption, regardless of those who believe otherwise or who claim that man has no rights at all. Because each individual has a right to his life, it stands to reason that he has every right to defend his life. In addition, he has every right to sustain his life, which indicates that he has a right to work, to prosper, to supply his every need, which leads to his right to property and all the fruits of his labor. Every individual has a right to do whatever is necessary in order to sustain, protect, and continue his life, so long as he does not aggress or infringe on the same rights due all other individuals.[167]

On his website, Barnett writes,

> Freedom does not happen due to politics or constitutions; it can only exist in the minds of individuals.[168]

The excerpt from Barnett's book offers an elegant restatement of the natural rights theory discussed throughout this work. His statement above serves as a reminder that you yourself are the source of individual liberty; it arises from your capacity to think and reason, not from any external authority.

2024, Poverty

One of humanity's most remarkable yet underappreciated achievements is the dramatic reduction in extreme poverty worldwide. In 1981, 44 percent of the global population lived on less than $2.15 per day, a condition defined as extreme poverty (adjusted for inflation and for differences in the cost of living between countries). By 2024, this figure had plummeted to just 8.6 percent, representing a transformative shift in the human condition.

The data supporting this accomplishment is available from several sources, including the World Bank,[169] the United Nations,[170] and Our World in Data.[171]

The decline in extreme poverty is a result of the advance of individual liberty and economic freedom. China and India, once obstructed by centralized economic control, embraced deregulation, privatization, and trade liberalization, spurring rapid economic growth. The fall of the Berlin Wall in 1989 symbolized the collapse of communist regimes across Eastern Europe, paving the way for advances in individual liberty and economic freedom. Similarly, the dissolution of the Soviet Union in 1991 ended decades of oppressive central planning, which allowed former Soviet states to adopt more open economies, thus fostering entrepreneurship, investment, and improved living standards.

When discussing poverty, we would do well to bear in mind this important reminder from Per Bylund, a professor of economics at Oklahoma State University:

> What causes poverty? Nothing. It's the original state, the default, and starting point. The real question is: What causes prosperity?

Did you know that extreme poverty has declined so dramatically in such a short time? Individual liberty and economic freedom have lifted billions of people out of extreme poverty in less than two generations! This should be headline news, a widely known fact celebrated as one of humanity's most outstanding achievements. Is it possible that this is an "inconvenient truth" counter to the worldview promoted by the collectivists and central planners?

The twenty-first century has given us powerful new tools to advance individual liberty. Today, an army of authors, podcasters, social media influencers, and activists are amplifying the message of individual liberty, thanks to access to more ways to share ideas than at any other time in history. We now even have a form of money beyond government control that is immune to inflation!

Further ahead, we will discuss how to use these powerful tools to advance individual liberty and defeat the agents of tyranny. But first, we will examine three philosophies that present the most significant challenge to individual liberty.

8

THE CURRENT CRISIS

The first quarter of the twenty-first century has witnessed the rise of authoritarian influence across all segments of society. Major institutions—including the media, news, arts, education, politics, government, corporate leadership, and religion—are increasingly dominated by advocates of collectivism and centralized control. Propaganda and censorship are now widespread across all major institutions. In the United States, support for socialism is nearing historic highs, while radical new ideologies are spreading rapidly. Proposed solutions to society's problems—whether real or imaginary—invariably involve central planning and wealth redistribution. In this chapter, we'll examine the three philosophies that have given rise to the current crisis.

The Long March Through the Institutions

What has been called the "takeover of the institutions" was a deliberate strategy systematically articulated by Antonio Francesco Gramsci (1891–1937), a founder and, at one time, the leader of the Italian Communist Party. While imprisoned by Benito Mussolini's regime from 1926 until his death in 1937, he wrote *Prison Notebooks*, over 3,000 pages of history and political theory.

Gramsci not only opposed bourgeois values (what today we might call "traditional values" or "morality") but also emphasized that these values, however longstanding, were neither inevitable nor necessary. Unlike Lenin, who viewed culture as secondary to political struggles, Gramsci saw culture as central. He argued that political power alone was insufficient without cultural power. For Gramsci, cultural dominance was essential to achieving true power. He recognized that a class could not secure dominance through economic pursuits or brute force alone. Instead, it required a more nuanced approach: demonstrating intellectual and moral leadership, building alliances, and sometimes making compromises. His ultimate goal was to dismantle bourgeois values, including respect for private property and individual liberty, by reshaping the culture itself.

According to Gramsci, for a socialist political triumph to have any lasting impact, socialist values would need to infiltrate all institutions of society, not simply the government. "In the new order," he wrote, "Socialism will triumph by first capturing the culture via infiltration of schools, universities, churches, and the media by transforming the consciousness of society. … Socialism is precisely the religion that must overwhelm Christianity."

Gramsci's vision has allowed socialism to endure and thrive from the early twentieth century to the present. Without his approach, a narrow focus on economic policy alone would likely have consigned socialism to the dustbin of history. Economically, socialism has failed everywhere, often with horrific consequences: Tens of millions have starved, and millions more have been murdered in efforts to "re-educate" populations into becoming the so-called "New Socialist Man." By shifting focus beyond economics, Gramsci's agenda enabled socialism to permeate and influence every aspect of society.

In 1967, German sociologist and student political activist Rudi Dutschke coined the phrase "the long march through the institutions." This was his strategic blueprint for initiating revolutionary conditions, which aimed to dismantle capitalist society by infiltrating various social institutions. Dutschke promoted undermining the established institutions while working within them: doing the mundane tasks associated with the job—e.g., learning how to program and use computers, how to teach at all levels of education, how to use mass media, how to organize production, how to design, etc.—while gradually moving the institution in the desired direction and maintaining one's revolutionary consciousness while working alongside ordinary workers. The term "long march" wasn't mere rhetoric; it was a tribute to the prolonged endeavors of the Chinese communists, epitomized by their literal march across China.

The strategies laid down by figures like Gramsci and Dutschke remain a testament to the multifaceted nature of the communist manifestos: They do not intend merely to change governments and economic systems but instead to attempt to transform the very souls of societies.

Critical Theory

Another factor contributing to the current erosion of individual liberty is the widespread acceptance of critical theory within academia. Marxism divides societies into classes of oppressors and the oppressed. Karl Marx identified the bourgeoisie (the capitalists or business owners) as the oppressors and the proletariat (the working class) as the oppressed. When conflict between the bourgeoisie and the proletariat did not spark a worldwide revolution, frustrated Marxists re-examined their premises.

In the 1920s, a post-Marxist school of philosophy emerged at Goethe University in Frankfurt, Germany, formally established as the Institute of Social Research and later known as the Frankfurt School. Prominent members of this school of thought were Max Horkheimer, Theodor Adorno, Herbert Marcuse, Walter Benjamin, Erich Fromm, and Jürgen Habermas. The Frankfurt School developed what was called "critical theory" as the new method for dividing society. Racial and ethnic minorities, alongside "the poor," would become the oppressed, while racial and ethnic majorities, along with "the rich," would be the oppressors.

The term "critical" highlights the theory's liberation goal: It critiques society with the intention of freeing individuals from domination. This stands in contrast to traditional theory, which prioritizes objectivity and neutrality. The use of "critical" underscores its focus on examining society, culture, and institutions through a lens of critique. Horkheimer defined critical theory in 1937 as a theory that "seeks human emancipation from slavery" and "acts as a liberating influence."

Frankfurt School scholars were forced out of Germany by the Nazis and eventually welcomed at Columbia University. At the time of this writing, critical theory—along with its recent reformulation, critical race theory—is playing a more significant role than ever in dividing society.

Herbert Marcuse, the German-born philosopher, was among the most influential members of the Frankfurt School. His critiques often pierced the heart of conventional liberalism, most controversially via his "Repressive Tolerance" hypothesis, published in 1965.

Marcuse argued that the classical liberal concept of tolerance, which allowed for the free expression of all ideas and opinions, served to reinforce the existing power structure and maintain the status quo. According to Marcuse, in a society where there is an unequal distribution of power and wealth, the notion of "equal" or "neutral" tolerance has the effect of perpetuating the dominant ideology, further repressing the oppressed. He believed that the ruling class, with the help of the media and other institutions, used the idea of tolerance to maintain their power and control over the masses while suppressing any dissenting voices that threatened their authority. To Marcuse, property rights are not considered safeguards of natural rights and human dignity but as tools of oppression that preserve inequality. Individual liberty is dismissed as illusory, market choices framed as mere disguises for deeper domination. By rejecting natural law and objective truth, critical theory erodes the very foundation on which individual liberty and property rights depend.

In Marcuse's view, therefore, true freedom could be achieved only through "liberating tolerance," which would actively promote and encourage alternative, dissenting viewpoints while challenging the dominant ideology. This would involve a form of "discriminatory tolerance," in which the oppressed are given more latitude to express their views than the oppressors in order to redress the power imbalance. This concept is used to justify spreading collectivist propaganda and censoring opinions that oppose collectivism, often using labels like "disinformation" and "misinformation."

Postmodernism

The third factor that accounts for the current advance of tyranny is that postmodern philosophy, or postmodernism, was also welcomed into the world of academia. Postmodernism was founded in the late 1960s in France, taking inspiration from the likes of Nietzsche, Kierkegaard, and Heidegger. A maverick group of thinkers, led by Jacques Derrida, Michel Foucault, Jean-François Lyotard, and Jean Baudrillard, began to radically dismantle the established paradigms of modern philosophy. By the 1980s, these audacious ideas had not only traversed the Atlantic to find a haven in America but also garnered a global following.

This movement questions ideas that have dominated thinking since the seventeenth century. It challenges Enlightenment rationalism, which emphasizes reason and universal truths. Postmodernism emphasizes the notion that truth is not absolute but rather varies according to individual perspectives. In other words, "reality" is not something we can experience directly; instead, it is shaped by our minds and cultural context. Claims of objective truth or knowledge are viewed as simplistic and misleading.

Influenced by critical theory, postmodernism argues that knowledge and moral systems are not fixed or universal but are shaped by political, historical, and cultural factors. It often critiques traditional ideas about truth, morality, human nature, and progress, seeing them as tied to power structures. Postmodernism embraces concepts such as relativism (the belief that truth depends on context and that language defines truth), pluralism (accepting many viewpoints), and skepticism about claims of certainty. Key ideas such as deconstruction and post-structuralism originate from this tradition, which often questions the concept of an objective, unchanging reality or the reliability of reason.

An essential figure in this movement was Richard McKay Rorty. A graduate of the University of Chicago (BA and MA) and Yale (PhD), his academic career included work at Princeton, the University of Virginia, and Stanford.

Rorty rejected the long-held idea that accurate mental pictures of objects in the outside world are a prerequisite for knowledge. He argued instead that knowledge is an internal and linguistic affair; knowledge relates only to our own language. According to Rorty, language is made up of vocabularies that are temporary and historical, and he concluded that "since vocabularies are made by human beings, so are truths."

According to postmodernism, there are no objective moral values or normative facts. It is impossible to speak meaningfully about an independently existing reality, as reality depends on social and linguistic circumstances. Having rejected the notion of an independently existing reality, postmodernism denies that reason or any other method is a means of acquiring direct knowledge of that reality. In essence, language constitutes reality, rather than merely attempting to represent it.

In postmodernism, individual liberty and property rights are not recognized as universal or natural principles. Instead, they are treated as fluid, culturally contingent, and ultimately illegitimate narratives that serve existing hierarchies. By dissolving objective truth and natural law, postmodernism erodes the foundation upon which individual liberty and property can be consistently defended—leaving them vulnerable to reinterpretation or outright rejection in the name of new power structures.

Postmodern accounts of human nature are consistently collectivist, holding that individuals' identities are constructed largely by their social-linguistic groups. Postmodern themes in ethics and politics are characterized by an identification with and sympathy for the groups perceived to be oppressed, as well as a necessity to battle on their behalf.

Social Justice: Putting It All Together

The concept of social justice has taken on new, distinct features. Whereas the campus Free Speech Movement was a hallmark of social justice in the 1960s, violent skirmishes waged against free speech and academic freedom are now associated with the term "social justice."

The fusion of critical theory and postmodern philosophy, amplified by the long march through the institutions, has produced a new social justice creed that revolves around identity and grievance, rejecting universal truths in favor of subjective "lived experiences." Its central tenet is intersectionality—an oppression-ranking system that measures moral standing by the compounded disadvantages of one's identity categories. This framework inverts the traditional social hierarchy, elevating those deemed most oppressed to the highest moral authority while delegitimizing those considered privileged. Under the new social justice creed, individual liberty is redefined as collective liberation from oppression rather than personal sovereignty and the absence of coercion. The individual exists only to serve the group. Property rights are viewed as barriers to equity, valid only when they advance redistributive or collective justice. In this framework, liberty and property are not universal rights but conditional privileges, filtered through hierarchies of victimhood and privilege and legitimized only when they serve "equity" as defined by the movement's elites.

The new social justice creed manipulates personal characteristics to group individuals into categories of the oppressed, who are then encouraged to identify and accuse their oppressors. This process is a modernized version of Marx's bourgeois-versus-proletariat framework, substituting identity categories for economic class. The result is a perpetual cycle of division—one that grants political and cultural elites the power to divide and conquer the population through the ever-expanding mechanisms of government.

This stands in sharp contrast to the classical liberal and natural-rights traditions, which uphold individual liberty and property as the moral foundation of a just society, immune to collective claims.

The long march through the institutions has provided collectivists with the opportunity to control public discourse using the methods prescribed by critical theory. Propaganda favoring the collectivist doctrine is promoted throughout all institutions, and opposition to collectivist doctrine is censored and/or labeled as misinformation or disinformation. Finally, using postmodernist methods, collectivists define long-held beliefs as merely products of political, historical, or cultural narratives and hierarchies. By redefining vocabulary, postmodernists undermine and seek to eliminate long-held beliefs, replacing them with new ones to be enforced by ostracism and censorship.

Individual liberty and property rights have no place in the society envisioned by those supporting the "long march through the institutions," critical theory, and postmodernism. While differing in focus, all three philosophies converge in their rejection of individual liberty. The long march aims to dismantle the bourgeois values that safeguard individual liberty and property. Critical theory views these principles not as protections of human dignity but as tools of domination, casting law, family, and the economy as instruments of oppression. Postmodernism goes further, denying objective truth and universal principles altogether and reducing individual liberty and property rights to mere constructs or "narratives of power." Once stripped of their foundation in natural law and reframed as mechanisms of exploitation, individual rights lose all meaning.

Ultimately, each ideology attempts to subordinate individual sovereignty to a shifting collective will, leaving no possibility for resisting coercion. The next chapter will outline a plan to defeat these philosophies.

9

WHAT MUST BE DONE

In the first six chapters, you studied the fundamental philosophy of individual liberty. Congratulations, that is an exceptional achievement! You are now a member of a small group of individuals who have learned the Forbidden Idea. I hope this knowledge eases your frustration and despair and gives you the strength to rise above the political and economic fray.

In Chapter 7, you explored the history of individual liberty, which reveals humanity's greatest triumph: breaking free from the grip of tyrants. Chapter 8, with its account of today's opposition to liberty, may have felt discouraging—but take heart. This chapter will place a battle plan in your hands, illuminate a path through the darkness of tyranny, and recommend actions to advance individual liberty with clarity and confidence.

I'd like to share one final philosophical quotation with you before we dive into strategy. Keep in mind this advice from Albert Camus:

> The only way to deal with an unfree world is to become so absolutely free that your very existence is an act of rebellion.

After studying the philosophy and history of individual liberty, I believe that I am now living up to Camus's advice, which suggests that my existence is an act of rebellion. This achievement brings me a sense of peace and happiness. I hope reading this book has brought you the same.

Now, on to the battle plan. First, continue your education in the philosophy and history of individual liberty. This book is intentionally written to be (relatively) short and easy to understand. There are many more books and essays out there that will broaden and deepen your understanding of this philosophy. For guidance, I suggest you visit my curated reading list, The Root of Liberty,[172] which you can find online and at the end of this book under Further Reading. Start with the Essential Reading List: twelve essays and books that provide the background information on the topics covered in this book.

Next, learn and apply the Breitbart doctrine: Politics is downstream from culture.[173] To change politics, you must help change the culture. This means that you can advance individual liberty by serving as a passionate advocate for it and persuading others to do the same. Once the culture changes, politics will follow.

You are surrounded by and deeply immersed in intimate groups that I will refer to as "little platoons."[174] These little platoons are made up of your family, neighbors, friends, coworkers, co-volunteers, church members, and other associates. Members of these little platoons know you and respect you. Share the philosophy and history of individual liberty with them. You don't need to initiate conversations about politics, economics, history, or philosophy—but when the opportunity arises, don't hesitate to share your views. Take your time to clearly and calmly explain the core principles that you have learned: Individual liberty—the absence of coercion—is grounded in natural law, self-ownership, the non-aggression principle, and negative rights. Remember that the table of contents of this book outlines these fundamental principles of individual liberty. If you need a refresher, a quick glance at the first six chapter titles may help jog your memory. After explaining the core principles, discuss the heroes and events from history that advanced individual liberty, as described in Chapter 7. Speaking out is our method of resisting the censorship promoted by critical theory.

Conversations will naturally shift toward real-world applications of the philosophy of individual liberty. When they do, remind others that the constitutional limits placed on the federal government have clearly failed to prevent the expansion of its power. What began as a tightly constrained system has grown into the largest, most expensive, and most powerful government in human history. In the real world, the progress of individual liberty can be measured by the size of government. When government expands, individual liberty recedes. When government grows larger, the individual becomes smaller. In contrast, individual liberty flourishes when government contracts.

The goal of the individual liberty movement should be to reduce government spending at the federal, state, and local levels, thereby reducing the size and intrusions of government. Note that reducing spending does not mean simply slowing the rate of increase; it means spending less in the current year than was spent in the previous year.

Explain to your little platoons that federal spending lies largely beyond our direct control, which makes exposing the problem even more urgent. Reducing spending is the emergency brake needed to stop the runaway train of government. Yet attempts to change, amend, or cut spending are consistently defeated by politicians, bureaucrats, and beneficiaries of government programs. Measures such as tax cuts, balanced budget laws, and debt ceilings have had no effect on slowing the growth of government.

Federal spending grows easily because the Federal Reserve (the Fed) can create money (fiat currency) out of thin air. This power fuels unchecked government expansion. Ending the Fed would drive a stake through the heart of the liberty-devouring federal regulatory system. However, if the Federal Reserve persists, any genuine attempt to control spending is doomed to fail. Say it as often as possible: End the Fed![175]

Also explain to your little platoons that when government reduces or halts spending on a program, if that program is necessary, individuals or groups step in to meet the demand for its services or goods. My favorite explanation of this phenomenon comes from Frédéric Bastiat, who, in *The Law* (1850), responded to the same justifications for government spending that we hear today:

> Socialism, like the ancient ideas from which it springs, confuses the distinction between government and society. As a result of this, every time we object to a thing being done by government, the socialists conclude that we object to its being done at all. We disapprove of state education. Then the socialists say that we are opposed to any education. We object to a state religion. Then the socialists say that we want no religion at all. We object to a state-enforced equality. Then they say that we are against equality. And so on, and so on. It is as if the socialists were to accuse us of not wanting persons to eat because we do not want the state to raise grain.[176]

Your little platoons can repeat Bastiat's message: Saying that government should not provide a service does not mean the service shouldn't exist. Likewise, opposing government provision of a good doesn't mean the good shouldn't be available. Under economic freedom, individuals choose which goods and services they want, and others decide whether it's in their self-interest to offer them. It's not about denying needs but about respecting voluntary exchange and individual choice.

When asked, "What about people who can't afford those goods or services?" you can respond with this point: If these are true necessities—not luxuries or nonessentials—then civil society will respond through voluntary charity. Voluntary cooperation has consistently outperformed government coercion in the past and will continue to do so in the future.

After your little platoons have been exposed to and understand the fundamental principles of individual liberty, they will be ready to accept more advanced and provocative messages. Here are a few examples:

Taxation is theft.

War is mass murder.

All government regulations are ultimately enforced by violence.

You've already studied these topics—presented by various authors, philosophers, and economists—in Chapter 7. Remember, cutting spending reduces or even eliminates the three government violations of individual liberty listed above.

Once you inspire your little platoons to speak out for cutting government spending, they will carry that message to their own little platoons. From there, it will spread outward, each group igniting another, until a groundswell of voices rises across the country. This movement does not wait for permission or rely on central command; it grows because free people, acting in their own circles, are willing to share the truth. As this wave of persuasion swells, politicians will no longer be able to ignore it—and some will adopt it into their political platform.

You only need to shift the worldview of three to ten percent of persuadable, voting-age people in decisive regions to have an impact on election results.[177,178] Do not be concerned that your platoons seem small and powerless. Take heart in the advice of Margaret Mead:

> Never doubt that a small group of thoughtful, committed citizens can change the world; indeed, it's the only thing that ever has.

Work locally to create change for both today and the future. Influence spending decisions through your school board, park district, or municipal government.

Build or support alternative institutions. Launch or back independent schools, news outlets, art collectives, and publishing platforms—parallel institutions that resist cultural capture. This is how we will counterbalance the long march through the institutions.

Support cultural creators. Writers, musicians, filmmakers, and comedians shape imagination and values. By supporting them, you can help spread ideas that touch both hearts and minds.

Work to allow or expand options for school choice, including vouchers, education savings accounts, tax-credit scholarships, individual tax credits and deductions, charter schools, magnet schools, open enrollment, online academies, homeschooling, microschools, and special needs scholarship programs. The most important and impactful action you can take right now is to remove your children from the government school system. If you are looking for a place to start, consider the Ron Paul Curriculum.[179]

Whether or not you have children in the government school system, work to change the curriculum. Engage in reform through textbook selection, school board elections, and curriculum oversight. What the next generation internalizes as "normal" will shape the future. Reading Chapter 7 of this book has introduced you to several organizations that produce educational literature and media. You and your little platoons can recommend that these be incorporated into your local school curriculum: "The Tuttle Twins" from the Libertas Network,[180] "Bring FEE to your classroom" from the Foundation for Economic Education,[181] "The Mises Academy" from the Mises Institute,[182] and "Liberty Classroom" from Tom Woods.[183]

School choice and curriculum reform offer our best chance to counter postmodernism. Once its doctrines are no longer propagated through education, the philosophy will collapse under the weight of its own absurdity.

There is a strong network of local organizations that advances individual liberty. You can join this network by supporting a state policy think tank. These organizations advance individual liberty through legislation, litigation, political engagement, investigative journalism, and leadership training. Every state has at least one, and they are listed in the State Policy Network directory.[184]

We do not have the luxury of only associating with our little platoons. In many situations, we will be exposed to conversations in which someone advocates for central planning, the expansion of government regulation, wealth redistribution, or other violations of individual liberty and property rights. If you find yourself in a similar situation, resolve to champion individual liberty in all aspects of human endeavors—never concede any ground, never surrender any issue, and never apologize for any statement made in the defense or advancement of individual liberty. Adopt the motto from the family crest of Ludwig von Mises:

Do not give in to evil but proceed ever more boldly against it.

If you find yourself in a discussion with opponents of individual liberty, focus on asking questions. Don't be sarcastic or try to set traps; ask sincerely with the goal of understanding their philosophy. I ask questions to genuinely see if they might be right and I might be wrong. For example, if someone supports government regulation, ask them about the specifics of the regulations they favor and, most importantly, where they believe government derives the authority to enact and enforce them. Since every regulation ultimately relies on coercion, ask whether they also endorse the use of violence to enforce those regulations.

In advancing individual liberty, don't let the perfect become the enemy of the good. If there's a chance to cut spending, support it—even if it falls short of a full repeal. Always advocate for complete repeal, but don't pass up smaller victories along the way.

The same applies to regulations: If you can lessen their adverse effects, take that step while still pressing for full repeal. Small wins build momentum toward ultimate success.

Give this your serious consideration: You cannot wait for the "right" time to oppose tyranny. Life will always be full of family, school, work, and countless obligations. The time to act is now—even if only in a small way.

Individual liberty is a beautiful and elegant ideal based on truths discovered, defined, and defended over thousands of years by some of mankind's greatest intellectuals. By standing on the shoulders of these giants, we will advance individual liberty to greater heights and overcome its tyrannical adversaries. Our thoughts, words, and actions will inspire others to promote individual liberty and will change our culture. When the culture changes, politics will follow. With unwavering commitment to our principles and a passionate determination to inspire others, we will achieve individual liberty in our lifetime.

UPWARD TO LIBERTY!

ACKNOWLEDGMENTS

271

This book owes its clarity and brevity to the exceptional contributions of Thomas E. Woods Jr., whose meticulous editing and encouragement helped transform my rough outline into a book. The guidance and resources provided through his Author Academy were instrumental.[185] I am profoundly grateful for Tom's unwavering dedication to excellence and his steadfast commitment to advancing individual liberty.

I also extend my heartfelt thanks to Mark C. Coleman for his time and effort in editing the initial draft of this book.

QUOTATIONS

Government, with its laws and regulations more numerous than the hairs of an ox, is a vicious oppressor of the individual, and more to be feared than fierce tigers. —Lao Tzu, *Tao Te Ching*, 500 B.C.

The more corrupt the state, the more numerous the laws. —Tacitus (Roman Senator), *Annals*, 117 A.D.

Resolve to serve no more, and you are at once freed. I do not ask that you place hands upon the tyrant to topple him over, but simply that you support him no longer; then you will behold him, like a great Colossus whose pedestal has been pulled away, fall of his own weight and break into pieces. —Etienne de La Boetie, *The Politics of Obedience*, 1552

If the safety of the people be the supreme law, and this safety extend to, and consist in, the preservation of their liberties, goods, lands, and lives, that law must necessarily be the root and the beginning, as well as the end and the limit, of all magisterial power, and all laws must be subservient and subordinate to it. —Algernon Sidney, *Discourses Concerning Government*, 1698

All human constitutions are subject to corruption, and must perish, unless they are timely renewed, and reduced to their first principles. —Algernon Sidney, *Discourses Concerning Government*, 1698

No man can confer upon others that which he has not in himself. —Algernon Sidney, *Discourses Concerning Government*, 1698

Man will never be free until the last king is strangled with the entrails of the last priest. —Denis Diderot

It is dangerous to be right in matters on which the established authorities are wrong. —Voltaire, *Le Siècle de Louis XIV*, 1751

It is forbidden to kill; therefore, all murderers are punished unless they kill in large numbers and to the sound of trumpets. —Voltaire, *Questions sur les Miracles*, 1765

Those who can make you believe absurdities can make you commit atrocities. —Voltaire, *Questions sur les Miracles*, 1765

It is not from the benevolence of the butcher, the brewer, or the baker that we expect our dinner, but from their regard to their own interest. We address ourselves not to their humanity but to their self-love, and never talk to them of our own necessities but of their advantages. —Adam Smith, *The Wealth of Nations*, Book IV, Chapter II, 1776

Society in every state is a blessing, but government, even in its best state, is but a necessary evil; in its worst state an intolerable one: for when we suffer, or are exposed to the same miseries by a government, which we might expect in a country without government, our calamity is heightened by reflecting that we furnish the means by which we suffer. —Thomas Paine, *Common Sense*, 1776

Tyranny, like hell, is not easily conquered; yet we have this consolation with us, that the harder the conflict, the more glorious the triumph. —Thomas Paine, *Common Sense*, 1776

The tree of liberty must be refreshed from time to time with the blood of patriots and tyrants. —Thomas Jefferson, letter to William Stephens Smith, 1787

The natural progress of things is for liberty to yield and government to gain ground. —Thomas Jefferson, letter to Edward Carrington, 1788

Where there is liberty there is no violence, and where there is violence there is no liberty. —Immanuel Kant, *The Metaphysics of Morals*, 1797

I have sworn upon the altar of God eternal hostility against every form of tyranny over the mind of man. —Thomas Jefferson, letter to Dr. Benjamin Rush, 1800

A wise and frugal Government, which shall restrain men from injuring one another, shall leave them otherwise free to regulate their own pursuits of industry and improvement, and shall not take from the mouth of labor the bread it has earned. —Thomas Jefferson, from his first inaugural address, 1801

None are more hopelessly enslaved than those who falsely believe they are free. —Johann Wolfgang von Goethe, *Elective Affinities*, 1809

The farmer and manufacturer can no more live without profit than the laborer without wages. —David Ricardo, *On the Principles of Political Economy and Taxation*, 1817

The pursuit of wealth generally diverts men of great talents and of great passions from the pursuit of power, and it very frequently happens that a man does not undertake to direct the fortune of the State until he has discovered his incompetence to conduct his own affairs. —Alexis de Tocqueville, *Democracy in America*, 1835

The State is the great fiction through which everyone endeavors to live at the expense of everyone else. —Frédéric Bastiat, *The State*, 1848

Everyone wants to live at the expense of the state. They forget that the state lives at the expense of everyone. —Frédéric Bastiat, *The State*, 1848

There is only one difference between a bad economist and a good one: the bad economist confines himself to the visible effect; the good economist takes into account both the effect that can be seen and those effects that must be foreseen. —Frédéric Bastiat, "That Which Is Seen, and That Which Is Not Seen," 1849

The production of security should, in the interests of the consumers of this intangible commodity, remain subject to the law of free competition. Whence it follows: That no government should have the right to prevent another government from going into competition with it, or to require consumers of security to come exclusively to it for this commodity. —Gustav de Molinari, *The Production of Security*, 1849

Life, liberty, and property do not exist because men have made laws. On the contrary, it was the fact that life, liberty, and property existed beforehand that caused men to make laws in the first place. —Frédéric Bastiat, *The Law*, 1850

But how is this legal plunder to be identified? Quite simply. See if the law takes from some persons what belongs to them, and gives it to other persons to whom it does not belong. See if the law benefits one citizen at the expense of another by doing what the citizen himself cannot do without committing a crime. —Frédéric Bastiat, *The Law*, 1850

Socialism, like the ancient ideas from which it springs, confuses the distinction between government and society. As a result of this, every time we object to a thing being done by government, the socialists conclude that we object to its being done at all. We disapprove of state education. Then the socialists say that we are opposed to any education. We object to a state religion. Then the socialists say that we want no religion at all. We object to a state-enforced equality. Then they say that we are against equality. And so on, and so on. It is as if the socialists were to accuse us of not wanting persons to eat because we do not want the state to raise grain. —Frédéric Bastiat, *The Law*, 1850

I believe that my theory is correct; for whatever be the question upon which I am arguing, whether it be religious, philosophical, political, or economical; whether it affects well-being, morality, equality, right, justice, progress, responsibility, property, labor, exchange, capital, wages, taxes, population, credit, or Government; at whatever point of the scientific horizon I start from, I invariably come to the same thing—the solution of the social problem is in liberty. —Frédéric Bastiat, *The Law*, 1850

The sole end for which mankind are warranted, individually or collectively, in interfering with the liberty of action of any of their number, is self-protection. That the only purpose for which power can be rightfully exercised over any member of a civilized community, against his will, is to prevent harm to others. His own good, either physical or moral, is not a sufficient warrant. —John Stewart Mill, *On Liberty*, 1859

We have the right, as individuals, to give away as much of our own money as we please in charity; but as members of Congress, we have no right so to appropriate a dollar of the public money. —Colonel David Crockett, *Not Yours to Give*, 1867

The principle that the majority have a right to rule the minority, practically resolves all government into a mere contest between two bodies of men, as to which of them shall be masters and which of them shall be slaves. —Lysander Spooner, *No Treason. No. 1*, 1867

A man is none the less a slave because he is allowed to choose a new master once in a term of years. —Lysander Spooner, *No Treason. No. 6*, 1867

But whether the Constitution really be one thing, or another, this much is certain—that it has either authorized such a government as we have had, or has been powerless to prevent it. In either case, it is unfit to exist. —Lysander Spooner, *No Treason. No. 6*, 1867

The will of the people cannot make just that which is unjust. —Lord Acton, *The History of Freedom in Antiquity*, 1877

It is easier to find people fit to govern themselves than people fit to govern others. —Lord Acton, letter to Mandell Creighton, 1881

…you will not make people wiser and better by taking liberty of action from them. A man can only learn when he is free to act. It is the consequences of his own actions, and the consequences of these same actions as he sees them in other persons, that teach him. —Auberon Herbert, *The Right and Wrong of Compulsion by the State*, 1885

You tell me a majority has a right to decide as they like for their fellow-men. What majority? 21 to 20? 20 to 5? 20 to 1? But why any majority? What is there in numbers that can possibly make any opinion or decision better or more valid, or which can transfer the body and mind of one man into the keeping of another man? —Auberon Herbert, *The Right and Wrong of Compulsion by the State*, 1885

There cannot possibly be two supreme laws. Either the will of the majority or the rights of the individual are the highest law of our existence; one, whichever one it is to be, must yield in presence of the other. —Auberon Herbert, *The Right and Wrong of Compulsion by the State*, 1885

Whatever party names we may give ourselves, this is the question always waiting for an answer: Do you believe in force and authority, or do you believe in liberty? —Auberon Herbert, *The Right and Wrong of Compulsion by the State*, 1885

Liberty is not a means to a higher political end. It is itself the highest political end. —Lord Acton, letter to Mary Gladstone, 1887

Power tends to corrupt, and absolute power corrupts absolutely. —Lord Acton, letter to Mandell Creighton, 1887

I contend that for a nation to try to tax itself into prosperity is like a man standing in a bucket and trying to lift himself up by the handle. —Winston Churchill, speech to the British House of Commons, 1904

I disapprove of what you say, but I will defend to the death your right to say it. —Evelyn Beatrice Hall, *The Friends of Voltaire*, 1906

There are two fundamentally opposed means whereby man, requiring sustenance, is impelled to obtain the necessary means for satisfying his desires. These are work and robbery, one's own labor and the forcible appropriation of the labor of others. … I propose in the following discussion to call one's own labor and the equivalent exchange of one's own labor for the labor of others the "economic means" for the satisfaction of needs, while the unrequited appropriation of the labor of others will be called the "political means." —Franz Oppenheimer, *The State*, 1908

At first, the conquerors usually looted and murdered their victims and then went on to find others. After centuries, however, the conquering

tribes decided to settle down among their victims; instead of killing them, they regularized and rendered the loot permanent, settling down to rule their victims on a long-range basis. The annual tribute became "taxes," and the land of the peasants was parceled out among the warlords to become subject of annual feudal rent. In this way, a state and a ruling class emerged from previously stateless societies. ... The conqueror in the first stage is like the bear, who for the purpose of robbing the beehive, destroys it. In the second stage, he is like the beekeeper, who leaves the bees enough honey to carry them through the winter.
—Franz Oppenheimer, *The State*, 1908

You can no more win a war than you can win an earthquake.
—Jeannette Rankin

Do not give in to evil but proceed ever more boldly against it.
—Ludwig von Mises (his motto)

War is the health of the state. —Randolph Bourne, *The State*, 1918

Today, however, we have to say that a state is a human community that (successfully) claims the monopoly of the legitimate use of physical force within a given territory. —Max Weber, "Politics as Vocation," 1919

All rational action is in the first place individual action. Only the individual thinks. Only the individual reasons. Only the individual acts.
—Ludwig von Mises, *Socialism*, 1922

In fact, Socialism is not in the least what it pretends to be. It is not the pioneer of a better and finer world, but the spoiler of what thousands of years of civilization have created. It does not build, it destroys. For destruction is the essence of it. —Ludwig von Mises, *Socialism*, 1922

There is simply no other choice than this: either to abstain from interference in the free play of the market, or to delegate the entire management of production and distribution to the government. Either capitalism or socialism: there exists no middle way. —Ludwig von Mises, *Liberalism: In the Classical Tradition*, 1927

We allow other parties to exist. However, the fundamental principle that distinguishes us from the West is as follows: one party rules, and all the others are in jail! —Mikhail Tomsky, in the November 13, 1927, issue of the Russian newspaper *Trud* (Labor)

Everything within the State, nothing outside the State, nothing against the State. —Benito Mussolini, from a speech delivered to the Italian Chamber of Deputies on December 9, 1928

Democracy is the theory that the common people know what they want, and deserve to get it good and hard. —H.L. Mencken

Society will have to live for the State, man for the governmental machine. And as after all it is only a machine, whose existence and maintenance depend on the vital supports around it, the State, after sucking out the very marrow of society, will be left bloodless, a skeleton, dead with that rusty death of machinery, more gruesome than the death of a living organism. Such was the lamentable fate of ancient civilization. —José Ortega y Gasset, *The Revolt of the Masses*, 1930

It is unfortunately none too well understood that, just as the State has no money of its own, so it has no power of its own. All the power it has is what society gives it, plus what it confiscates from time to time on one pretext or another; there is no other source from which State power can be drawn. Therefore, every assumption of State power, whether by gift or seizure, leaves society with so much less power; there is never, nor can there be, any strengthening of State power without a corresponding and roughly equivalent depletion of social power. —Albert Jay Nock, *Our Enemy, the State*, 1935

The State claims and exercises the monopoly of crime. … It forbids private murder, but itself organizes murder on a colossal scale. It punishes private theft, but itself lays unscrupulous hands on anything it wants. —Albert Jay Nock, *Our Enemy, the State*, 1935

Either we believe that the State exists to serve the individual or that the individual exists to serve the State. —Ayn Rand, a letter to John Temple Graves, 1936

Every Communist must grasp the truth, "Political power grows out of the barrel of a gun." Our principle is that the Party commands the gun, and the gun must never be allowed to command the Party. —Mao Zedong, from a speech he delivered at the Anti-Japanese Military and Political University in November 1938

But what is freedom? Freedom from what? There is nothing to take a man's freedom away from him, save other men. To be free, a man must be free of his brothers. That is freedom. That and nothing else. —Ayn Rand, *Anthem*, 1938

If you give the State power to do something for you, you give it an exact equivalent of power to do something to you. —Isabel Paterson and W.J. Cameron

First, they ignore you, then they ridicule you, then they fight you, then you win. —Mahatma Gandhi

The champions of socialism call themselves progressives, but they recommend a system which is characterized by rigid observance of routine and by a resistance to every kind of improvement. They call themselves liberals, but they are intent upon abolishing liberty. They call themselves democrats, but they yearn for dictatorship. They call themselves revolutionaries, but they want to make the government omnipotent. They promise the blessings of the Garden of Eden, but they plan to transform the world into a gigantic post office. Every man but one a subordinate clerk in a bureau. —Ludwig von Mises, *Bureaucracy*, 1944

The ultimate basis of an all-around bureaucratic system is violence. —Ludwig von Mises, *Bureaucracy*, 1944

He who is unfit to serve his fellow citizens wants to rule them. —Ludwig von Mises, *Bureaucracy*, 1944

The principle that the end justifies the means is in individualist ethics regarded as the denial of all morals. In collectivist ethics it becomes necessarily the supreme rule. —F.A. Hayek, *The Road to Serfdom*, 1944

Socialism is a philosophy of failure, the creed of ignorance, and the gospel of envy; its inherent virtue is the equal sharing of misery. —Winston Churchill, speech during the General Election campaign, 1945

There is all the difference in the world between treating people equally and attempting to make them equal. —F.A. Hayek, *Individualism: True and False*, 1945

The ideas which now pass for brilliant innovations and advances are in fact mere revivals of ancient errors, and a further proof of the dictum that those who are ignorant of the past are condemned to repeat it. —Henry Hazlitt, *Economics in One Lesson*, 1946

It is the Communists' intention to make people think that personal success is somehow achieved at the expense of others. It is the communists' aim to discourage all personal effort and to drive men into a hopeless, dispirited, gray herd of robots who have lost all personal ambition, who are easy to rule, willing to obey and willing to exist in selfless servitude to the State. —Ayn Rand, "Screen Guide for Americans," 1947

Men in government, therefore, should be those who aim at making government as unnecessary as possible. Contraction, not expansion, should be the aim. —Leonard E. Read, *Pattern for Revolt*, 1948

A man who chooses between drinking a glass of milk and a glass of a solution of potassium cyanide does not choose between two beverages; he chooses between life and death. A society that chooses between capitalism and socialism does not choose between two social systems; it chooses between social cooperation and the disintegration of society. Socialism is not an alternative to capitalism; it is an alternative to any system under which men can live as human beings. —Ludwig von Mises, *Human Action*, 1949

Once the principle is admitted that it is the duty of the government to protect the individual against his own foolishness, no serious objections can be advanced against further encroachments. —Ludwig Von Mises, *Human Action*, 1949

The wavelike movement affecting the economic system, the recurrence of periods of boom which are followed by periods of depression, is the unavoidable outcome of the attempts, repeated again and again, to lower the gross market rate of interest by means of credit expansion. There is no means of avoiding the final collapse of a boom brought about by credit expansion. The alternative is only whether the crisis should come sooner as the result of a voluntary abandonment of further credit expansion, or later as a final and total catastrophe of the currency system involved. —Ludwig Von Mises, *Human Action*, 1949

The only way to deal with an unfree world is to become so absolutely free that your very existence is an act of rebellion. —Albert Camus

Capitalism is essentially a system of mass production for the satisfaction of the needs of the masses. It pours a horn of plenty upon the common man. It has raised the average standard of living to a height never dreamed of in earlier ages. It has made accessible to millions of people enjoyments which a few generations ago were only within the reach of a small elite. —Ludwig von Mises, *The Anti-Capitalistic Mentality*, 1956

They loathe capitalism because it has assigned to this other man the position they themselves would like to have. —Ludwig von Mises, *The Anti-Capitalistic Mentality*, 1956

The bulk of public programs are designed primarily to benefit the middle classes but are financed by taxes paid primarily by the upper and lower classes. —Aaron Director

I swear by my life and my love of it that I will never live for the sake of another man, nor ask another man to live for mine. —Ayn Rand, John Galt's oath in *Atlas Shrugged*, 1957

Government is essentially the negation of liberty. —Ludwig von Mises, *Liberty and Property*, 1958

When a self-governing people confer upon their government the power to take from some and give to others, the process will not stop until the last bone of the last taxpayer is picked bare. —Howard E. Kershner

What's really terrifying is when you realize that bureaucracy isn't simply a growth on the body of the State. If it were only that, it could be cut off. No, bureaucracy is the very essence of the State. —Vasily Grossman, *Life and Fate*, 1959

Liberty not only means that the individual has both the opportunity and the burden of choice; it also means that he must bear the consequences of his actions. Liberty and responsibility are inseparable. —F.A. Hayek, *The Constitution of Liberty*, 1960

The state has transformed judicial review from a limiting device to another instrument for conferring legitimacy on the government's actions. —Charles Lund Black Jr., *The People and the Court: Judicial Review in a Democracy*, 1960

Individual responsibility—facing the consequences of one's actions—is a prerequisite for a free society. —F.A. Hayek, *The Constitution of Liberty*, 1960

Perhaps the fact that we have seen millions voting themselves into complete dependence on a tyrant has made our generation understand that to choose one's government is not necessarily to secure freedom. —F.A. Hayek, *The Constitution of Liberty*, 1960

Freedom is never more than one generation away from extinction. We didn't pass it to our children in the bloodstream. It must be fought for, protected, and handed on for them to do the same. —Ronald Reagan, an address to the Phoenix Chamber of Commerce, 1961

Planning other people's actions means to prevent them from planning for themselves, means to deprive them of their essentially human quality, means enslaving them. —Ludwig von Mises, *The Ultimate Foundation of Economic Science: An Essay on Method*, 1962

A major source of objection to a free economy is precisely that it gives people what they want instead of what a particular group thinks they ought to want. Underlying most arguments against the free market is a lack of belief in freedom itself. —Milton Friedman, *Capitalism and Freedom*, 1962

Inflation is always and everywhere a monetary phenomenon in the sense that it is and can be produced only by a more rapid increase in the quantity of money than in output. —Milton Friedman, from a lecture at the Council for Economic Education in Bombay, India, 1963

Extremism in defense of liberty is no vice. Tolerance in the face of tyranny is no virtue. —Barry Goldwater, from his acceptance speech at the Republican National Convention, 1964

We are fast approaching the stage of the ultimate inversion: the stage where the government is free to do anything it pleases while the citizens may act only by permission, which is the stage of the darkest periods of human history—the stage of rule by brute force. —Ayn Rand, *The Virtue of Selfishness*, 1964

Pick at random any three letters from the alphabet, put them in any order, and you will have an acronym designating a federal agency we can do without. —Milton Friedman

The natural tendency of government, once in charge of money, is to inflate and to destroy the value of the currency. —Murray Rothbard, *What Has Government Done to Our Money?*, 1964

The smallest minority on earth is the individual. Those who deny individual rights cannot claim to be defenders of minorities. —Ayn Rand, *Capitalism: The Unknown Ideal*, 1966

Foggy metaphors, sloppy images, unfocused poetry, and equivocations such as "a hungry man is not free" do not alter the fact that only political power is the power of physical coercion and that freedom in a political context has only one meaning, the absence of physical coercion. —Ayn Rand, *Capitalism: The Unknown Ideal*, 1966

The "private sector" of the economy is, in fact, the voluntary sector; and … the "public sector" is, in fact, the coercive sector. The voluntary sector is made up of goods and services for which people voluntarily spend the money they have earned. The coercive sector is made up of the goods and services that are provided, regardless of the wishes of the individual, out of taxes that are seized from him. —Henry Hazlitt, *Man vs. the Welfare State*, 1969

The government has nothing to give to anybody that it doesn't first take from someone else. —Henry Hazlitt, *Man vs. the Welfare State*, 1969

Of all tyrannies, a tyranny sincerely exercised for the good of its victims may be the most oppressive. It would be better to live under robber barons than under omnipotent moral busybodies. The robber baron's cruelty may sometimes sleep, his cupidity may at some point be satiated; but those who torment us for our own good will torment us without end for they do so with the approval of their own conscience. —C.S. Lewis, *God in the Dock*, 1970

In many cases, rent control appears to be the most efficient technique presently known to destroy a city—except for bombing. —Carl Assar Eugén Lindbeck, *The Political Economy of the New Left*, 1971

The libertarian creed rests upon one central axiom: that no man or group of men may aggress against the person or property of anyone else. This may be called the "non-aggression axiom." "Aggression" is defined as the initiation of the use or threat of physical violence against the person or property of anyone else. —Murray N. Rothbard, *For a New Liberty: The Libertarian Manifesto*, 1973

A claim for equality of material position can be met only by a government with totalitarian powers. —F.A. Hayek, *Law, Legislation, and Liberty*, 1976

The idea of a strictly limited constitutional State was a noble experiment that failed, even under the most favorable and propitious circumstances. —Murray N. Rothbard, *For a New Liberty: The Libertarian Manifesto*, 1973

The more power the state has, the more it attracts people who want to use that power for their own ends. —David D. Friedman, *The Machinery of Freedom: Guide to a Radical Capitalism*, 1973

The direct use of physical force is so poor a solution to the problem of limited resources that it is commonly employed only by small children and great nations. —David D. Friedman, *The Machinery of Freedom: Guide to a Radical Capitalism*, 1973

The libertarian insists that whether or not such practices are supported by the majority of the population is not germane to their nature: that, regardless of popular sanction, War is Mass Murder, Conscription is Slavery, and Taxation is Robbery. —Murray N. Rothbard, *For a New Liberty: The Libertarian Manifesto*, 1973

If you pay people not to work and tax them when they do, don't be surprised if you get unemployment. —Milton Friedman

Hence, in education as well as in all other activities, the more that government decisions replace private decision-making, the more various groups will be at each other's throats in a desperate race to see to it that the one and only decision in each vital area goes its own way. —Murray N. Rothbard, *For a New Liberty: The Libertarian Manifesto*, 1973

In trying freedom, in abolishing the State, we have nothing to lose and everything to gain. —Murray N. Rothbard, *For a New Liberty: The Libertarian Manifesto*, 1973

Only we can replace the governance of men by the administration of things. —Murray N. Rothbard, *Egalitarianism as a Revolt Against Nature and Other Essays*, 1974

One of the great mistakes is to judge policies and programs by their intentions rather than their results. —Milton Friedman, from an interview on *The Open Mind*, 1975

Most economic fallacies derive from the tendency to assume that there is a fixed pie, that one party can gain only at the expense of another. —Milton Friedman, *Free to Choose*, 1980

The most basic question is not what is best, but who shall decide what is best. —Thomas Sowell, *Knowledge and Decisions*, 1980

Keep your eye on one thing and one thing only—how much government is spending. Because that's the true tax. Every budget is balanced. There is no such thing as an unbalanced federal budget. You're paying for it. If you're not paying for it in the form of explicit taxes, you're paying for it in the form of inflation, or in the form of borrowing. —Milton Friedman, from an interview on *Idea Channel*, 1980

A society that puts equality—in the sense of equality of outcome—ahead of freedom will end up with neither equality nor freedom. ... On the other hand, a society that puts freedom first will, as a happy by-product, end up with both greater freedom and greater equality. —Milton Friedman, *Free to Choose*, 1980

Government is not the solution to our problem; government is the problem. —Ronald Reagan, from his first inaugural address, 1981

If the government were to take over the Sahara Desert, there would be a shortage of sand in five years. —Milton Friedman

Taxation is theft, purely and simply even though it is theft on a grand and colossal scale which no acknowledged criminals could hope to match. It is a compulsory seizure of the property of the State's inhabitants, or subjects. —Murray N. Rothbard, *The Ethics of Liberty*, 1982

The curious task of economics is to demonstrate to men how little they really know about what they imagine they can design. —F.A. Hayek, *The Fatal Conceit: The Errors of Socialism*, 1988

Human beings are born with different capacities. If they are free, they are not equal. And if they are equal, they are not free. —Aleksandr Solzhenitsyn

Taxation is the price we pay for failing to build a civilized society. The higher the tax level, the greater the failure. A centrally planned totalitarian state is a complete failure of civilization, while a totally voluntary society is its ultimate success. —Mark Skousen, "Persuasion vs. Force," 1991

The first lesson of economics is scarcity: There is never enough of anything to satisfy all those who want it. The first lesson of politics is to disregard the first lesson of economics. —Thomas Sowell, *Is Reality Optional? And Other Essays*, 1993

Truth is treason in the empire of lies. —Dr. Ron Paul

Anarchism is not a romantic fable but the hardheaded realization, based on five thousand years of experience, that we cannot entrust the management of our lives to kings, priests, politicians, generals, and county commissioners. —Edward Abbey, *Confessions of a Barbarian*, 1994

The fewer things politicians control, the less it matters who controls the politicians. —Dr. Mary Ruwart

The fact is that there is no such thing as a government of law and not people. The law is an amalgam of contradictory rules and counter-rules expressed in inherently vague language that can yield a legitimate legal argument for any desired conclusion. For this reason, as long as the law remains a state monopoly, it will always reflect the political ideology of those invested with decision-making power. —John Hasnas, "The Myth of the Rule of Law," 1995

I have never understood why it is "greed" to want to keep the money you have earned but not greed to want to take somebody else's money. —Thomas Sowell, *Barbarians Inside the Gates and Other Controversial Essays*, 1999

It is hard to imagine a more stupid or more dangerous way of making decisions than by putting those decisions in the hands of people who pay no price for being wrong. —Thomas Sowell, *Wake Up, Parents!*, 2000

It is absurd to believe that an agency which may tax without consent can be a property protector. Likewise, it is absurd to believe that an agency with legislative powers can preserve law and order. —Hans-Hermann Hoppe, *Democracy: The God That Failed*, 2001

Only a crisis, real or perceived, produces real change. When that crisis occurs, the actions that are taken depend on the ideas that are lying around. That, I believe, is our basic function: to develop alternatives to existing policies, to keep them alive and available until the politically impossible becomes politically inevitable. —Milton Friedman, *Capitalism and Freedom: Fortieth Anniversary Edition*, 2002

To those who believe government is a necessary evil: you're half right. —Robert P. Murphy, *Chaos Theory*, 2002

…unmask the State and showcase it for what it really is: an institution run by gangs of murderers, plunderers and thieves, surrounded by willing executioners, propagandists, sycophants, crooks, liars, clowns, charlatans, dupes and useful idiots—an institution that dirties and taints everything it touches. —Hans-Hermann Hoppe, from his keynote address at the Property and Freedom Society's fifth anniversary meeting, 2006

The government exists outside the matrix of exchange. There are no market prices for the goods and services it endeavors to produce. The revenue it receives is not a reward for social service but rather money extracted from the public by force. It is not spent with an eye to return on investment. As a result there is no means for the government to calculate its own profits and losses. Its inability to calculate with attention to economic rationality is the downfall of governments everywhere. Its decision-making is ultimately economically arbitrary and politically motivated. —Llewellyn H. Rockwell Jr., *The Left, the Right, and the State*, 2008

Prior to capitalism, the way people amassed great wealth was by looting, plundering and enslaving their fellow man. Capitalism made it possible to become wealthy by serving your fellow man. —Walter E. Williams, *I Love Greed*, 2012

The real goal should be reduced government spending, rather than balanced budgets achieved by ever rising tax rates to cover ever rising spending. —Thomas Sowell, from an interview with John Hawkins, 2012

The transformation of charity into legal entitlement has produced donors without love and recipients without gratitude. —Antonin Scalia, *Is Capitalism or Socialism More Conducive to Christian Virtue?*, 2013

When it comes to U.S. foreign policy, no matter who you vote for, you always wind up getting John McCain. —Thomas E. Woods Jr.

This idea that individuals can be and should be sacrificed for the "greater good" is the essence of the fascist/socialist/collectivist philosophy. —Thomas J. DiLorenzo, *The Problem with Socialism*, 2016

The soul-crushing misery, the mass exodus to get out, the endless broken promises so endemic to socialism simply cannot be dismissed as the failures of a few bad people. There's something rotten in the system itself. Indeed, the very ideas from which it springs are rotten. At socialism's core is end-justifies-the-means, moral relativist, anti-individual and collectivist rubbish. Bad people are everywhere, but nothing brings them forth and licenses them to do evil more thoroughly than concentrated power and the subordination of morality to the service of a statist ideology. That is the essence of the socialist vision, the iron fist within the velvet glove that belies all the happy talk to the contrary. —Lawrence W. Reed

What causes poverty? Nothing. It's the original state, the default and starting point. The real question is: What causes prosperity? —Per Bylund, *The Pete Quinones Show*, Episode 276, 2019

When people get used to preferential treatment, equal treatment seems like discrimination. —Thomas Sowell

FURTHER READING

A comprehensive library on the fundamental principles of individual liberty is available at the following website:

www.TheRootOfLiberty.com

Follow the brief instructions on the home page, then begin the Essential Reading List.

The books and essays from The Root of Liberty website are listed below:

The Essential Reading List

"I Pencil," Leonard Read
"That Which Is Seen, and that Which Is Not Seen," Frédéric Bastiat
"The Candlemakers' Petition," Frédéric Bastiat
The Law, Frédéric Bastiat
The Politics of Obedience: The Discourse of Voluntary Servitude, Étienne de la Boétie
Not Yours to Give, Colonel David Crockett
The Road to Serfdom, F.A. Hayek
"The Tale of a Slave" (excerpt from *Anarchy, State, and Utopia*), Robert Nozick
The State, Franz Oppenheimer
"The Myth of the Rule of Law," John Hasnas
The Right and Wrong of Compulsion by the State, Auberon Herbert

For a New Liberty: The Libertarian Manifesto, Murray N. Rothbard

<u>The Full Reading List</u>

No Treason: No. 1, No. 2: "The Constitution," No. 6: "The Constitution
    of no Authority," Lysander Spooner
1984, George Orwell
Liberalism: In the Classical Tradition, Ludwig von Mises
The Fatal Conceit: The Errors of Socialism, F.A. Hayek
The Creature from Jekyll Island, G. Edward Griffin
Basic Economics, Thomas Sowell
A Theory of Socialism and Capitalism, Hans-Hermann Hoppe
Animal Farm, George Orwell
The Ethics of Liberty, Murray N. Rothbard
Anarchy, State, and Utopia, Robert Nozick
Dumbing Us Down, John Taylor Gatto
"Anatomy of the State," Murray N. Rothbard
America's Counter-Revolution: The Constitution Revisited, Sheldon Richman
33 Questions About American History You're Not Supposed to Ask,
    Thomas E. Woods Jr.
A Conflict of Visions, Thomas Sowell
Anthem, Ayn Rand
"Bitcoin: A Peer-to-Peer Electronic Cash System," Satoshi Nakamoto
Apocalypse Never: Why Environmental Alarmism Hurts Us All, Michael
    Shellenberger
Capitalism and Freedom, Milton Friedman
Chaos Theory: Two Essays on Market Anarchy, Robert P. Murphy
Atlas Shrugged, Ayn Rand
Cool It: The Skeptical Environmentalist's Guide to Global Warming,
    Bjørn Lomborg
Crisis and Leviathan, Robert Higgs
The Economics and Ethics of Private Property, Hans-Hermann Hoppe
Anything That's Peaceful, Leonard Read
Egalitarianism as a Revolt Against Nature and Other Essays, Murray
    N. Rothbard
Free to Choose, Milton Friedman
Give Me Liberty, Rose Wilder Lane
Democracy: The God That Failed, Hans-Hermann Hoppe

Global Warming Skepticism for Busy People, Roy Spencer

Modern Times, Paul Johnson

"Persuasion vs. Force," Mark Skousen

Rollback: Repealing Big Government Before the Coming Fiscal Collapse, Thomas E. Woods Jr.

The Black Book of Communism, Stéphane Courtois and others

Discourses Concerning Government, Algernon Sidney

Civil Rights: Rhetoric or Reality?, Thomas Sowell

Defending the Undefendable, Walter Block

Capitalism: The Unknown Ideal, Ayn Rand

The Moral Case for Fossil Fuels, Alex Epstein

The Intellectuals and Socialism, F.A. Hayek

The Machinery of Freedom, David Friedman

The Middle of the Road Leads to Socialism, Ludwig von Mises

The Most Dangerous Superstition, Larken Rose

Fossil Future: Why Global Human Flourishing Requires More Oil, Alex Epstein

"War Is a Racket," Smedley Butler

The Politically Incorrect Guide to American History, Thomas E. Woods Jr.

The Privatization of Roads and Highways, Walter Block

The Problem of Political Authority: An Examination of the Right to Coerce and the Duty to Obey, Michael Huemer

Nullification: How to Resist Federal Tyranny in the 21st Century, Thomas E. Woods Jr.

Socialism, Ludwig von Mises

The Bitcoin Standard: The Decentralized Alternative to Central Banking, Saifedean Ammous

The Communist Manifesto, Karl Marx and Friedrich Engels

The Fountainhead, Ayn Rand

The Constitution of Liberty, F.A. Hayek

The Production of Security, Gustave de Molinari

The Skeptical Environmentalist: Measuring the Real State of the World, Bjørn Lomborg

The State Against Blacks, Walter Williams

The Moon Is a Harsh Mistress, Robert Heinlein

Real Dissent: A Libertarian Sets Fire to the Index Card of Allowable Opinion, Thomas E. Woods Jr.
The Fiat Standard, Saifedean Ammous
The Revolution: A Manifesto, Ron Paul
The Philosophical Origins of Austrian Economics, David Gordon
What Has Government Done to Our Money?, Murray N. Rothbard
Fahrenheit 451, Ray Bradbury
Our Enemy, the State, Albert Jay Nock
The Rothbard Reader, Murray N. Rothbard
Two Treatises of Government, John Locke
When Money Dies, Adam Fergusson
A Treatise on Political Economy, Jean Baptiste Say
Against Intellectual Property, N. Stephan Kinsella
America's Great Depression, Murray N. Rothbard
The Wizards of Ozymandias, Butler Shaffer
The Virtue of Selfishness, Ayn Rand
Brave New World, Aldous Huxley
The Voluntaryist Handbook, Keith Knight
Conceived in Liberty, Murray N. Rothbard
Economics in One Lesson, Henry Hazlitt
Fake Invisible Catastrophes and Threats of Doom, Patrick Moore
I'd Push the Button, Leonard E. Read
Money, Bank Credit, and Economic Cycles, Jesús Huerta de Soto
Omnipotent Government: The Rise of the Total State and Total War, Ludwig von Mises
Rules for Radicals: A Pragmatic Primer for Realistic Radicals, Saul Alinsky
Springtime for Snowflakes: 'Social Justice' and Its Postmodern Parentage, Michael Rectenwald
Superabundance: The Story of Population Growth, Gale L. Pooley and Marian L. Tupy
The Case Against the Fed, Murray N. Rothbard
The Church and the Market, Thomas E. Woods Jr.
"The Friedman Doctrine: The Social Responsibility of Business is to Increase Its Profits," Milton Friedman
The Theory of Money and Credit, Ludwig von Mises
"Twentieth Century Motor Company" (excerpt from *Atlas Shrugged*), Ayn Rand

A Brief Enquiry into the True Nature and Character of Our Federal Government, Abel Upshur

A Liberty Primer, Alan Burris

"An Arrow Against All Tyrants," Richard Overton

An Austrian Perspective on the History of Economic Thought, Murray N. Rothbard

Applied Economics, Thomas Sowell

Back on the Road to Serfdom: The Resurgence of Statism, Thomas E. Woods Jr.

Beyond Politics: The Roots of Government Failure, Randy T. Simmons

Beyond Woke, Michael Rectenwald

Boundaries of Order: Private Property as a Social System, Butler Shaffer

Cato's Letters, Thomas Gordon and John Trenchard

Choice: Cooperation, Enterprise, and Human Action, Robert P. Murphy

City of God, St. Augustine

On the Duty of Civil Disobedience, Henry David Thoreau

Common Sense, Thomas Paine

Critique of Pure Reason, Immanuel Kant

Das Kapital, Karl Marx

Delusions of Power: New Explorations of the State, War, and Economy, Robert Higgs

Democracy in America, Alexis de Tocqueville

Diary of a Psychosis: How Public Health Disgraced Itself During COVID Mania, Thomas E. Woods Jr.

Discovery, Capitalism, and Distributive Justice, Israel M. Kirzner

Disquisition on Government, John C. Calhoun

Economic Freedom of the World, James Gwartney

Economic Policy: Thoughts for Today and Tomorrow, Ludwig von Mises

Economic Sophisms, Frédéric Bastiat

Education: Free and Compulsory, Murray N. Rothbard

End the Fed, Ron Paul

Essays, Moral, Political, and Literary, David Hume

Explaining Postmodernism: Skepticism and Socialism from Rousseau to Foucault, Stephen R. C. Hicks

False Alarm: How Climate Change Panic Costs Us Trillions, Bjørn Lomborg

Francisco d'Anconia's speech: "Money is the root of all good" (excerpt from *Atlas Shrugged*), Ayn Rand

Freedom and the Law, Bruno Leoni
Freedom's Progress?: A History of Political Thought, Gerard Casey
From Mutual Aid to the Welfare State: Fraternal Societies and Social Services, 1890–1967, David T. Beito
Give Me a Break, John Stossel
Great Wars and Great Leaders: A Libertarian Rebuttal, Ralph Raico
Green Fraud: Why the Green New Deal Is Even Worse than You Think, Marc Morano
Harmonies of Political Economy, Frédéric Bastiat
Healing Our World, Mary Ruwart
Hot Talk, Cold Science: Global Warming's Unfinished Debate, S. Fred Singer
How an Economy Grows and Why It Crashes, Peter Schiff
How Inflation Destroys Civilization, Jörg Guido Hülsmann
How to Think About the Economy, Per Bylund
Human Action, Ludwig von Mises
In Defense of Global Capitalism, Johan Norberg
Kant's Principles of Politics, Including His Essay on Perpetual Peace, Immanuel Kant
Knowledge and Decisions, Thomas Sowell
Laissez-Faire Banking, Kevin Dowd
Lessons for the Young Economist, Robert Murphy
Lessons for the Young Economist Teacher's Manual, Robert Murphy
Letter from Thomas Burke to Richard Caswell, Thomas Burke
Liberalism Caused the Great Enrichment, Deirdre McCloskey
Liberty Defined, Ron Paul
Lord of the Flies, William Golding
Losing Ground: American Social Policy, 1950–1980, Charles Murray
Lost Rights, James Bovard
Man, Economy, and State, with Power and Market, Murray N. Rothbard
Market Anarchism as Constitutionalism, Roderick T. Long
Meltdown: The Classic Free-Market Analysis of the 2008 Financial Crisis, Thomas E. Woods Jr.
Mises: The Last Knight of Liberalism, Jörg Guido Hülsmann
Nothing to Fear: A Bright Future for Fossil Fuels, Donn Dears
On Power: The Natural History of Its Growth, Bertrand de Jouvenel
On Tyranny: Twenty Lessons from the Twentieth Century, Timothy Snyder
One Day in the Life of Ivan Denisovich, Aleksandr Solzhenitsyn

Politics, Aristotle

Principles of Economics, Saifedean Ammous

Private Property and Collective Ownership, James A. Sadowsky, S.J.

Production of Money on the Market, Jeffrey M. Herbener

Race and Culture, Thomas Sowell

Radicals for Capitalism, Brian Doherty

Refounding America, Terry Easton and Ashton Ellis

Report from Iron Mountain, Leonard C. Lewin

Suicide of the West, James Burnham

Terms of Engagement: How Our Courts Should Enforce the Constitution's Promise of Limited Government, Clark M. Neily III

The Adventures of Jonathan Gullible, Ken Schoolland

The Apology of Socrates, Plato

The Austrian School, Jesús Huerta de Soto

The Austrian Theory of the Trade Cycle and Other Essays, Richard M. Ebeling

The Best of Burke: Selected Writings and Speeches of Edmund Burke, Peter J. Stanlis

The Bottomless Well: The Twilight of Fuel, Peter W. Huber and Mark P. Mills

The Conscience of a Conservative, Barry Goldwater

The Conservative Mind, Russell Kirk

The Costs of War: America's Pyrrhic Victories, Abraham Kaplan

The Discovery of Freedom, Rose Wilder Lane

The Diversity Delusion: How Race and Gender Pandering Corrupt the University and Undermine Our Culture, Heather Mac Donald

The Essential von Mises, Murray N. Rothbard

The Ethics of Money Production, Jörg Guido Hülsmann

The Forgotten Depression: 1921, James Grant

The Forgotten Man, William Graham Sumner

The Free Market and Its Enemies: Pseudo-Science, Socialism, and Inflation, Ludwig von Mises

The Global Currency Plot, Thorsten Polleit

The God of the Machine, Isabel Paterson

The Great Deformation: The Corruption of Capitalism in America, David A. Stockman

The Great War, Hunt Tooley

The Gulag Archipelago, Vol. 1, 2, and 3, Aleksandr Solzhenitsyn
The Harvest of Sorrow, Robert Conquest
The Incredible Bread Machine, R.W. Grant
The Invisible Heart, Russell Roberts
The Left, the Right, and the State, Lew Rockwell
The Logic of Freedom, Laura Davidson
The Making of Modern Economics, Mark Skousen
The Man Versus the State, Herbert Spencer
The Mandibles: A Family, 2029–2047, Lionel Shriver
The Market for Liberty, Morris and Linda Tannehill
The Mystery of Banking, Murray N. Rothbard
The Myth of Left and Right: How the Political Spectrum Misleads and Harms America, Verlan Lewis and Hyrum Lewis
The Myth of Neutral Taxation, Murray N. Rothbard
The Myth of the Rational Voter, Bryan Caplan
The Nature of Man and His Government, Robert LeFevre
The Panic of 1819, Murray N. Rothbard
The Politically Incorrect Guide to Climate Change, Marc Morano
The Politically Incorrect Guide to the Constitution, Kevin Gutzman
The Principles of Ethics, Vol. 1 and 2, Herbert Spencer
The Quest for Community: A Study in the Ethics of Order and Freedom, Robert Nisbet
The Republic, Plato
The Republic and the Laws, Cicero
The Society of Tomorrow, Gustave de Molinari
The Theory of Moral Sentiments, Adam Smith
The Tuttle Twins book series, Connor Boyack and Elijah Stanfield
The Use of Knowledge in Society, F.A. Hayek
The Wealth of Nations, Adam Smith
The White Man's Burden, William Easterly
The Works and Correspondence of David Ricardo, Vol. 1: Principles of Political Economy and Taxation, David Ricardo
The Works of Voltaire, Vol. 1 (*Candide*), Voltaire
The Virtue of Selfishness, Ayn Rand
To Serve and Protect: Privatization and Community in Criminal Justice, Bruce L. Benson
War, Peace, and the State, Murray N. Rothbard

Warning to the West, Aleksandr Solzhenitsyn

We the Living, Ayn Rand

We Who Dared to Say No to War: American Antiwar Writing from 1812 to Now, Thomas E. Woods Jr.

Whatever Happened to Penny Candy?, Richard J. Maybury

While You Slept, John T. Flynn

Who Killed the Constitution?: The Federal Government vs. American Liberty from World War I to Barack Obama, Thomas E. Woods Jr.

Why Liberalism Works: How True Liberal Values Produce a Freer, More Equal, Prosperous World for All, Deirdre McCloskey

Why Liberty, Marc Guttman

Why Not Capitalism?, Jason Brennan

Why Not Socialism?, G.A. Cohen

NOTES

1   Lord Acton, Letter to Mary Gladstone, April 5, 1887.

2   Frédéric Bastiat, The Law (Paris: Guillaumin, 1850).

3   Aristotle, *Metaphysics*, 350 B.C.

4   Thomas Aquinas, *Summa Contra Gentiles* (1259–65; reprint, Turin: Marietti, 1961).

5   John Locke, *Second Treatise on Government* (London: Awnsham Churchill, 1689).

6   Henry David Thoreau, *"Civil Disobedience"* (original lecture "The Rights and Duties of the Individual in Relation to Government," 1848; published as *Resistance to Civil Government*, in *Æsthetic Papers*, ed. Elizabeth P. Peabody, 1849).

7   Bertrand de Jouvenel, *On Power: The Natural History of Its Growth*, trans. J.F. Huntington (New York: Viking Press, 1949)

8   Ludwig von Mises, *Human Action: A Treatise on Economics* (New Haven: Yale University Press, 1949).

9   Friedrich A. Hayek, *The Constitution of Liberty* (Chicago: University of Chicago Press, 1960).

10   Ayn Rand, "Introducing Objectivism," *Los Angeles Times*, June 17, 1962.

11   Ayn Rand, *Atlas Shrugged* (New York: Random House, 1957).

12   Ayn Rand, *Capitalism: The Unknown Ideal* (New York: New American Library, 1966).

13   Milton Friedman, *Capitalism and Freedom* (Chicago: University of Chicago Press, 1962).

14   Ronald Reagan, *"A Time for Choosing,"* speech delivered on behalf of Barry Goldwater, October 27, 1964, Los Angeles, CA, broadcast on NBC.

15   Murray N. Rothbard, *For a New Liberty: The Libertarian Manifesto* (New York: Macmillan, 1973).

16   Dr. Ron Paul, *Liberty Defined: 50 Essential Issues that Affect Our Freedom* (New York: Grand Central Publishing, 2011).

17 Ayn Rand's philosophy, known as Objectivism, inspired the creation of numerous organizations. One such group is the Prometheus Foundation, managed by Carl Barney and Craig Biddle. The referenced passage is from a 2019 article titled "LIBERTY, What Is It? Why Is It Good? On What Does It Depend?"

18 Grant Babcock, "What Is a Libertarian?," Libertarianism.org, accessed September 27, 2025, https://www.libertarianism.org/what-is-a-libertarian.

19 Ludwig von Mises, *Socialism: An Economic and Sociological Analysis*, trans. J. Kahane (London: Jonathan Cape, 1936).

20 Rothbard, *For a New Liberty: The Libertarian Manifesto*.

21 Leonard E. Read, *Students of Liberty* (Irvington-on-Hudson, NY: Foundation for Economic Education, 1950).

22 John Locke, *Two Treatises of Government* (London: Awnsham Churchill, 1689).

23 Bastiat, *The Law*.

24 Hayek, *The Constitution of Liberty*.

25 Friedman, *Capitalism and Freedom*.

26 Murray N. Rothbard, *The Ethics of Liberty* (Atlantic Highlands, NJ: Humanities Press, 1982).

27 Ludwig von Mises, *Liberty and Property* (Princeton, NJ: Van Nostrand, 1958).

28 F. A. Harper, remarks at the Mont Pelerin Society meeting, St. Moritz, Switzerland, September 4, 1957.

29 Bastiat, *The Law*.

30 Rothbard, *The Ethics of Liberty*.

31 Locke, *Two Treatises of Government*, 1689.

32 William Roper, *The Life of Sir Thomas More* (1557; repr., London: Cassell.

33 Ayn Rand, *The Virtue of Selfishness: A New Concept of Egoism* (New York: New American Library, 1964).

34 Rothbard, *For a New Liberty: The Libertarian Manifesto*.

35 Rothbard, *The Ethics of Liberty*.

36 Portions of this chapter have been adapted from Ken Schoolland, *The Philosophy of Liberty*, YouTube video, 5:15, posted by "Ken Schoolland," March 16, 2014, https://www.youtube.com/watch?v=M9srplWe_QQ..

37 Locke, *Two Treatises of Government*.

38 Rothbard, *The Ethics of Liberty*.

39 Rothbard, *For a New Liberty: The Libertarian Manifesto*.

40   Ayn Rand, "The Virtue of Selfishness: A New Concept of Egoism" (New York: New American Library, 1964).

41   Herbert Spencer, *Social Statics: or, The Conditions Essential to Human Happiness Specified, and the First of Them Developed* (London: John Chapman, 1851).

42   Roderick T. Long, "Slavery Contracts and Inalienable Rights: A Formulation," *Formulations* 2, no. 2 (Winter 1994–95). (Reprinted online at the Center for a Stateless Society, Jan. 3, 2013.)

43   David Friedman, *The Machinery of Freedom: Guide to a Radical Capitalism* (New Rochelle, NY: Arlington House, 1973).

44   James A. Sadowsky, "Private Property and Collective Ownership," in *Property in a Humane Economy*, ed. Samuel L. Blumenfeld (La Salle, IL: Open Court, 1974), 79–92.

45   https://www.sumerianshakespeare.com/xpag39/urukagina, accessed September 27, 2025.

46   "Online Library of Liberty," accessed September 27, 2025, https://oll.libertyfund.org/pages/images-of-liberty-and-power-amagi-symbol-liberty-fund-logo.

47   Hammurabi, The Code of Hammurabi, trans. L. W. King (London: Luzac and Co., 1902).

48   Hammurabi, Code of Hammurabi.

49   "Samuel: Last of the Judges," Learn Religions, accessed September 27, 2025, https://www.learnreligions.com/samuel-last-of-the-judges-701161.

50   Holy Bible: New Living Translation, 1 Samuel 8, accessed September 27, 2025, https://www.bible.com/bible/116/1SA.8.NLT.

51   Murray N. Rothbard, "The Ancient Chinese Libertarian Tradition," Mises Daily, April 15, 2022, accessed September 27, 2025, https://mises.org/mises-daily/ancient-chinese-libertarian-tradition.

52   Lao Tzu, *Tao Te Ching*, taoism.net, accessed September 27, 2025, https://taoism.net/tao-te-ching-online-translation/.

53   Paul MacCotter, *Medieval Ireland: Territorial, Political and Economic Divisions* (Dublin: Four Courts Press, 2014).

54   Richard Kraut, *How to Read Plato* (London: Granta Books, 2008).

55   Aristotle, Rhetoric, trans. W. Rhys Roberts, in *The Complete Works of Aristotle: The Revised Oxford Translation*, ed. Jonathan Barnes, vol. 2 (Princeton, NJ: Princeton University Press, 1984), I.10.

56   Aristotle, Rhetoric, trans. W. Rhys Roberts, in *The Complete Works of Aristotle: The Revised Oxford Translation*, ed. Jonathan Barnes, vol. 2 (Princeton, NJ: Princeton University Press, 1984), I.5.

57   Aristotle, Rhetoric, trans. W. Rhys Roberts, in *The Complete Works of Aristotle: The Revised Oxford Translation*, ed. Jonathan Barnes, vol. 2 (Princeton, NJ: Princeton University Press, 1984), I.4.

58   Murray N. Rothbard, *An Austrian Perspective on the History of Economic Thought*, vol. 1, *Economic Thought Before Adam Smith* (Aldershot, UK: Edward Elgar, 1995).

59   Zhuangzi, *The Complete Works of Chuang Tzu*, trans. Burton Watson (New York: Columbia University Press, 1968).

60   Cicero, *De Officiis*, trans. Walter Miller (Cambridge, MA: Harvard University Press, 1913).

61   Cicero, *De Legibus*, trans. Clinton W. Keyes (Cambridge, MA: Harvard University Press, 1928).

62   Tacitus, *The Annals of Imperial Rome*, trans. Michael Grant (London: Penguin Books, 1956).

63   Augustine of Hippo, *The City of God*, trans. Henry Bettenson (London: Penguin Books, 1972).

64   Justinian I, *The Institutes of Justinian*, trans. J. B. Moyle, 5th ed. (Oxford: Clarendon Press, 1913).

65   *Magna Carta*, trans. National Archives (PDF), accessed September 27, 2025, https://www.archives.gov/files/press/press-kits/magna-carta/magna-carta-translation.pdf

66   Thomas Aquinas, *Summa Contra Gentiles* (c. 1259–65; repr., Turin: Marietti, 1961).

67   Thomas Aquinas, *Summa Theologica*, trans. Fathers of the English Dominican Province, 5 vols. (New York: Benziger Bros., 1947).

68   Niccolò Machiavelli, *The Prince*, trans. George Bull (London: Penguin Books, 1961).

69   Francisco de Vitoria, Political Writings, ed. Anthony Pagden and Jeremy Lawrance (Cambridge: Cambridge University Press, 1991), 233–40.

70   Étienne de La Boétie, *The Discourse of Voluntary Servitude*, trans. Harry Kurz (Indianapolis: Liberty Fund, 1975).

71   George Buchanan, *A Dialogue on the Law of Kingship among the Scots: De Jure Regni apud Scotos*, ed. Roger A. Mason and Martin S. Smith

(Farnham, UK: Ashgate; repr., Cambridge: Cambridge University Press, 2012).

72 Robert Bellarmine, *On Temporal and Spiritual Authority: De Laicis*, trans. R.W. Dyson (Indianapolis: Liberty Fund, 2012).

73 "Petition of Right," Liberty Fund: Online Library of Liberty, accessed September 27, 2025, https://oll.libertyfund.org/pages/1628-petition-of-right.

74 Richard Overton, *The Commoners' Complaint* (London, 1647).

75 Locke, *Second Treatise of Government.*

76 Algernon Sidney, *Discourses Concerning Government* (London: 1698).

77 Marquis de Condorcet, *Sketch for a Historical Picture of the Progress of the Human Mind*, trans. June Barraclough (Westport, CT: Hyperion Press, 1979).

78 Adam Smith, *An Inquiry into the Nature and Causes of the Wealth of Nations* (London: W. Strahan and T. Cadell, 1776).

79 Smith, *Wealth of Nations.*

80 *The Massachusetts Body of Liberties* (1641; repr., Boston: Massachusetts Historical Society, 1843).

81 John Dickinson, *Letters from a Farmer in Pennsylvania to the Inhabitants of the British Colonies* (Philadelphia: David Hall and William Sellers, 1768).

82 "Declaration and Resolves of the 1st Continental Congress," Liberty Fund: *Online Library of Liberty*, accessed September 27, 2025, https://oll.libertyfund.org/pages/1774-declaration-and-resolves-of-the-1st-continental-congress.

83 "Olive Branch Petition," *World History Encyclopedia*, accessed September 27, 2025, https://www.worldhistory.org/article/2351/olive-branch-petition/.

84 "Proclamation of Rebellion (King George III)," *American History Central*, accessed September 27, 2025, https://www.americanhistorycentral.com/documents/proclamation-of-rebellion-king-george-iii-text/.

85 Thomas Paine, *Common Sense* (Philadelphia: R. Bell, 1776).

86 John Locke, *An Essay Concerning Human Understanding* (London: Thomas Basset, 1690).

87 "Articles of Confederation," *National Archives*, accessed September 27, 2025, https://www.archives.gov/milestone-documents/articles-of-confederation.

88   "Treaty of Paris," *National Archives* / Milestone Documents, accessed September 27, 2025, https://www.archives.gov/milestone-documents/treaty-of-paris.

89   Albert Jay Nock, *Our Enemy, the State* (New York: William Morrow, 1935).

90   Patrick Newman, "A Case Study in State Conquest: The Federalists' Constitution," YouTube video, 47:15, posted by "Mises Institute," October 12, 2024, https://youtu.be/-fLO5V_vtiA?si=doffRbU4bAVD84By.

91   JoJohn G. Grove, "A Maxim for Power-Skeptical Conservatism," Law & Liberty, November 23, 2021, accessed September 27, 2025, https://law-liberty.org/a-maxim-for-power-skeptical-conservatism/.

92   Thomas Jefferson to William Stephens Smith, November 13, 1787, in The Papers of Thomas Jefferson, ed. Julian P. Boyd, vol. 12 (Princeton, NJ: Princeton University Press, 1955), 356–57.

93   David Hume, *Essays, Moral, Political, and Literary* (London: A. Millar, 1758).

94   Thomas Jefferson to Samuel Kercheval, April 12, 1816, in *The Papers of Thomas Jefferson*, ed. Julian P. Boyd et al., vol. 30 (Princeton, NJ: Princeton University Press, 1983), 370–71, https://founders.archives.gov/documents/Jefferson/01-30-02-0370-0004.

95   "Virginia Resolves," *The Avalon Project*, Yale Law School, accessed September 27, 2025, https://avalon.law.yale.edu/18th_century/virres.asp.

96   "Kentucky Resolves (1798)," *The Avalon Project*, Yale Law School, accessed September 27, 2025, https://avalon.law.yale.edu/18th_century/kenres.asp.

97   Bastiat, *The Law*.

98   Frédéric Bastiat, "That Which Is Seen, and That Which Is Not Seen," in *Selected Essays on Political Economy*, trans. Seymour Cain (Irvington-on-Hudson, NY: Foundation for Economic Education, 1964)

99   Jean-Baptiste Say, *A Treatise on Political Economy; or, The Production, Distribution and Consumption of Wealth*, trans. C.R. Prinsep (London: Longman, Hurst, Rees, Orme, and Brown, 1821).

100   Lysander Spooner, *No Treason. No. VI. The Constitution of No Authority* (Boston: 1870).

101   Herbert Spencer, *Social Statics: or, The Conditions Essential to Human Happiness Specified, and the First of Them Developed* (London: John Chapman, 1851).

102 Herbert Spencer, "The Sins of Legislators," The Contemporary Review 18 (1871).

103 Alexis de Tocqueville, *Democracy in America*, trans. Henry Reeve, rev. Francis Bowen (Cambridge, MA: Sever and Francis, 1862).

104 William Graham Sumner, "The Forgotten Man," in *The Forgotten Man and Other Essays*, ed. Albert Galloway Keller (New Haven, CT: Yale University Press, 1918).

105 Gustave de Molinari, *The Production of Security*, trans. J. Huston McCulloch (New York: Center for Libertarian Studies, 1977).

106 Auberon Herbert, *The Right and Wrong of Compulsion by the State* (London: Williams and Norgate, 1885).

107 Franz Oppenheimer, *The State*, trans. John M. Gitterman (New York: Vanguard Press, 1922).

108 Max Weber, "Politics as a Vocation," in *From Max Weber: Essays in Sociology*, trans. and ed. H.H. Gerth and C. Wright Mills (New York: Oxford University Press, 1946).

109 Nock, *Our Enemy, the State*.

110 H. L. Mencken, *Notes on Democracy* (New York: Alfred A. Knopf, 1926).

111 Ludwig von Mises, *The Theory of Money and Credit*, trans. H. E. Batson (London: Jonathan Cape, 1934).

112 Ludwig von Mises, "Cyclical Changes in Business Conditions," Quarterly Journal of Austrian Economics 1, no. 3 (1943)

113 Ludwig von Mises, *Human Action: A Treatise on Economics* (New Haven, CT: Yale University Press, 1949).

114 Ludwig von Mises, *Liberalism: In the Classical Tradition*, trans. Ralph Raico, ed. Arthur Goddard (Irvington-on-Hudson, NY: Foundation for Economic Education, 1962).

115 Ludwig von Mises, "Profit and Loss," in *Planning for Freedom and Other Essays and Addresses* (South Holland, IL: Libertarian Press, 1951).

116 Ludwig von Mises, *Liberty and Property* (London: Institute of Economic Affairs, 1959).

117 Henry Hazlitt, *Economics in One Lesson* (New York: Harper and Brothers, 1946).

118 F.A. Hayek, *The Constitution of Liberty* (Chicago: University of Chicago Press, 1960).

119 F.A. Hayek, *Law, Legislation, and Liberty*, 3 vols. (Chicago: University of Chicago Press, 1973–79).

120 F.A. Hayek, *The Fatal Conceit: The Errors of Socialism*, ed. W. W. Bartley III (Chicago: University of Chicago Press, 1988).

121 "Jekyll Island Conference," Federal Reserve History, accessed September 27, 2025, https://www.federalreservehistory.org/essays/jekyll-island-conference#duc.

122 Randolph Bourne, "War Is the Health of the State," in Untimely Papers (New York: B. W. Huebsch, 1919).

123 Ayn Rand, *Anthem* (London: Cassell, 1938).

124 Ayn Rand, *Atlas Shrugged* (New York: Random House, 1957).

125 Ayn Rand, *Capitalism: The Unknown Ideal* (New York: New American Library, 1966).

126 Rand, *Atlas Shrugged*, Part III, Chapter VII, "This Is John Galt Speaking."

127 Foundation for Economic Education, FEE, accessed September 27, 2025, https://fee.org/.

128 Friedman, *Capitalism and Freedom*.

129 Friedman, *Capitalism and Freedom*.

130 Friedman, *Capitalism and Freedom*.

131 Milton Friedman and Rose Friedman, *Free to Choose: A Personal Statement* (New York: Harcourt Brace Jovanovich, 1980).

132 The Libertarian Forum (New York: Karl Hess and Murray N. Rothbard, 1969–1984).

133 Murray N. Rothbard, *Anatomy of the State* (Los Angeles: Rampart College, 1974).

134 Murray N. Rothbard, *Conceived in Liberty*, 4 vols. (New Rochelle, NY: Arlington House, 1975–79).

135 Rothbard, *For a New Liberty*.

136 Murray N. Rothbard, *The Ethics of Liberty* (Atlantic Highlands, NJ: Humanities Press, 1982).

137 Rothbard, *The Ethics of Liberty*.

138 Thomas Sowell, *Knowledge and Decisions* (New York: Basic Books, 1980).

139 Thomas Sowell, *A Conflict of Visions: Ideological Origins of Political Struggles* (New York: William Morrow, 1987).

140 Thomas Sowell, *Is Reality Optional? And Other Essays* (Stanford, CA: Hoover Institution Press, 1993).

141 Thomas Sowell, *Barbarians Inside the Gates and Other Controversial Essays* (Stanford, CA: Hoover Institution Press, 1999).

142 Thomas Sowell, *Wake Up, Parents!* (Stanford, CA: Hoover Institution Press, 2000).

143 Walter Block, *Defending the Undefendable* (New York: Fleet Press, 1976).

144 *The Adventures of Jonathan Gullible: A Free Market Odyssey*, JonathanGullible.com, accessed September 27, 2025, https://www.jonathangullible.com/.

145 SPN, accessed September 27, 2025, https://spn.org/

146 https://spn.org/directory/

147 https://repository.law.wisc.edu/s/uwlaw/ark:/86871/w126362d

148 John Taylor Gatto, *Dumbing Us Down: The Hidden Curriculum of Compulsory Schooling* (Philadelphia: New Society Publishers, 1992).

149 Grassroot Institute of Hawaii, GrassrootInstitute.org, accessed September 27, 2025, https://www.grassrootinstitute.org/

150 Property & Freedom Society, accessed September 27, 2025, https://propertyandfreedom.org/

151 Mark Skousen, "Persuasion vs. Force," *The Freeman* 41, no. 5 (May 1991).

152 FreedomFest, accessed September 27, 2025, https://freedomfest.com/.

153 Jörg Guido Hülsmann, *The Ethics of Money Production* (Auburn, AL: Ludwig von Mises Institute, 2008).

154 "The Bob Murphy Show," accessed September 27, 2025, https://www.bobmurphyshow.com/

155 Human Action Podcast, Mises Institute, accessed September 27, 2025, https://mises.org/podcasts/human-action-podcast

156 Ron Paul, *Liberty Defined: 50 Essential Issues That Affect Our Freedom* (New York: Grand Central Publishing, 2011).

157 libertas.org, accessed September 27, 2025, https://libertas.org/

158 "Mises Institute," accessed September 27, 2025, https://mises.org/

159 Llewellyn H. Rockwell Jr., *The Left, the Right, and the State* (Auburn, AL: Ludwig von Mises Institute, 2008).

160 TomWoods.com, accessed September 27, 2025, https://tomwoods.com/

161 Liberty Classroom, accessed September 27, 2025, https://libertyclassroom.com/

162 Tom School of Life, accessed September 27, 2025, https://tomschooloflife.com/

163 Thomas J. DiLorenzo, *The Problem with Socialism* (Washington, DC: Regnery Publishing, 2016).

164 Libertarian Institute, accessed September 27, 2025, https://libertarianin-stitute.org/

165 https://scotthortonacademy.com/

166 Free the People, accessed September 27, 2025, https://freethepeople.org/

167 Gary D. Barnett, "There Is No Limit to State Power, and There Never Has Been!," September 8, 2023, https://garydbarnett.substack.com/p/there-is-no-limit-to-state-power-and-there-never-has-been.

168 Gary D. Barnett, accessed September 27, 2025, https://www.garydbarnett.com/

169 "Poverty," *World Bank Open Data*, https://data360.worldbank.org/en/indicator/WB_PIP_HEADCOUNT_LMIC?view=trend&average=WLD.

170 "Ending Poverty," *United Nations*, accessed September 27, 2025, https://www.un.org/en/global-issues/ending-poverty.

171 "The Share and Number of People Living in Extreme Poverty," *Our World in Data*, accessed September 27, 2025, https://ourworldindata.org/grapher/the-share-and-number-of-people-living-in-extreme-poverty.

172 "The Root of Liberty," accessed September 27, 2025, https://www.the-rootofliberty.com/

173 "Politics Is Downstream from Culture, Part 1: Right Turn to Narrative," Hedgehog Review, accessed September 27, 2025, https://hedgehogreview.com/web-features/infernal-machine/posts/politics-is-downstream-from-culture-part-1-right-turn-to-narrative.

174 Edmund Burke, *Reflections on the Revolution in France* (London: J. Dodsley, 1790).

175 Ron Paul, *End the Fed* (New York: Grand Central Publishing, 2009).

176 Bastiat, *The Law*.

177 Claudia Kann, Kevin Arceneaux, Daniel Hopkins, and Tiffany Barnes, "Persuadable Voters Decided the 2022 Midterm: Abortion Rights and Issues-Based Frameworks for Elections," *PLOS ONE* 19, no. 1 (January 2024): e0294047, https://doi.org/10.1371/journal.pone.0294047. See also "2016 Presidential Election Results," *Washington Post*, November 2016, https://www.washingtonpost.com/graphics/politics/2016-election/swing-state-margins/

178 J. Xie, S. Sreenivasan, G. Korniss, W. Zhang, C. Lim, and B.K. Szymanski, "Social Consensus through the Influence of Committed Minorities," Physical Review E 84, no. 1 (2011): 011130, https://doi.org/10.1103/PhysRevE.84.011130.

[179]   Ron Paul Curriculum, accessed September 27, 2025, https://www.ron-paulcurriculum.com/

[180]   Tuttle Twins, accessed September 27, 2025, https://tuttletwins.com/

[181]   "FEE Classroom," *Foundation for Economic Education*, accessed September 27, 2025, https://fee.org/classroom/#start.

[182]   "Mises Academy," accessed September 27, 2025, https://academy.mises.org/

[183]   "Liberty Classroom," accessed September 27, 2025, https://libertyclassroom.com/

[184]   "SPN Directory," *SPN*, accessed September 27, 2025, https://spn.org/directory/

[185]   "Woods Author Academy," accessed September 27, 2025, https://woodsauthoracademy.com/